A QUIET REALITY

A CHAPLAIN'S JOURNEY INTO BABYLON, IRAQ
WITH THE I MARINE EXPEDITIONARY FORCE

EMILIO MARRERO, JR.

A QUIET REALITY

A CHAPLAIN'S JOURNEY INTO BABYLON, IRAQ
WITH THE I MARINE EXPEDITIONARY FORCE

EMILIO MARRERO, JR.

FaithWalk Publishing
an imprint of CSS Publishing
Lima, Ohio

A QUIET REALITY

FIRST EDITION
Copyright © 2009 by
Dr. Emilio Marrero Jr.

DISCLAIMER
THE OPINIONS AND CONCLUSIONS EXPRESSED HEREIN ARE THOSE OF THE INDIVIDUAL AUTHOR AND DO NOT NECESSARILY REPRESENT THE VIEWS OF EITHER THE DEPARTMENT OF DEFENSE OR ANY OTHER GOVERNMENTAL AGENCY.

Names and descriptions have been changed throughout this book to preserve the privacy of individuals.

Most scripture quotations are from the Holy Bible, New International Version. Copyright © 1973, 1978, 1984 International Bible Society. Used by permission of Zondervan Bible Publishers. All rights reserved.

Scripture quotations marked (NASB) are from the New American Standard Bible © 1960, 1962, 1963, 1968, 1971, 1972, 1973, 1975, 1977 by The Lockman Foundation. Used by permission.

14   13   12   11   10   09   6   5   4   3   2   1

Library of Congress Cataloging-in-Publication Data

Marrero, Emilio.
    A quiet reality : a chaplain's journey into Babylon, Iraq with the 1st Marine Expeditionary Force / Emilio Marrero, Jr. — 1st ed.
    p. cm.
    ISBN-13: 978-0-7880-2617-1 (perfect bound : alk. paper)
    ISBN-10: 0-7880-2617-8 (perfect bound : alk. paper)
    1. Marrero, Emilio. 2. Iraq War, 2003—Personal narratives, American. 3. Iraq War, 2003—Chaplains. 4. Iraq War, 2003—Religious aspects. 5. United States. Marine Expeditionary Force, 1st. 6. Persian Gulf War, 1991—Personal narratives, American. 7. Military chaplains—United States—Biography. 8. United States. Marine Corps—Chaplains—Biography. 9. United States. Navy—Chaplains—Biography. 10. Baptists—United States—Clergy—Biography. I. Title.
DS79.76.M363 2009
956.7044'37092—dc22

                                                                    2008055360

ISBN-13: 978-0-7880-2617-1
ISBN-10: 0-7880-2617-8   PRINTED IN USA

Inspiring! An intriguing blend of comfort and challenge, cooperation, and conflict. A great description of the tensions and conflicts in Iraq from the round level ... in Babylon they acted as ambassadors of respect and kindness, gently firm but approachable, principled, persuasive, and culturally competent. You will love the closing chapter which is personally revealing and riveting! An intimate message of hope that needs to be shared.

Rear Admiral Darold Bigger (Retired)
Former Director of Religious Programs
for the Navy, Marine Corps, Coast Guard,
and Merchant Marine Reserve

The Rev. Dr. Emilio Marrero, a Navy Chaplain recounts his experiences of being a chaplain during the Kuwait and Iraqi wars. He takes us along on his journey of ministerial service to men and women on the front lines of battle. Along this journey we confront the conflicts, fears, and bravery that is demanded of people who wear the uniform of our military and those who choose to be clergy to them. Through Chaplain Marrero's journey you come to understand much of what our troops face when under the conditions of war or violence. You can come to understand how they struggle to do good as they try to insure their self and fellow soldiers survival. Unlike any ministry book you have read Chaplain Marrero's narrative will inform you of how many decisions are made and of the men and women who enforce them. You will be informed of the tensions that are inherent in warfare and that make the role of a clergyperson both conflictive and rewarding. You will begin to appreciate the service of our military, the role of clergy, and how we, as Americans, must begin to understand military service. Chaplain Marrero provides insight into their role in our modern and global context; even in the hell of war many of our troops are compassionate, risking life and limb not just for us in America but for the Iraqi civilians, for their Iraqi culture, and all of civilization in the saving of Babylon. This book is highly recommended if you are interested in another perspective on the Iraqi war, if you are a person of faith, or a person who is thinking of a calling to ministry.

The Reverend Luis Cortes, Jr.
President
Esperanza USA
4261 North 5th Street
Philadelphia, PA 19140

From the Bronx to the Rivers of Babylon, the "Mayor of Babylon," Chaplain Emilio Marrero, tells a fascinating story of war, compassion, struggles, faith, and ancient biblical history in a country that we read about daily — Iraq. As he describes the different events it is obvious he continues to carry out the order of his Marine Commanding Officer, "Take care of my Marines." He tells the true story of saving Babylon for civilization. Strongly recommended, a must read — **A Quiet Reality** is a different view of the war, the people, and the accomplishments made in that part of the world.

Rear Admiral Fred Metz, US Navy (Retired)
Naval Aviator

This work is dedicated to all the men and women of this nation who courageously answer the call to service, subjecting their lives to their nation's call while not knowing what will be asked of them; to the families that love them and support them during these journeys of faith as did my wife, Wanda, and my children, Tabitha and Emilio; and to this great nation, the United States of America, which guarantees me the freedom to express my views, serve with honor, and defend liberty.

A special thank you to my parents, Emilio and Isabel Marrero, who while poor, gave me a priceless possession — faith and hope.

Last, but not least, to God almighty, who called me out of the masses to serve by caring for those around me with a message of redemption and hope.
Semper Fidelis

Table Of Contents

Acknowledgments

In the fall of 2004, after having returned from my second tour in Iraq, I'd often accompany Brigadier General James L. Williams, the Commanding General for the 1st Marine Expeditionary Force (Rear) in Camp Pendleton, on his visits to San Diego's Balboa Naval Hospital as he visited our wounded Marines and Sailors. General Williams would consistently encourage these young recovering warriors to take the time to tell their story. He'd emphasize the need for them to honor their experience by sharing it with their loved ones or with veterans in their community. He understood the impact of unlocking their memories and sharing their thoughts and emotions with others in their healing journey. Yet, he also knew that many of them did not feel ready for this task so he would *gently order* them to at least journal. It was a piece of advice I enthusiastically affirmed and repeated to the wounded warriors as well as with those returning Marines and Sailors who were having difficulty with their transitions. It was a piece of advice I genuinely offered up but didn't apply to myself.

Life continued on in its usual fashion and at times I found myself sharing tidbits of moments here and there. Those who heard some of my accounts in sermons or sea stories would encourage me to write. My father-in-law, Dr. Ted Villafana, would often ask me when I was going to write my story and I can recall saying that I didn't have much to tell. Over the years I have been encouraged by my wife, Wanda; a few fellow chaplains; and other friends to take the time to write down my experiences. At their behest I found myself sitting down to write only to end in frustration unsure of where to begin, what to write, and often wondered if it even mattered.

In March 2006, the British Broadcasting Company sought to get an apology by Colonel John Coleman for our presence in Babylon during 2003. Colonel Coleman's staff tracked me down in Okinawa and asked me to jot down a few facts on the timeline of events in order to respond to BBC's inquiries. I did as he asked and forwarded it to his staff only to learn a month later of the article claiming Marines were apologizing for having irreversibly damaged Babylon. This event opened a floodgate of emotions in me and as a result I began to systematically jot down my thoughts, reflections, and memories. I was appalled at the idea that we were being called on to apologize, and we were explicitly castigated. We had been demonized for an act of moral courage that I believed was being obscured and intentionally misrepresented.

I set out to see if I could weave my notes into a story that allowed the reader a glimpse into the quiet realities of this war. These are events not often captured in other writings, the efforts ignored and diminished by a thrill-seeking media. This is not meant to be an exhaustive or authoritative historical accounting of the events mentioned but rather a very personal glimpse from my perspective that resulted in an emotional journey that caused me to grow in my faith walk in my journey as a pastor and a man.

I'd like to take a moment and thank Dirk Wierenga and the folks from Faithwalk Publishers for believing in this project and agreeing to publish it after so many rejections from others. I can't thank Becky Allen and her editorial staff at CSS Publishing enough for their skilled craftsmanship and professionalism. I wish to recognize my son, Emilio, and his creative contribution to this work as he worked so diligently on designing the front cover. I was urged to pursue my initial efforts by my sister and her husband, Enid and Mario Burgos, who read my first drafts and were so encouraging as they demanded that I keep writing and emailing new chapters to them. I would be negligent if I didn't recognize Religious Program Specialist Chief Petty Officer Andrew Stanley, my RP Senior Enlisted Advisor at Navy Expeditionary Combat Command who, while deployed to Iraq with Riverine Squadron 3, took his personal time to read my manuscript on his laptop and provided me with some invaluable feedback. Most of all, I'd like to recognize Wanda for her ongoing loving encouragement and keeping this at the forefront of our conversations. She knows this was an unsettled event for me, and she understands the value of journaling and writing better than I do. Her undying enthusiasm and passion in life helped me to give this the attention it demanded during those nights after work and those quiet weekends in Okinawa.

Without the help of those who have encouraged me and those who toiled over this manuscript this would have been simply a collection of thoughts and memories tucked away in a drawer and in the crevices of my mind. I thank them for their talents and their long hours to help make this a reality for me.

I hope you will take the journey with me in the pages ahead and be drawn into this story as I share moments, thoughts, and hopes. You will find yourself caught in a current of random thoughts as I reflect on the events, the thoughts that tied the past with the present, and as I dared to peer into the hearts and minds of those around me. Many books on Operation Iraqi Freedom will focus on the raw emotion, violent nature, or political turmoil that has defined this event in history, but I hope to walk you through the same events in a quieter way as they unfold through interpersonal relationships. I hope in these writings you seek to understand my struggle as I sought to interpret my reality through the heart of a pastor and the life of a Naval Officer and as I attempt to be moored in my faith while engaging in man's ugliest venture. Americans and Iraqis alike have been changed by the events of this war, some very obviously via confrontational and violent combat, but the quiet reality is that many more were impacted in a very deep way through a much quieter unfolding of reality as our cultures clashed at times and gingerly touched at others. I learned that there is a faith that can breathe life into us in the most of the mundane or adulterated situations that can inspire us to do more than we dare to envision. It is this faith that encourages me to look toward tomorrow with anticipation and hope.

Semper Fidelis,
Emilio Marrero, Jr.

Foreword

In this book you'll find an intriguing blend of comfort and challenge, cooperation and conflict. Written by a Navy Chaplain, it reflects both cultural and religious diversity and boldly describes the truth as he experienced it.

War is a terrible thing; to that nearly every war veteran will attest. Some of my civilian friends seem surprised when I tell them that nearly all the military personnel with whom I have served dread war and wish to avoid it. Because the military prepares to fight if necessary, some presume that military personnel want war. But those who prepare for war understand clearly its consequences and the personal trauma war causes.

We usually associate the costs of war with lives lost or bodies and minds wounded or maimed. Those personal consequences are certainly painful and substantiate the effort to avoid war whenever possible. Other risks and consequences exist as well.

One of those is the risk to historical artifacts and sites. While compared to the physical and mental consequences of war, this may seem more an inconvenience than a tragedy. But when human beings lose their sense of origin, when they cannot root themselves in a past, when they become aimless wanderers preoccupied only with the present, they risk losing the moral, ethical, and cultural underpinnings that preserve their society. The chaotic lawless result has been illustrated by several doomsday novels and movies, all of which make the point that losing the long-preserved testimony and treasures of history is no menial loss at all.

Iraq faced such consequences and experienced some of that rootlessness after the overthrow of the Saddam Hussein regime. The looting of some precious reminders of ancient civilization did occur, but there were intentional efforts to reverse and recover those losses. One outstanding example is the concerted effort of the US Marine unit that settled near the site of ancient Babylon. Iraqi looters invaded this site until the Marines arrived and reversed the deterioration that had taken place.

As Director of Religious Programs for the Navy, Marine Corps, Coast Guard, and Merchant Marine Reserve, I had the privilege of visiting our troops in Iraq. During the summer of 2003 I saw what the Marines accomplished at Babylon. The site of the ancient city was protected, merchants were busy again, and there appeared to be a cooperative and productive spirit among all those whose interactions had been imposed on them by the war.

The military leaders who recognized the historical significance of the place they commanded and who seized the opportunity to protect that heritage for future generations need to be applauded. We read or watch the romantic chronicle of General Patton's intervention on behalf of the Lipizzaner horses of the Spanish riding school in Vienna during World War II. The story of what Marines did in Babylon, in what is often called the cradle of human civilization, has even more profound and far-reaching implications. To find a military unit willing to invest itself for the good of others, to see young Marines enthralled by the significance of this site, to see believers awed by walking where biblical persons walked, was inspiring. That men and women in uniform would devote so much time, effort, and attention to the good of a conquered nation demonstrates the constructive, considerate, and benevolent side of the military.

As point man in this effort, Chaplain Marrero was uniquely suited to this task. His Puerto Rican energy and New York City determination prepared him well for his assignment in Babylon. There he had to cope with intercultural tensions, religious suspicion and hostility, conflicting goals and perceptions, economic distress, being an outsider who was imposing rules, and all this for those with high hopes for quick progress toward personal and communal success.

Chaplain Marrero acted in the established tradition of Chaplain Support for Community Relations projects. His was a much more complicated, delicate, demanding, and long-term undertaking. He became known as the Mayor of Babylon because of his ongoing responsibilities and the depth of his investment in the well-being of the site and the people nearby. He and those who worked with him illustrate the best of our nation's servants. In Babylon

16

they acted as ambassadors of respect and kindness, gently firm but approachable, principled, persuasive, and culturally competent. They reflect a crucial but little-heard side of the Iraq story.

Darold Bigger
Rear Admiral, Chaplain Corps
US Navy Reserve (Ret)

Chapter One

My First Night In Iraq

Have I not commanded you? Be strong and courageous.
Do not be terrified; do not be discouraged, for the Lord
your God will be with you wherever you go.
— Joshua 1:9

I opened my eyes as wide as I could, hoping that the wider I exposed my eyeballs the more light I might be able to absorb — but I failed miserably as I saw nothing. The blackness of the night was thick and regardless of what I did with my eyes or how I moved my head I could see nothing. Had I been standing still in a quiet room this may not have proven so disheartening but it took on a new sense of urgency as I sat in the front seat of a Humvee[1] traveling at thirty miles per hour at 2 a.m. as part of a convoy under tactical conditions. In Marine speak it meant no headlights, spearheading into the heart of Iraq. My driver and bodyguard, RP2[2] Donnell Stephens, a bright, conscientious, and dedicated young family man from South Central Los Angeles, was mumbling under his breath as he struggled to keep the only set of night vision goggles between us affixed to his face while we headed down this highway in total darkness.

Anxiety increases exponentially when your primary sense fails you. When my eyes could no longer interpret the world for me, I tried to make my other senses compensate. I could smell the heavy putrid smell of diesel exhaust emanating from the vehicles to my right. At times when we slowed down I even smelled the blunted heavy canvas that oft covers our gear in other vehicles nearby. I heard the clatter of heavy machinery and visualized through momentary blindness that the vehicles passing our small Humvee were either tanks or Amphibious Assault Vehicles ten times our size and density. The sound of the passing hunks of steel was deafening but muted by fear as vehicle after vehicle passed us on the road. We stuck to our lane in the blackness of night. Our goal was simple, keep the convoy together without killing ourselves in a major traffic accident. I held my hands up to my face on occasion to see if the darkness had faded by any measure but it did not. What I could not see I felt. The proximity of my hand was somehow perceivable in the same way I felt the heavy dense steel pass by to my right.

On most occasions the vast majority of us in the vehicles had no real idea of where we were or where we were heading. It was standard operating procedure to have an orientation brief prior to departure. Waypoints and destinations were provided to drivers and security personnel during these short meetings but the rest of us were clueless. Small headsets affixed to the driver's head by a headband were provided but often the message was garbled or the surrounding traffic noise muted the radio transmission.

Our destinies on these convoys were completely in the hands of the Convoy Commander and those few selected individuals throughout the column who planned it. Everyone else stayed as close as possible to the vehicle ahead of them. No one wanted to be the one to lose the convoy before them. The convoy stretched out for miles as vehicles loaded with tons of equipment in all shapes and sizes moved along dreadfully slowly with the melodic motion of an accordion. Distances expanded between vehicles and then there would be a mad dash to close the gap with short sprints forcing everyone to race ahead and catch up. Panic set in on driver and passenger alike deathly afraid that we would be the sorry idiots to be cut off by another vehicle or that in a momentary act of inattention we would merge into the wrong lane and end up following the wrong convoy taking with us all those who followed us.

The boredom of long slow convoys is challenging as you fight with sleep and struggle to remain alert. Traveling in the dark during an invasion is unnerving, to describe it mildly. After all, you're driving into a combat situation with no situational awareness. You attempt to be professional and stay alert hoping to be ready in the event of an attack while at the same time fighting exhaustion and heat or cold. Then there are those moments when all is quiet and you've allowed yourself to be lulled into a distant place when a sudden flash and thundering boom orders the cold rush of adrenaline to be injected through your veins while you attempt to decipher whether the sound was friendly or foe. At the other end of the spectrum, the battle between exhaustion and vigilance takes on a new dimension when the unknown entices your psyche to start exploring all the possible scenarios that can unfold before you and the demons of wild fantasy play out in your mind as you attempt to be ready for any scenario that may arise.

On this night I would look forward to the occasional burning hulk of an Iraqi vehicle or some distant burning oil pipe. In them I was granted a temporary reprieve from darkness, and sight, though clouded, was momentarily regained. In those short moments of light we rested our anxiety and grew confident of our place in this massive migration of weaponry. We could see a few vehicles ahead of us as well as those other convoys of mechanized infantry and artillery alongside as they passed us.

I remember passing through a town at one point and inhaling that combined smell of burning charcoal and gunpowder. Hundreds of vehicles came through this small town, and we could see the orange embers of a fading fire in the periphery. The closer we came to the dying embers, the more we could see. All of a sudden RP2 Stephens caught something with his night vision goggles (NVGs) and threw a warning my way, "Watch your right side chaplain, there's someone there!" I was spooked and frustrated because I could see nothing and then out of nowhere as we grew closer to a secondary light in the background there emerged the Iraqi shadow, just a few feet away from where I sat. His shadow depicted a beaten man, with drooping shoulders and a hanging head. The shadow shuffled past me and he was the only person I saw in the eighteen hours of that convoy.

This was my second invasion. Twelve years earlier I accompanied Marines into combat during Desert Storm in 1991 where we moved under the cover of blackness through the northern Saudi Arabian desert into Kuwait and on into the Kuwait International Airport. Tactical convoys haven't changed much since those days. I remember kicking off at about 2:30 a.m. in the dark and my young driver, RPSN David Thompson, had the most difficult time keeping his eyes on the truck's cat eyes in front of us. Cat eyes were what we called the dimly lit, tiny reflective lights on the back of the Humvees and trucks when we traveled under tactical conditions with no lights. They are the size of a nickel and you literally have to be directly behind them at five feet or less to see them clearly. It was dark; the cat-eyes were properly illuminated but the dust from driving over the sand made them almost impossible to see. I kept yelling at him, "Stay close, Thompson, stay close! Hit that bumper if you have to but don't lose that truck!" At the same time I was praying fervently, "Lord, please don't let us get lost out here, we have another fifteen vehicles following us."

We drove on with that constant sense of frustration all night long. It was the darkest night I've ever seen and all the while it was raining oil from the Kuwaiti sabotaged oil wells, making it that much more difficult to see through our windshield. The droplets of oil got into everything and the smell of petrol overpowered whatever sweet or foul smell the desert may have had to offer.

When we started our trek that night it was just the 35 or so vehicles in our convoy. Unlike the modern convoy of the 2003 invasion, which was primarily on a freeway. The 1991 journey was through the desert and true to form I was totally unaware of where we were. Through that night I prayed without ceasing, afraid that some Iraqi tank or patrol would stumble upon us or have the presence of mind to outflank us and hit us broadside. Though I couldn't see them I'd often hear the unique sounds of AH-1W Cobras flying overhead — on one occasion I could have sworn that the attack helicopter was directly overhead when he released his Hellfire missile. The missile whooshed away tearing the fabric of the sky to find its target. On our immediate horizon the sky lit up and the most intense, thundering, crushing sound that I've ever heard reverberated within my bones filled the sky and completely overwhelmed us.

In the breaking of day, the sun began to permeate through the armor of darkness and shades of light allowed us to see beyond ourselves. As the sun rose, I was amazed. I unzipped the side plastic window of the Humvee so I could see past the oil-covered plastic and I took in a sight that has never left me to this day. As far as I could see to my right, there were convoys like mine following in line moving north, paralleled to our convoy. I asked RPSN

Thompson to unzip his window and to our amazement they were there, too, column after column of vehicles as far as the human eye could see. We were a massive force moving north, in unison, and in the light our true strength was revealed in a uniquely clear and powerful way. As the sun climbed higher I could see with greater clarity. To my right, two columns over, was a five-ton truck with its canopy removed and its bed loaded with Marines.

One of those Marines positioned himself toward the front of the truck bed, right behind the cab, and with all his might he held on to a large American flag that waved violently and boldly against the rising sun. The blood red and stark white stripes contrasted sharply against the pale browns and yellows of the desert. It demanded all attention for miles around and I imagine that like I, having emerged out of a dark and anxious night, those colors waving so brightly inspired every American whose eyes were privileged to such a sight on that morning. Helicopters screamed across the sky in a hurry to the front and appeared like angels guarding us from above and for a sweet moment juxtaposed against that flag all of my fear dissipated.

In the dark, I was like Elijah in 1 Kings 19, overcome with fear and afraid of the frailty this life often brings us. I was a young father at the time and I grieved more than anything else not being able to return to my beautiful wife, Wanda, and our children, Tabitha and Emilio. In the darkness, whether it's the darkness of night, the darkness of depression, or the darkness of sin when we are in rebellion against God, we always presume we are alone. Yet we must learn that it is one of the greatest lies Satan plants deep within our consciousness. Elijah believed he was alone but in God's gentle but direct manner he informed Elijah of his misperception.

> The Lord said, "Go back the way you came, and go to the Desert of Damascus. When you get there, anoint Hazael king over Aram. Also, anoint Jehu son of Nimshi king over Israel, and anoint Elisha son of Shaphat from Abel Meholah to succeed you as prophet. Jehu will put to death any who escape the sword of Hazael, and Elisha will put to death any who escape the sword of Jehu. Yet

I reserve seven thousand in Israel — all whose knees
have not bowed down to Baal and all whose mouths
have not kissed him."   — 1 Kings 19:15-18

Like Elijah who had erroneously perceived his demise in low numbers, I was fooled by the lack of vision the darkness had robbed from me. It all served as a metaphor to our spiritual condition. With the rising of the sun it was clearly revealed to me that I was far from being alone or isolated but in fact I had been surrounded by friendly forces all through the night. I was in the company of thousands — tens of thousands — hundreds of thousands who moved north as liberators to free a nation and end tyranny in this region. This was perhaps a once in a lifetime experience, so I thought.

So here I was once again, twelve years later accompanying the brave young men and women of the US Marine Corps crossing yet another part of the same desert, traveling from the northern Kuwaiti desert into southern Iraq on our way to Baghdad. Just a few days prior, as we headed north on the Kuwait highway, a large convoy of white armored personnel carriers caught my eye. First their unique color captured my attention and then the obvious intrigued me — they were headed in the opposite direction from where everything was happening. I turned my head and stared at their large emboldened letters plastered on their vehicles that read "UN" as they faded away toward Kuwait City in the south and we headed north — a sure sign of failed diplomacy.

As dawn broke we began to arrive at our new location in the desert, well inside of Iraq. Marines were placed at different locations to guide the convoy to our predetermined positions designed to set up a tactical presence and establish a temporary base. With the arrival of the day came the task to dig in and establish our work and living spaces. The command element immediately began to establish their tactical operations center from where our Commanding General, Lieutenant General James Conway, would continue to quarterback all of the Marine forces engaged in this operation.

The night came quickly and by day's end I realized I had not slept in over 32 hours. The area was secured and I unabashedly

24

climbed into my private two-man tent for a moment of sanctuary and a deep desire to sleep. The days of going without sleep endlessly were behind me — this old guy by Marine Corps standards was pretty beat. I kept my boots and uniform on and threw the sleeping bag and flak jacket over me. I began my gentle descent into sleep when I heard, "Chaplain, chaplain where are you?"

My selfish and exhausted flesh tempted me to ignore it and succumb to the sleep but instead I yelled out, "Over here. Who's looking for the chaplain?" As I unzipped my tent and looked out I met the Sergeant Major's red lit flashlight. "Chaplain, hurry there's a need for you at one of our sites nearby!" He was obviously excited and concerned so I curiously asked, "What happened?"

The Sergeant Major went on to explain that one of our units from Task Force Tarawa from Camp Lejeune, got into a heavy fight in a place called An Nasiriyah. "Grab your stuff, chaplain, the surgical team doesn't have a chaplain and we can use you there." I turned and called out to RP2 Stephens. We followed the Sergeant Major to a waiting Humvee and climbed into the two backseats. The front seats were backlit only against the computer screens of the Blue Force tracker in the vehicle. We had no idea, once again, who was taking us to the surgical unit but we climbed in and headed out. We engaged in some small talk in the shadows and once again submitted ourselves into their hands as we left the security of our new compound and trucked up and down the ravines of the desert in search of the surgical site.

It proved relatively easy to find after a few tense minutes of darkness. Ahead of us we could see the white glow of the external lights being used to light up the trauma area just outside the surgical tents. CH-46 helicopters were coming in and dropping off the wounded. It was indeed a surreal sight as the entire area was covered in hovering dust from the approaching helos[4] and the soft white lights seemed to burst off the sand particles in the sky against the deep blackness behind it.

The surgical area was surprisingly loud and hectic. Helos were coming in and covering the area with waves of dust. The surgical teams were yelling out orders and running back and forth between the triage area and the treatment area. To the untrained eye it all appeared so random and hectic but in reality it was a very well controlled dance with chaos. I stepped out of the Humvee and instinctively headed toward the brilliantly lit triage area where I was met enthusiastically by the towering figure of Hospitalman Master Chief Robert Elliot, who was simply addressed as Master Chief. The vast amount of blood over his torso and stomach area on his surgical apron immediately caught my attention. I continued toward him and received a warm greeting from the Master Chief. As I became oriented to the situation I came to discover that the seven wounded patients being treated in the triage area were all Iraqis.

I saw some of this in Desert Storm but in all honesty I've seen so much more of it this time around. It always amazes me how conscientiously we as a military force make such sincere gestures to treat our wounded humanely, even the outright enemy. Don't get me wrong, we don't treat them like VIPs. We posted Marines and Sailors at a stone's throw from their tables and pointed shotguns and M-16s at them throughout their stay. In the meantime our corpsmen, nurses, and doctors worked feverishly to attend to their wounds and discomfort. I saw a young corpsman walking around offering them ice chips while attempting to communicate to see if they were comfortable. The seriously wounded had already been taken inside for surgery and these were those who could afford to wait. No matter how often you witness this dynamic, one cannot be but impressed with the level of humanity evidenced on this night — especially in light of the fact that we just lost some of our own.

Master Chief pointed me to Force Sergeant Major William T. Kinney and told me I would be needed right away toward the back of the makeshift compound. RP2 Stephens and I walked toward the container that sat in a darkened corner within the perimeter of the surgical team's camp. There were a handful of Marines standing around and one did not need light to feel their collective broken hearts. When Sergeant Major Kinney saw me, he called the Marines together and led me to the opening of the container where seven of our young Marines were laid unceremoniously inside their black body bags on shelves within the container. "Come around, Marines, the chaplain is going to do his thing — come listen," prodded the Sergeant Major in a caring, but firm, voice.

Herein lies the paradox that chaplains have to live with while serving in the military — the vast majority of folks associate you + with death. In sharp contrast, chaplains believe they represent eternal life. In the midst of such crisis, chaplains are often called upon to minister to the dead and we struggle with this reality. During much of my career as a Navy chaplain I have dedicated myself to teaching my Marines and Sailors to call upon me as early as possible during the onset of an oncoming crisis. I want them to use me as a resource while there is an opportunity for communication, reflection, and spiritual healing. Perhaps the reasoning for being called upon during times of death is that most service members understand that chaplains in all branches of the US military share a common core principle, "Nurture the living, care for the wounded, and honor the dead." It provides a clear concise statement for our theology of ministry and guides us in our pursuit for ministry in the most of nontraditional settings. Yet many tend to focus on the portion related to "honoring the dead" and immediately refer to us during these sad times often forgetting the first two elements, "nurture the living and care for the wounded."

I am a Baptist minister, an American Baptist to be exact. In my theological framework, humanity has until its last breath to respond to the loving call of God. In this framework we see humanity like a rebellious teenager struggling to define their existence away from God. We believe that there comes a time of spiritual maturity where the rebellious teenager sheds the anger and misconceptions attributed to God, and they begin to look for a mature understanding of life's meaning and therein seek peace with God. This peace in my framework involves a call to repentance when we rebel against the design of God and a seeking to restore their relationship with a God who desires to have a personal, interactive relationship with humanity. I believe God is an all encompassing and gracefully forgiving God. In this theological framework, I believe God gives an invitation to humanity and in an act of love he actually limits his own power over humanity in order to allow humanity to be able to genuinely respond freely, to accept or reject God. I also believe that the response to this invitation can be done with great fanfare in a large church with as much credibility and authenticity as it can

27

be done in a whispering confession during one's last breath only to be heard by God. For this reason, I dare not ever judge who has made the confession of heart or not. However, in this framework there is no accommodation for those who have already died. Upon death, the decision to relate or not to relate to God has been sealed. Unlike other faiths where the dead are believed to be transported to a way station or a state of sleep for future opportunities of reconciliation with God, Baptists and the vast majority of Protestant Christians have no such provisions.

There I stood with half a dozen young Marines in a dark combat zone grieving for their friends, their brethren in arms, and perhaps questioning their own mortality — what could I offer them with integrity that would be genuine to me and to them when they called upon me to minister to their dead comrades? I wanted to be relevant to the moment; I wished to be real and honest. I had no idea what their spiritual traditions might be. I decided to lead them in a prayer on their behalf, on behalf of the family of the deceased, and in an attempt to momentarily honor with dignity those who have been killed. I called them together and I knelt down over the closest body bag to me not yet placed in the container and placed my hand on the top of the bag.

I had consciously chosen not to open the bag, not knowing the condition of the deceased. I did not wish to further traumatize the young men around me in the event the body happened to be disfigured or burned, so I opted to pray for each Marine without unzipping the bags. However, when my hand touched the first bag I could feel the contour of the young Marine's face through the heavy plastic. My hand looked for a place to rest and I could feel the bridge of his nose and then the forehead. The immense reality of the moment shook me to my core, for while I was confident that I was prepared to do this, I realized that as soon as that bag ceased to be a bag and it took its proper form as the lost life of a young man I was overridden by emotion.

I could not speak. I attempted to force the words out and I stuttered a low gasp. In the dark I allowed a tear to well in my eyes. I felt brokenness in my heart and I pleaded to God with humble emotion and a spirit of gentle advocacy a heartfelt prayer in the likes of: "Gracious and loving Lord, in your grace receive this young man into your hands, forgive us all of our sins, show us compassion during these days of war. Be with the poor families who do not yet know that their son is gone and grant them comfort and peace that only you can provide. Walk with us and give us strength and courage. We rely on your promise that you walk with us until the end of time. In your holy name we pray. Amen."

I laid hands on each deceased Marine and said a similar whispered prayer. With each prayer spoken quietly under my breath I also pleaded silently for mercy upon those there with me and the many others out there on this violent night. I prayed for each deceased Marine, as much for them as for their families and especially for those that stood behind me. I could not help but think of the agony I would feel if I learned of my son's death. Sending your child to war does not prepare you in any way for the real possibility of death. It is something that happens to other people. I believe most people cope in a state of denial until the knock on the door from men and women in uniform shatters that fantasy. I moved from Marine to Marine that night knowing that to the young Marines behind me it raised a great deal of questions and they watched in what perhaps felt to them a painful eternity. When I was done praying I invited them to stay there and honor their comrades and support one another. I wanted so badly to tend to each of them but the screams from inside the adjacent surgical tent reminded me that there were more to attend to, so I was escorted hurriedly to see the ones that were wounded.

I was met by a medical team member who led me from the container to the back door of the treatment room. We walked into a brightly lit room that immediately reminded me of the thousands of hours of *M*A*S*H* reruns I had watched with my family on those quiet and peaceful evenings. At the opposite end of the treatment room there were three people working on a Marine. I stepped toward them, avoiding the puddles of blood on the floor and the gear that was strewn about. One of the attendants called to us and asked us if we would mind clearing the way. I turned to RP2 Stephens and asked him to pick up the 782 gear, what Marines call their suspenders attached to a web belt with ammo, canteens, and first-aid kit. He reached down to grab the flak jacket and was unmistakably surprised by the fact that it was weighed down with blood. When he lifted it up toward him blood poured out of it onto the deck. He looked at me and said, "What do I do with this?" With no real clear idea I returned with a blank look and one of the attendants retorted, "Put it in one of those plastic bags behind you and stick it in the corner."

I turned to face the Marine on the bed and was granted an undesired lesson in the human anatomy. His leg was propped up and bent at the knee, with his foot resting on the bed. The attendants were cleaning the wound where all of the outer skin of his left leg from his knee down to his ankle was missing. I could see the various muscles with utmost clarity. His screams of pain brought me back to him after having been momentarily affixed psychologically to his leg, so I hurried to his side. I gave him my hand to hold as he struggled with the pain and I then took a position by his head and spoke softly in his ear, "Son, I'm the chaplain and I want to pray for you — is there anything I can specifically pray for?" Without hesitation, thought, or prompting he grimaced in pain and turned to me and said, "Chaplain, pray for my wife and daughter and my Marines who are still out there in the fight. I want to go back out to join them."

Every generation has its doubts of the generation that follows in its footsteps. In the Marine Corps and Navy we joke and revel on the attributes of the "Old Corps" or "Old Navy," implying that those of us who went before suffered greater distress than the new generation of today. We, the older generation, often wonder if the new generation in this age of iPods, video games, and instant gratification possess the necessary fortitude to endure tragedy, disappointment, and hardships like combat. On this day in a surgical room in Iraq, I began to realize that in fact this generation possesses within its rank those who have the uncommon valor and courage of heroes past. In times as this when the measure of a man is determined by how he responds in the rawness of pain and harsh circumstances, this young man's virtues emerged clearly as he focused not on his leg, the blood he lost, or his pain but he was determinedly focused on his family — his family at home and his

30

family here. I can't share all of the stories of selfless acts conducted by these young men who in peacetime make officers worry because of their childish antics, naive presumptions, and ignorant rantings. But in the heat of battle, in the face of death, they face the events with courage and lean on one another in a way rarely accommodated anywhere else in our society.

In the Judeo-Christian scriptures, we find the events of David's kingdom in the book of 2 Samuel, chapter 11 where David sends his soldiers off to war under the leadership of Joab. While his army is off in combat, David in one of his weakest moments catches a glimpse of Bathsheba, the wife of one of his officers, Uriah the Hittite, and David seduces her. Aware of his breach and the fact that she sent word to David of her pregnancy, David attempted to hide his sin by sending for Uriah and asking for a status report on the war. When Uriah completed his report. David granted him permission to go home and be with his wife, David was hoping that by Uriah sleeping with his wife, he could conceal the betrayal he had committed. However, Uriah being the man of honor and the warrior brethren that he was departed from the king's presence, went to the servant's quarters, and did not lie with his wife. The following morning, David tried to confirm his plan and asked Uriah of his stay with his wife. Uriah answered, "The ark and Israel and Judah are staying in tents, and my master Joab and my lord's men are camped in the open fields. How could I go to my house to eat and drink and lie with my wife? As surely as you live, I will not do such a thing!" The event ends poorly for Uriah the Hittite as David, out of frustration and in an attempt to continue to conceal his sin, sent him back to the war with orders to be sent to the very front of the battle for a sure death.

This account clearly juxtaposes the weak, self-serving, and dishonorable leader David had become in his kingdom against the character of Uriah who personified the honor of a selfless and committed warrior. To a degree, Uriah represented to David what he, David, had been years earlier to the people of Israel but yet in his disobedience and self-serving fashion had come to abandon. Metaphorically, as David killed Uriah, he, in reality, was killing himself and the image he had once represented as the Warrior King. Ironically, David's actions catapulted Uriah from obscurity and on into eternal recognition in the written word of scripture. The secret he so intensely wished to hide became the very characteristic, which defined his kingdom and stature in biblical history. In contrast, this simple yet honorable obscure officer became the personification of what it means to be a warrior of honor.

In their moments, like Uriah, many of these obscure young men make decisions, statements, and act out on convictions in ways that honor Uriah and the rest of us who wear the cloth of our nation and desire to passionately serve faithfully and well. When such honor is exhibited in its raw state, in action, it supersedes all things said and inspires others to act in similar fashion because selfless honor resonates with the character of God instilled within our soul.

During the next thirty minutes by the Marine's side, I was able to see him stabilized and his wounds tended. As the medical team worked on him, he shared his story of how a rocket propelled grenade (RPG) screamed by him and tore the flesh off his leg. He recounted the intensity of the battle at An Nasiriyah and interrupted himself over and over again with disgust in realizing that this was inconvenient in that it kept him from returning to the battlefield with his brother Marines.

In my humble opinion, he was extremely fortunate to have escaped alive. I learned three days later that twelve Marines had lost their lives that night in a savagely intense firefight with Iraqi Fedayeen Saddam (Saddam's "Men of Sacrifice") militia on a bridge across the Euphrates in An Nasiriyah coupled with the tragedy of a possible friendly fire from one of our own aircraft. We'd also learned that in the midst of all this, in that same vicinity, an Army convoy from the Army's 507th Maintenance Company had been ambushed and that twelve soldiers were unaccounted for and were believed to have been taken prisoner. This was the same ambush that later in the war became famously associated with PVT Jessica Lynch. This war was already very different from the last war — it wasn't going to end in 100 hours.

For the next hour, I walked around the compound and had the opportunity to talk offline with a few Marines and Sailors. The helos were still coming in to pick up the wounded, American and Iraqi, to transport them to the Fleet Medical Hospital that was tucked behind us in the tactical layout. With the passing hours, the adrenaline filtered out of my system and exhaustion began to tug at me. All of the helos were gone and so were the wounded. The triage area had been cleared and was eerily quiet as it lay ready to receive more casualties. Those of us not on duty for the rest of the night scrambled for a portable cot or a place in a Humvee to call it a night.

I collapsed onto a cot that Sergeant Major Kinney found for me. I looked up into the sky and noticed a dimly lit desert night. I paused long enough to remember that it was March 23, my father's birthday. He had died a couple years prior. It was also my youngest sister's birthday. I sure hoped Enid, my sister, had a better day than I did. I paused and shot a quick but genuine plea for peace in prayer; consciously thought of Wanda, my wife, our relationship, our children, Tabitha and Emilio; recapped the emotions of the day, shed a tear, and fell into a deep sleep under the open sky.

---

1. The popularized name for the government tactical vehicle officially known as the M998 High Mobility Multipurpose Wheeled Vehicle (HMMWV or pronounced Humvee).

2. RP is the Navy Military Occupational Specialty acronym that is given to young men and women who serve in the Navy as Religious Program Specialists. Their basic duties during peacetime include administrative and clerical support of chaplains but when assigned to the Fleet Marine Force, they also serve as combat drivers and force protection (similar to a bodyguard) to the unarmed chaplain.

3. "Helo" is Marine Corps vernacular for helicopter.

Chapter Two

Connections

Search me, O God, and know my heart; test me and
know my anxious thoughts. — Psalm 139:23

Two weeks passed since that bloody night at An Nasiriyah. Coalition Forces made tremendous gains in their movement up toward Baghdad. We survived the "Mother of all Sandstorms" which was a feat in itself. Pvt. Jessica Lynch was rescued in An Nasiriyah, and the infamous Iraqi Information minister aka Baghdad Bob or Muhammed Saeed Al-Sahaaf, continued to defiantly declare that Coalition forces were being repelled on all fronts as we surrounded him.

One might naturally presume that by being in the center of a war it would be relatively easy to gather information. Such a conclusion is not true. Units engaged in operations received information pertaining to their movements and specific situation. There were those who were privileged to be higher in the "food chain" due to their rank and position and in turn obviously had better access to information than most. You know, that "need to know" rule. For the average Marine or Sailor the only readily available information were the occasional brief summaries from their commanders, snippets from radio reports, or the usual misinformation based on wild rumors from within the ranks Marines called the "Lance Corporal network."

In carrying out my duties as a chaplain, I walked about the camp regularly. The Navy calls this "ministry of presence." I didn't always cover the entire camp but I found my way through certain sections or various units sporadically to change things up for me and the troops. The purpose of these walks was predominantly to advertise my accessibility to them as their pastor and to help me gauge how they were feeling. Regardless of your rank, when Marines and Sailors note you are a chaplain they have a tendency to share with you what they really think — on average most Marines interact 80% of the time in one-way conversations with their superiors: Superiors talk and you listen. When a chaplain comes around, the focus is usually on the Marine and not the chaplain so for the most part they revel at the opportunity to share what they're thinking when asked.

In my walks throughout the camp I would normally make time to stop by the Marine Expeditionary Force (MEF)[1] Operations Center commonly referred to as the MOC. I'd inconspicuously blend into the back of the tent and take in portions of the daily intelligence briefs covering events of the past twelve hours. These partial snippets of information would often satisfy my personal need for some current events but rarely did they grant me enough data to comprise a full mosaic. There were regular meetings, at least twice a day, that comprehensively summarized our progress for the Commanding General but these briefs were normally reserved for the very senior officers and those other officers involved with watch sections neither of which applied to me.

My other resource for viable information was a portable radio. I had learned during Desert Storm how difficult it was to get any real news during an operation like this and how frustrating it was to feel part of an information vacuum. This time around I came prepared and I purchased a hand-cranked, regenerating, short-wave portable radio and kept it close to me. I depended on reports from "Voice of America" and the BBC to get updated regularly throughout the day. I do have to admit that at times I felt like listening to the BBC proved to be an exercise in temperance. I truly appreciate the difficulty journalists face as they struggle to be objective. I wholeheartedly support the role of the free press and their presence in operations such as OPERATION IRAQI FREEDOM. I also wholeheartedly believe in the role journalism plays in keeping a democracy informed while also serving as a venue of accountability for the public trust. I just had a difficult time appreciating melodramatic, often exaggerated ill-informed accounts that bordered on editorials rather than straightforward reports.

Despite the frustration and exercise in temperance I continued to play my radio daily. I intentionally placed my tent between the

location

36

medical tent and the chow tent where we enjoyed one hot meal per day in the evenings. I normally placed the radio on the hood of my Humvee during our hot meal at dinner and listened to reports roll in. Many of the Marines would collect their paper tray and squat around the Humvee to listen. Listening to the radio quelled some of that desire to be informed but it also proved to be entertaining. I enjoyed hearing the editorial remarks and emotional outbursts often flung at the radio broadcasters when the troops felt the reporting evolved into negative or misinformed editorials.

Information is invaluable and obviously missed when not readily available. This was not just true for me but I found it to be true for many Marines and Sailors. One of my roles as chaplain is to gauge the morale of the troops. I discovered that as I visited small units and talked to Marines, their morale level usually directly correlated to how well they felt they were being kept in the "know." The finest Generals, Commanding Officers, Sergeants Major, and small unit leaders were usually the ones who would take the time to provide the Marines with a sense of situational awareness by taking advantage of school circles. This is an impromptu classroom time in the field where the Marines would form a circle around the speaker. The leader used this time to provide updates to attempt to inspire the Marines, and to build camaraderie. This builds trust. When Marines trust their equipment, their training, and their leaders their morale skyrockets and fortifies them with a powerful level of resiliency in the most difficult of times. These factors contribute to the strength of the unit and the resiliency of the individual even against Combat Operational Stress (COS) or Post Traumatic Stress Disorder (PTSD). Information is a part of this. This doesn't mean that Marines expect a comprehensive download of every issue that is evolving, but if they are given courtesy uplinks it helps them stay connected.

Well-informed Marines and Sailors have no need to circulate rumors because they have solid information. This may be an overstatement because no matter how well informed your Marines will be, there will *always* be rumors. It is part of the lore of being in the military. The difference will be that a poorly informed team may circulate rumors that call into question the mission, the character of a leader, or the veracity of leadership as opposed to having a well-informed team that trusts its leaders but entertains itself by circulating rumors on trivial matters like being shipped home after the war on a Carnival Cruise Line™ with all the beer you can drink.

In an effort to compliment the Commanding Officers' efforts in keeping our Marines and Sailors informed, I continued to pursue my quest for relevant data, a quest as much for me as it was for them. When I came upon solid, unclassified nuggets of truth I would be sure to visit Marines who were on guard duty, resting from a patrol, or those assigned to isolated areas and I'd share some of this news with them. It was a way of connecting them and bringing them into the "know." It also became a way in which I could empower a young sergeant or team leader by sharing some info with them that allowed him or her to share it with their people. Information is power and when used properly it can be power that proactively binds people together under these circumstances.

To fill in some of the blanks, I took time to chat with Marines engaged in the G-2 (Intelligence) or G-3 (Operations) sections. There was only one television on the compound and it was located in the MOC. Lieutenant General Conway preferred *Fox News* so those of us who enjoyed access to the MOC would come by daily and take in five or ten minutes of news. It was not rare to find the television on mute as other matters were being discussed in the ops center. Those of us catching a glance at the news would take in the pictures and videos of what the rest of the forces were experiencing. In the end, I'd take the tidbits of information provided by the staff in the MOC for they held the greatest currency of credibility, coupled with the usually encouraging and optimistic prognostications from *Fox News* and weigh those against the dramatic and sometimes dismaying interpretations offered on the BBC. When I would weave all of this together I felt pretty confident that I had a decent picture of events and interpretations.

I consider myself pretty open-minded or sensible, and for that reason I made a conscientious effort to gather data and listen to both Fox and the BBC. I desired to be fair and realistic in how I saw this so that I may temper words and attitudes carefully when I would speak publicly in a sermon or when I spoke privately with

Marines and Sailors during those quiet moments of doubt and questioning. I believed that by simply being there with them I had earned some level of trust but at the same time I didn't wish to flippantly negate that trust with words that would be perceived as prejudiced, one way or another. I didn't want to speak words that might erroneously classify me as the spokesman for the party line or be tempted to resort to falling back on religious slogans. The quest to be relevant and real as a member of the clergy was a constant consideration as I attempted to interact with a generation of unchurched men and women in an age of postmodernism. This generation tends to be suspect of organized religion, yet embrace matters of spirituality as very relevant and important. I conscientiously struggled internally in that I did not wish to be perceived as being a loyally blinded cheerleader, while at the same time, I wanted to clearly be true to the fundamental message of hope that I represented as a member of the clergy and the evangelical message I represented. Gathering data was a way to engage in critical self-reflection. It was an attempt to feel tethered to the rest of the world back home and a means to connect with the Marines and Sailors who were as hungry as I was for news on the war.

Contrary to the presumption of many, not all Marines and Sailors are right leaning conservatives. These young men and women in uniform may appear to be a monolithic society on the outside but when one delves into the ranks one discovers a wide diversity of ideas and spirit. It has been said time and time again that the uniformed services are a reflection of American society. This is a very real truth that has been affirmed within me through experience and observation over my past 28 years of service in uniform.

The Marines and Sailors today continue to represent the neighborhoods of America and when they come together and willingly share in the rigors of military life, they represent all that is uniquely priceless with this country. To the surprise of many, this is also reflected in their politics, their faith, and their values. I've walked in on conversations where troops argued for and against the merits of the war, the politics of our nation, and expressed their frustration with Congress openly with one another. The fact that each one picks up their weapon and takes their place on the line or in the convoy voluntarily, allows them the right to express the passion of their hearts. Perhaps this is why bonds forged in combat are so strong and run so deep. There is something about submitting oneself to one's own mortality that grants us permission to expose ourselves in our truest of forms. We express our thoughts and opinions and we hear each other out regardless of whether we believe they are ramblings or articulated insights. Yet this can be done because there is love, a love that is not emotional, sexual, or squiggly but one rooted in the conscientious act where we swear loyalty to one another and give it currency with our lives. It is an act of *philos* love. It is the ultimate family, regardless of skin color or ethnicity.

It is here where small nuggets of information are an act of love and concern, where we find the means to stay connected with one another. These moments of communication, formal and informal, take on profound meaning. It is through these moments of communication where the connection to the mission and one another take place, where we find significance in what we are doing, and where we affirm one another.

Regardless of our political or philosophical leanings, what really connects us in an intimate fashion is the mission at hand. Journalists, lobbyists, and politicians may argue over the merit of the war and conclude that an exit strategy is mandated. Yet they speak with no real credibility for they have nothing at stake in the process. To some on the outside, the war in Iraq is akin to a chess game of opportunity as they seek to increase their posture in the public eye or gain the support of one group over another. They pontificate on matters that are ethereal to them and have no concrete impact except as they influence opinion polls. Mandating a pullout is a calculated step toward political or media career risk management as they attempt to prognosticate in a fashion that tickles the ears of the greater populace that is equally disengaged. They feed into the ideal notion of the general populace who on a notional level will always side with the imagery of peace over the stark reality of war without embracing to any real degree of reality what the first, second, or third levels of effect will produce. It is akin to seeking peace by pursuing a divorce in a troubled marriage rather than pursuing other courses of action that may be uncomfortable but may save the relationship.

Though our Marines come from all walks of life and political orientation there is something that connects them together — the impact they are making. President Ronald Reagan understood this when he stated, "Some people wonder all their lives if they've made a difference. The Marines don't have that problem." It is a statement rooted in the reality of events. In the midst of Iraq, your impact is not measured by gallop polls but by the smiles and tears of the Iraqis we came to serve and yet seem to be forgotten by the world. To stay and finish this mission isn't a polemically charged position to be admired by the masses but a spiritual struggle faced by young men and women who breathe life into US foreign policy. They are investing into the success of this mission like no other person who has commissioned them to this duty. They place their lives on the line to insure its success. To them, they are part of the classic struggle between good and evil. They are here to win and make a right of many wrongs. Winning isn't defined by a budget analysis, a drop in the opinion polls, or the lack of perseverance that desires to make it all go away. Winning here is about the fact that we came into these people's home, and we liberated them from a tyrant. In the process, we turned their lives upside down and we have to insure that when — not if, but when — we leave it must be a better place than what we found.

We can consciously and ethically argue that perhaps the way we came to be here was questionable at best. After all, we as a nation deviated from our own ethical parameters for justifying war and acted preemptively. We acted on intelligence that later proved to be by worst measures corruptible or at best wholly inadequate. Some would attest that the reasons for being engaged in this war are tenuous, the objectives were shortsighted, and the resources committed to accomplish the long-term mission vastly lacking. There are those who believe that the true war needed to be focused and completed in Afghanistan because of its link to 9/11 and that we prematurely engaged in Iraq to our own detriment. Regardless of where you may stand in your position on the Iraq war, one thing

41

is inevitably factual, we are engaged and we have to find a responsible and successful way in which to end our engagement. Regardless of whether we were right or wrong, the fact remains that we are there and as a result of our presence we as a nation have a moral responsibility to end this in a fashion that will benefit the local populace and our national interests. Admitting a mistake in past policy and procedures does not warrant abandoning a moral responsibility. For those proponents who continue to wave the flag of peace in the name of justice, I ask that we step back from the politics of this situation and look at this from an ethical and moral footing. If we care about justice, the poor, and the responsibility government has to its people then regardless of the cost we have no choice but to guarantee a safe transition. Some may declare this myopic but I dare say that it is the right thing to do. Our nation refers to the service of those who volunteer as a "service of sacrifice." If this is so, then we who serve cannot seek to bear the fruits of this honor without having paid our tithes of sacrifice. Our fate is entrusted to the wisdom and will of the general public and those who represent their will in government.

If the nation desires to mitigate its sacrifices then the nation as a whole needs to be slower to anger and slower to bear the sword of military action in place of abandoning diplomatic efforts and committing to warfare. Once we are committed to war, the servants in uniform are placed on the altar of sacrifice and the only justification for ending a war borne by the sacrifice of its servants should be a victory that guarantees a higher moral gain. Anything less is a fraudulent use of its people. It is imperative that we accept the reality that we created the current situation in Iraq and walking away from it now and abdicating our responsibilities to these people who depend on us is a greater moral offense than how we came to be here.

Winning in Iraq is about living up to our word as a nation and strengthening our credibility with the people in this region. In 1991, President George H.W. Bush encouraged the Kurds in the north and the Shiites in the south to rise up against Saddam but failed to support them once the uprising took hold. Local Iraqis reminded us of this broken promise whenever they grew weary of our pledges.

I believe this broken promise contributed in part to their hesitancy to support us in the early stages of 2003. As a nation, we have to build credibility in the region and in reality at home as well.

Winning in Iraq is also very much about the human element. Those of us who have seen their faces, walked in their homes, buried their dead, and fed their hungry can't turn our backs on them. We can't leave because it's deemed inconvenient by some back home. Walking away from a war may sound good in principle so we may appease our fantasy of pursuing an elusive peace but in the reality of Iraq where it is lived it is no longer about balancing universal principles but it is about the moral responsibility we have to this generation of Iraqis.

Winning in Iraq translates to commitment because we have friends, brothers, and sisters who wore the cloth of this nation, suffered great sacrifices, and gave to the point of death. A warrior understands that there is a value to be honored in their sacrifices so fear of death and the fantasy of peace are not enough to turn our backs on the mission or the people we have personally served. Of all the gripes and complaints I heard in the months I served with the Marines of I MEF, the one thing I rarely heard was a desire to abandon the mission. In resonance with this was the ongoing desire that the Iraqis have expressed openly to have us stay and finish what we started. They don't trust their own and it will take time for them to believe in the hope we offer. In the meantime, they beg us to stay and they lay their trust at our feet. For as much as we hated the desert, the insurgents, and the heat, we didn't want to leave any more than the Iraqis desired for us to leave.

When I think of the human condition in Iraq, I can't help but reflect back to the nation of Israel during the exodus under the leadership of Moses. They had endured over 300 years of slavery in Egypt and through a series of miraculous events orchestrated by God they gained their freedom as a people. In their wandering through the desert as per Exodus 16:3 we discover that it didn't take long for them to grow weary from the daunting task of self-rule and determination. They complained to Moses and even complained that they had been better off under the fist of Pharaoh's rule than under the free leadership of Moses. This very failure to grasp the responsibilities associated with free rule drove them toward their reliance on idols rooted in fear. This very same spirit of fear kept them as a people from entering the promise land when Joshua, Caleb, and the other ten spies returned to the nation and reported on the land God had promised. Those overwrought with fear saw themselves as grasshoppers (Numbers 13:33) and the Canaanites as giants. Their fear rooted in their oppression due to their time in slavery kept them from claiming their land. It was after this where they were doomed to wander for another generation until the new generation, rid of its personality of oppression and slavery, had risen to claim its new land.

The people of Iraq are no different in that after the past thirty years of oppression and tyrannical rule the average citizen cannot conceptualize a reality outside of their experience. To ask them to embrace democracy or believe in liberty is to ask them to commit to a conceptual premise that is not fathomable in their context. They are currently taking "baby steps" toward self-reliancy as they form a new government — an act we need to applaud and affirm. We need to give them time to grow out of such a spirit of oppression, and we need to provide that transition of stability since we are responsible for their current state of affairs regardless of how we came to be here.

---

1. A Marine Expeditionary Force (MEF) is the largest and most robust Marine Air Ground Task Force (MAGTF). A MAGTF combines air elements, ground combat elements, and logistical support elements under the command of a Lieutenant General (three-star general). A MEF can be comprised of one or more full Marine Aircraft Wings, one or more Force Service Support Groups, and one or more reinforced Infantry Divisions.

Chapter Three

Compassion Convoy

Even in darkness light dawns for the upright, for the gracious and compassionate and righteous man. Good will come to him who is generous and lends freely, who conducts his affairs with justice. Surely he will never be shaken; a righteous man will be remembered forever.
— Psalm 112:4-6

The Marines had advanced far north into cities like Al Kut and the outskirts of Baghdad so it was time to jump ahead once again and move our headquarters element. This meant another convoy. We were headed north to northeast toward a place called Numeniya but, unlike any normal trip, we were not taking the most direct or expedient route. Instead we were taking a roundabout route that took us north, northwest, and then easterly thus adding many hours to our travel time. The trade off was that the route was supposedly relatively secure. The equipment we carried was a compilation of very sensitive electronic instruments that allowed the Commanding General (CG) to maintain his expeditionary operations center. From this center the CG orchestrated and monitored all efforts made by Marines while remaining connected to other Coalition elements. Much of this was composed of high-tech gear that allowed him to communicate with his Generals and senior officers in the field while also processing huge streams of intelligence data. The last thing we wanted to do during these convoys was expose it to an unsecured environment and run the risk of having an RPG take it or any part of it out of commission.

Moving out was a massive undertaking. It included over 100 vehicles and a few hundred Marines. The preparatory briefs informed us that we would be passing some areas that were lightly populated so we were forewarned on the rules of engagement. I'd learned that we had some US AID Meals Ready to Eat (MRE) in the camp but since we were low on space it was rumored that we

Chaplains go soon to
check out Rumors –

may have to leave the pallets behind and resort to sending some vehicles back at a later time to pick them up, if at all. I discussed this issue with the I MEF Headquarters Group Commanding Officer, Colonel John Cunnings, who confirmed the rumor. I then proposed that we break the pallet and hand out the MRE packets to each of the Marines in the vehicles. This saved space and it would encourage the Marines to share them with the local children as we drove through areas in need. The Colonel thought it was a good idea and made it happen.

The drive initially lacked any character. The desert lay before us apparently void of any life or color. As the sun rose in the sky the more uncomfortable we became inside the confined spaces of the Humvee. Like frogs in a boiling pot, we slowly assimilated to a certain temperature tolerance point with our flak jackets, long-sleeved shirts, gloves, and helmets. Assimilation or not, there comes a point when you realize it's just downright hot and miserable. I wanted to open my mouth wide to gasp for air but to do so would be to invite more sand and dust into my system. I, like others, was convinced that if I would ever die out here my body would pour out sand during the first cut of an autopsy. Everyone was equipped with at least two bottled waters and we would make frequent stops to permit the troops to refill their water bottles, canteens, and camelbacks with water from the waterbulls[1] we pulled along. After a few hours on the open desert road, the waterbulls were no longer respites of cool water but instead they were filled with water hot enough to make tepid coffee.

In the late afternoon we crossed a small bridge and pulled into an area that opened up into a vast valley with a wide-open expanse on either side of us. At quick glance it just looked like more open, empty desert. Closer scrutiny revealed that throughout the open expanse of desert on both sides of the road there were small mud huts placed throughout the scenery. The road before us was as straight as I've ever seen a road leading directly into the horizon and over the edge of the world. To our left and to our right the open expanse was briefly given to change in character by what appeared to be cuts into the dirt and thus gave it the appearance of multiple layers in certain locations.

46

When our first trucks pulled across the remaining section of the blown-out bridge into this open road, we noticed a few families waiting by the intersection. They were dressed in the usual manner we had expected to see here in Iraq but they were covered in white dust. Our vehicles slowed down as we went past them and the children darted away from the sides of their parents and began to run alongside our vehicles yelling, "GI, American GI."

They took their fingers and partially brought them together in the way you prepare to handle a spoon or fork and then they would motion their hands toward their mouths — the nonverbal sign for food. Some children were more aggressive and came right up to our vehicles reaching in with open hands and frowning eyes.

The convoy was not allowed to stop, it was a security issue, but I noticed that we slowed down significantly enough to allow the children to jog alongside. A closer look at these children revealed sun-parched, dust-laden, hungry children. Their eyes screamed for mercy and their gestures begged for anything. These were Iraq's poor; probably the poorest of poor, most likely Shiites pushed into the wastelands of the south.

Their circumstances remind us of the reality we Americans so oft forget that is commonplace throughout the world. "There are currently 1.3 billion people in the world (22% of the world's population) currently living below the poverty line, 841 million souls are malnourished, and 880 million are without access to medical care. One billion people lack adequate shelter, 1.3 billion have no access to safe drinking water, and 2.6 billion go without sanitation. Among the children of the world, 150 million are malnourished. Each day 30,000 will die of preventable diseases."[2]

The Navy and Marine Corps have taken me places I would never have dreamed of visiting on my own. These trips have exposed me to some of the poorest places in the world. My life in the South Bronx in New York City was filled with gang and drug-infested neighborhoods where in all honesty I saw more corpses as a child growing up in the Bronx from gang warfare and drug deaths than I saw during Desert Storm in 1991. I was referred to as the city's poor but poor was such a relative term. I was poor in comparison to the very wealthy but compared to those in the South

Bronx at the time I was like everyone else around me. The term seemed irrelevant. We never went without food, though sometimes the best my mother could muster was white rice and an egg. The fact remained — we didn't go hungry. When all else failed, there were always free lunches and government cheese to obtain. Every year I received my one pair of Pro-Keds right before school began and a new pair of jeans. My dad had been a migrant worker from Puerto Rico in the late 1950s and counted himself fortunate to have a steady job loading trucks. He would leave 25 cents for each of us at least twice a week, which afforded us the great treat of a small brown paper bag full of penny and nickel candy from a local candy store, so life was good. In comparison to the 1.3 billion people in the world living below the poverty line, I had it very good.

The issue of poverty didn't become an issue for me until I went to high school in Midtown Manhattan. I tested and was accepted to the High School of Art & Design on 57th Street and Second Avenue just blocks away from the United Nations building. I took the subway every morning from the Bronx into Manhattan and it was then that I became very self-conscious of what I didn't have. When I compared myself to my neighbors in the Bronx there was no issue but when I entered the gates of the high school I knew I was in a different world. Midtown Manhattan was a world of Mercedes Benz, BMWs, and Rolls Royces. My world, on the other hand, was one of Chevy Impalas, Ford Pintos, and Falcons. My dress wasn't tattered in any way but it didn't match the modern styles of the creative and wealthier students around me. Truth be told, no one said anything to me about how I looked but that was exactly the problem — there weren't too many people to talk to in a tenth grade class of 1,200 students. I found a handful of other Puerto Rican and black students from the Bronx and they became my associates. In my ignorance I associated their economic wealth with their race and presumed that to be white meant you were wealthier. The reality was that I didn't take the time while in school to realize that some of the white students came from other parts of the city that suffered my same reality. I had a few white students who reached out. We were project buddies but unfortunately the deep friendships that are characterized to be so crucial and popular

48

in American movies during these high school years were not my reality. In retrospect, this was due to my own unrecognized racism, insecurity, and naïveté.

I developed a dual personality — at home and on the block I was laid back and comfortable. I enjoyed my friends and I was very much the diplomat, interacting amongst the many cliques and gangs in the neighborhood. In school, it was another story. I resented their wealth, their whiteness, and their privilege. In my mind it wasn't about race or racism it was about stature, wealth, and accessibility to resources. I was angry, reserved, and I worked hard at maintaining my distance. A part of me was ashamed. I got tired of making excuses for not having the proper art supplies. I grew to resent my parents for not having more. I went to work after school at age sixteen, determined to feel better but instead I grew isolated. In the end I became poor.

I grew to believe that my lack of fiscal resources somehow affected the character of who I was as a person. I began to feel less valued and became less invested. I grew angrier and angrier in those years and turned the anger inward. I became poor when I ceased to believe in myself, poor when I failed to trust in others, and poor when I lost my vision and hope. I interpreted not having a few bucks in my pocket and a few art tools as being sure signs of poverty but the true poverty lay in the emptiness of my soul, which I filled instead with anger.

I've had the blessing since then to travel around a great part of the world and I have seen places off the beaten path. I've learned that poverty is not restricted to any particular race. I've since discovered poverty in our backyard in the US outside of black and Latino neighborhoods. I've learn that in this world there are some people who are in deep poverty but their spirits cannot be crushed, and they walk this earth with a great sense of purpose and dignity. I've also seen a few who have been blessed with the riches of modern society with access to relative wealth; yet they walk in despair and alone — in poverty of spirit, a poverty of their own making. Here in Iraq I saw what I have not seen thus far in any other country I've visited in the past. I saw a population of people who lived in dire poverty and were wrestling with despair and losing the match.

They were severely poor in wealth and spirit. These people in the south were the first I've ever seen that walked with faces that lacked emotion, vibrancy, or hope. Even the children begged with a deep sadness and rarely smiled.

The truck in front of me was a new seven-ton truck with an open flatbed loaded down with gear and half a dozen Marines. Without hesitation, these Marines began to toss the yellow packets of meals off to the side of the road kicking up a cloud of dust upon impact. The children began to yell in gratitude and wrestled one another for the food.

Somehow, someway, the word was transmitted and as we moved forward I noticed that from the far reaches of the expansive desert more children began to emerge from those mud huts two and three football fields away. It was quite the sight to see them screaming, waving their arms, and running frantically toward the road clamoring not to be left without a gift.

Everyone in my Humvee had three yellow MRE packets each and we donated those quite quickly. When we noticed that more children were coming out of the desert we pulled out our own military MRE packets and began to distribute the tan packets. I had a small boy with big brown eyes and dark wavy hair matted to his skull with white desert dust wearing a knitted blue shirt run alongside and begged for water. He reminded me so much of my own son when he was six that I parted with reason and good judgment and gave him my cool water bottle.

It didn't take very long for the children to be in our rearview mirrors and we faced many more hours ahead. As the hours passed, the heat dissipated but hunger and thirst began to set in and we all sat quietly in the vehicle sharing the only food we had left between us — a bag of sunflower seeds preserved by the First Sergeant. To my amazement, I later discovered that this was not only true of us but it was a condition shared throughout the convoy. The vast majority of the troops gave everything they had — US AID meal packets, military packets, candy, snacks, and their water bottles. Without any fanfare, everyone gave everything they had while knowingly facing the remaining hours of the trip with little food and hot water in our waterbulls.

I Don't think so

On the quiet drive back to our next jump point I thought of the
irony of our circumstances in that the richest nation in the world
has committed its military to fight this war on behalf of some of
the poorest, most isolated, and abused people in the world. By far,
every Marine and Sailor, regardless of their social stature back in
the United States, is vastly wealthier in comparison to the average
Iraqi, especially these Shiites who lived in the southern desert. The
quiet reality was that scenes like this were repeated often throughout the landscape of Iraq but went unnoticed by the people in the
US. I hope that someday as Iraqis reflect on their experience and
recall moments like this that they may ask, "What compels a per-   *— Oil*
son who lives in relative comfort by world standards to leave behind their families, comfortable homes, and the relative safety of
their neighborhoods to travel around the world and endure sleep-
less nights, long hours in intense heat, and expose themselves to
such dangers as insurgent attacks, an improvised explosive device
(IED), or snipers in the name of freedom?"

I believe there are a few things that compel us. The first is
hope. We may be seen by some in this world as being arrogant or
compulsive but more than anything else they see us as naive because of the hope we carry deep within us. We truly believe that
giving people proper dignity and respect will ignite deep within
them a flame that will allow them to see a tomorrow of possibilities. The rags-to-riches account is not a story but an ethic weaved
into the American fabric of who we are as a people. Faith is yet
another factor. Though Americans may not be tremendously religious, we see ourselves as people of faith. We believe in a faith
that is personal, progressive, and life-changing. Compassion is another characteristic I hope they conclude compels us as a nation. It
has been my experience that we can be extremely self-absorbed as
a people but when we find ourselves face-to-face with genuine
needs we don't turn to others to meet the needs we observe; we
take the time to fill the need. We feel the need to fill the need because we believe in the sanctity of life and the rights endowed to
that life by God.

In the big scheme of things, I do hope that these small acts of
love and care genuinely exhibited by the most ordinary, young,

committed Americans shall have a lasting impact and thus super-
sede the violence and prejudice they've come to know as an ordinary part of their everyday existence in this hell on earth called
Iraq.

---

1. The M149 Water Trailer can carry 400 gallons of potable water. It is commonly referred to as a "Waterbull."

2. Right Reverend John Bryson Chane, Bishop of Washington, Diocese of Washington, Episcopal Church, Easter Sunday sermon at the Washington National
Cathedral, April 20, 2003.

Chapter Four

Baghdad Road

The Lord your God has blessed you in all the work of your hands. He has watched over your journey through this vast desert ... God has been with you, and you have not lacked anything. — Deuteronomy 2:7

Officially Baghdad fell into Coalition hands on April 5, 2003. Elements of the 1st Marine Division were well inside the city and rumors poured back to our location of discovered torture chambers and child prisons within the city. A week later, the focus shifted to Tikrit, the hometown of Saddam Hussein where pockets of resistance were reported to be most prevalent as Saddam Hussein loyalists held on to nostalgic notions.

Numeniya is about ninety miles southeast of Baghdad and where I MEF and many of its logistics elements staged themselves in direct support of the engaged units in and around the ring of Baghdad. For me, those weeks passed by dreadfully slow. In sharp contrast to my days in Desert Storm where we were constantly on the move and enjoyed a second row seat in the fight into Kuwait City, this time we were a little further back in the fight. The role of the headquarters unit at the MEF level is about strategy, orchestrating the execution, and managing resources. The "pointy end of the spear," as Marines refer to it, belonged to the combat arms like the mechanized infantry, artillery, armor, and combat engineers. In the air it was the helicopter pilots that got in close and those fast attack jets coming down to provide close air support. The vast majority of the rest of us were the supporting arms of the combat elements — a key and necessary element to the fight but nonetheless it was a little less sexy and a little further to the rear.

It should be noted that being in support of the combat arms does not necessarily correlate with safety. Modern warfare is about maneuver agility, the ability to identify the enemy's center of gravity, and maneuvering around to hit it directly at its weakest point.

In many cases, this means that the infantry attempts to find the enemy's center of gravity — its weakest or most crucial point — and then plows through and delivers a severe blowing punch. The momentum continues as the advancing forces attempt to "bite off the snake's head." In pressing forward so quickly it is not uncommon to create disenfranchised units along the way. These enemy units are often disconnected from its headquarters and disoriented. These same units are left in disarray and can end up along our flanks as we proceed behind the infantry.

In Desert Storm, this blow was delivered so dramatically and intensely that it completely demoralized the Iraqi soldiers causing many of these disoriented units to surrender en masse. I recall an incident just north of the Al-Wafra burning oil fields in Kuwait where our forces were moving from south to north. In an attempt to marry up with another element of our unit we attempted to travel independently in a two-vehicle convoy moving west to east. The winds had shifted and the heavy smoke from the oil fields obscured our vision. We couldn't see a thing so it didn't take long before we realized we were disoriented — actually lost. In our quest we discovered a small building connected to a tall tower and an adjacent parking lot. We pulled off the road into the parking lot and attempted to get our bearings. The forces just ahead of us moved on deeper into the dark smoke. We thought we had properly identified the road in front of the building on our map so we jumped back into our Humvee to continue our search. We drove down the road around 1.5 miles when we realized we were heading the wrong way on the map. We turned the vehicles around and headed back toward the building with the tower.

As we approached the small parking lot we noticed a great deal of commotion — there were about five Humvees and thirty Marines surrounding the building. We saw about twenty Iraqi soldiers walk out of the small building with their hands up in the air and lowering themselves onto their knees in the parking lot. I turned to RPSN Thompson and looked at him with utter astonishment. Had all of these soldiers been inside the building while we stopped to look at our directions? I wondered how many AK-47 rifles were pointed at our backs just waiting for us to take a step toward the

54

building or perhaps they were waiting patiently inside for someone to open the door and capture them so they wouldn't run the risk of being shot.

The young Marine lieutenant sat in the passenger side of his Humvee, stroked his side-mounted M60 machine gun, and informed us with a heavy Bostonian accent that they had just arrived and secured the area. In fact he must have concluded right away that we were very lost since somehow we managed to get in front of this infantry sweep for just a short while. He pointed us in the right direction and we sheepishly found our convoy just a few kilometers away, safely parked waiting for the area ahead to be cleared. To this day I often wonder if I would be able to recount these events if it weren't for the fact that the Iraqis were beaten to surrender in the early hours of the war.

This, however, proved not to be the case this time around. In Iraq, this time around, there were many reports of Iraqi troops feigning to surrender in order to get our troops to lower their defenses and then attempt a counterattack. The new mode of operandi for the vast majority of the military was to dissolve into the general public and hide underground. Some delivered attacks against our forces through local militias feeding the insurgency while others disappeared.

While all of this was going on I sat in a camp in An Numeniya and listened to debriefs. I spoke with a few Marines who were evacuated to the local hospital and chatted with those who would transit from Numeniya to other points in the area.

It was in Numeniya where I was approached by 1st Lieutenant Jacob Berry who asked if I happened to have any additional supplies that I could share with children or an extra blanket for a guest in our camp. I wasn't quite sure of his intent and he was pretty secretive but I complied. I had anticipated some interaction with children so I carried a box of colored pencils and a coloring book that my wife, Wanda, had provided for me. I also had a couple of extra "poncho liners" that were light camouflaged blankets for those cold desert nights. I handed all of the extra supplies over to Lieutenant Berry and figured I'd never see them again. A few days later he returned with my poncho liners and informed me that the guests we had been keeping so secretively in the camp were rumored to be the family that provided information that led to the rescue of Private Jessica Lynch. Later research revealed this to be Mohammed Odeh al-Rehaif along with his wife and five-year-old daughter who were later granted humanitarian asylum to the United States by April 28, 2003. It's amazing to realize that out here everyone does their part as best as they can and in the outplaying of life sometimes we intersect with historical events or people totally unbeknownst to us at the time.

With all that had happened in the month since the war kicked off, Easter week was upon us before I knew it. Palm Sunday services in our camp were well attended in a large tent that doubled as the chow hall. We invited Chaplain Gwudz, the Roman Catholic priest, to accompany us and we visited some of the wounded at a local field hospital down the road from our camp and provided Palm Sunday services to a group of Combat Engineers charged with laying an expeditionary bridge across a short expanse of the Tigris River just north of An Numeniya. In the spirit of Palm Sunday, Father Gwudz asked if it would be possible to gather a few palm branches from the local area. The Combat Engineers sent out a formal working party that pulled palm branches off some Iraqi palm grove and donated what seemed to be hundreds of palms for each of the Christian services held that morning. With palms in hand we headed out to the bridge site. Upon arrival to this forward position, the Roman Catholics gathered under a tree and we Protestant Christians went down by the river and held services on the bridge expanse itself. We engaged in our rituals of singing, praying, reading from the Bible, and sharing communion when I noticed a crowd of about twenty Iraqis standing quietly by the banks of the river observing us. As I spoke of the triumphant entry of Jesus into Jerusalem and his quest to enter our lives, I wondered then, as I did many a time during this deployment, what the observing Iraqis thought of our entry into their lives.

In the days to follow, the Marines began to pour out of Baghdad and move south while other Coalition Forces took their places throughout the city and in nearby provinces. The V Army Corps

56

moved into the Baghdad International Airport representing the senior Coalition Headquarters in Iraq. The Army now owned Baghdad and its V Army Corps was the senior military command. Chaplain Gwudz, the Roman Catholic priest who accompanied us to the river, was the highest-ranking chaplain in I Marine Expeditionary Force and I served as his Deputy Force Chaplain. In an attempt to coordinate efforts and establish an open channel of communication between the chaplains in the two highest echelons of command in the theater, we decided it would be appropriate to take a trip north to meet with Chaplain Douglas L. Carver, a Southern Baptist pastor serving as the V Army Corps Chaplain.

The trip north was a routine trip. We readied ourselves to head north in our two unarmored Humvees while escorted by members of 1st Force Reconnaissance in two of their Improved Fast Attack Vehicles. These are Mercedes Benz 4x4 off-road vehicles modified for the Marine Corps' Force Recon teams. They look like mini-SUVs on heavy testosterone. They were equipped with an M2-.50 caliber machine gun mounted directly behind the driver and passenger, a M240G 7.62 mm machine gun on a swivel rack sticking out of the front passenger's side. The vehicle was designed for three combatants. Those of us old enough to remember the early days of television in the '60s could not help but recall scenes of *Rat Patrol* when looking at these warriors. Unlike the rest of us equipped with the standard-issue Kevlar helmets and Interceptor Flak jackets these guys looked like a cross between a Harley biker and a dusty Starship Trooper with specially fitted helmets, goggles, pistols, and carbine rifles strapped to their frames. Their very presence added a major intimidation factor to our convoy that we were quite happy to have on our side.

Force Recon Marines are the "crème de la crème" in the eyes of many Marines. They carry the latest in technology, are trained to engage independently, and trained to be self-sufficient while being highly expeditionary. They have a solid reputation for being physically fit and highly professional. They are the eyes and ears of the Marine Corps and answer to the call for those highly specialized, low-density, high-demand operations. During our time in An Nasiriyah and An Numeniya, a few of them shared with me

57

that they were feeling pretty frustrated because they felt the war was passing them by. The gripes of a modern-day warrior for not getting enough of the fight were probably not too unfamiliarly similar to the complaints of a Spartan or a Roman Centurion on garrison duty in ages past. They noted, in frustration, that they were being utilized more as a reactionary force for the MEF Headquarters than as the over-the-horizon force they were trained to be.

"On the conventional or 'Green' side, the [recon] mission is to conduct Amphibious Reconnaissance, Deep Ground Reconnaissance, Battlespace Shaping, and surveillance to observe, identify, and report enemy activity. They conduct specialized terrain reconnaissance that includes hydrography, beaches, roads, bridges, routes, urban areas, helicopter landing zones (HLZ), airborne drop zones (DZ), and aircraft forward operating sites."[1] Yet to their dismay, while 1st Marine Division pulled far ahead of us and kinetically engaged the enemy some of Force Recon Marines sat out these fights during the initial stages of the war. The reality was that I didn't possess enough information to know whether this was a sudden doctrinal change, circumstantial adaptation, or simply the perception of a few anxious and very competitive Marines who desired to get in and see more of the fight. Regardless of the reason, the truth was that their perception interpreted this as very real and it led them to open frustration. In the face of this I marveled at these young Americans. The media seems to so often find the handful of soldiers who are very willing to express their dislike of the arduous and harsh conditions of the desert and of war, but here, the quiet reality is that morale suffers not because of the harshness of circumstances but the lack of it, the lack of engagement, and the fear that they will not get an opportunity to employ a profession that has demanded so much of them. When we asked for an escort north into the Baghdad International Airport compound we anticipated they wouldn't be too excited about babysitting two chaplains' vehicles on a routine mission but fortunately, contrary to our thoughts, they were happy to do it.

The journey north by northwest to the airport allowed us the opportunity to catch a glimpse of life outside and in Baghdad. The central region of Iraq is dramatically different from the open, endless, and dry expanse of the dusty south. The central region of Iraq was brightly colored with the sudden onset of green acres of farmland accented with towering palm tree groves and the flowing waters of the Euphrates and Tigris rivers. It became very clear that we were now at the very beginning of the Fertile Crescent's eastern border.

This was the ancient land of Abraham. He was known as Abram during the days of his travel through this region. Terah, Abraham's father, buried his son, Haran (Abraham's brother), in Ur of the Chaldeans, which is just north of modern Basra. Following the burial of Haran, the family headed north from Ur through the Fertile Crescent, probably through these very same rich lands in between the Euphrates and Tigris rivers, to a place called Haran in the far north. Today it lies in the approximate vicinity of modern day Jerabulus in Turkey. Terah died in Haran and it was there that Abraham received the call from God recorded in Genesis 12, and began a venture with his family and nephew, Lot.

> *The Lord had said to Abram, "Leave your country, your people and your father's household and go to the land I will show you ... So Abram left, as the Lord had told him; and Lot went with him. Abram was seventy-five years old when he set out from Haran."*
> — Genesis 12:1, 4 (NASB)

I often wondered what Abraham and his family might have seen 4,200 years ago compared to what is seen today. I imagine the terrain was not much different. The barren, open desert surrounded the respite laden narrow passageway of life nestled within the Fertile Crescent back then as it does today. I can imagine how the ancient Bedouins and travelers slowly trekked in caravans from the south to the north for weeks on end enduring the harshness of the dry desert and then suddenly coming to a place where life, represented in the green of vegetation, emerged so richly. I can see why an oasis would seem like an incredulous reality after having been deprived of color by the paleness of the brown chalky desert and the blinding reflection of the blaring sun. For those in the respite care of the Fertile Crescent, the desert sits out over the horizon in a foreboding fashion, serving as a constant testament of the dangers and harshness of life. Occasionally the power of the desert encroaches upon the peace found in the fields nourished by the rivers when the desert blows its sands with great force, temporarily blinding all life with the sting of its sailing sand as to remind us that we are never out of its gripping reach in this corner of the world.

This jaunt from An Numeniya exposed us to the gradual changes in clime, scenery, and living conditions in this region. In the initial pull out from our compound we passed hundreds of trucks, trailers, and logistics equipment. In a matter of days we turned this small farm area into a major military complex. In that short time, the little bit of green grass that had managed to survive this winter season had been crushed under the weight of heavy machinery and thousands of boots. The grass had perished and given way to white dust and sand that was easily blown about by the slightest breeze. Our massive presence in this serene area dwarfed the small village nearby and almost fooled us into feeling like we were back home in one of our large military bases except for the fact that at home we don't have the backdrop of Iraqi farmhouses nor the encroaching desert dust at our feet.

The first real indication of being outside the protection of a massive compound was the presence of our Marines at improvised checkpoints leading in and out of the base. Within the periphery of the checkpoint, Marines had carved out defensive observation posts in the soil, providing strategic vantage points intended to oversee the sentry's station. The sentries, sometimes two or three junior enlisted, normally stood in the middle of the road protected solely by strands of rolled barbed wire. Heavy machine guns were posted a few yards away in those discreetly placed observation posts providing the sentries with protective cover as they assessed the threat of oncoming traffic.

The Commanding General of the 1st Marine Division, Major General James N. Mattis, referred to this practice of redundant protection as "Guardian Angel." He emphatically called for an overlapping system of protective "over-watch" where Marines who appeared to the general public to be clearly exposed would in fact find themselves deep within a field of readily available firepower. This concept did two things, it provided over-watch security that allowed firepower to be accessible in defense of the more exposed sentries and it provided the exposed Marines with a sense of confidence that they in fact were not alone or arbitrarily endangered. Marines always talk of how they "take care of their own" and in this process it was tangibly clear. Marines were charged with literally watching another Marines' back. The name was quite *apropo*.

A few yards down from the sentry stood a gaggle of young Iraqi men dressed in western clothing waving their hands wildly at passing vehicles with wares in their hands. I instinctively noticed right away their house slippers and dusty, clay-laden feet as they attempted to sell their merchandise. Ordinarily this would not be what I would take notice of initially but in my conversations with Marines they shared that at times this was a way of being able to identify former Iraqi soldiers blending within the local populace. Evidently, according to some of the accounts, former soldiers or Fedayeen militia had been identified through their footwear. Most Iraqis wore sandals as it facilitated their need to remove their shoes during prayer, and it complimented their traditional or western dress but former soldiers held on to their boots. As we drew closer, I was surprised to discover that these men were selling bottles of whiskey and cigarettes! I turned to my driver and exclaimed my disbelief, "I thought this was a Muslim country?! Where did they get alcohol?" RP2 Stephens kept his eyes on the road but could only give me a laugh in the face of my incredulity and naiveté.

The road carried us to what appeared to be a small village center. The ground was heavily littered with brass casings and couplings from the use of heavy machine gun rounds. The brass caught rays of the sun and glistened against the road's black, dull asphalt and from within the green weeds that held their ground on the sidelines. The intersection was flanked by small buildings marked with holes and chips carved into their sides by the recent onslaught of gunfire. We drove through the intersection in silence as we attempted to picture the events that occurred here. The Humvee climbed onto a small overpass that revealed a part of the village center below us. Strewn to the side, in almost pristine condition, stood what appeared to be an abandoned Iraqi T-55 Soviet-era main battle tank that escaped damage. Across the street were the carcasses of a few cars that were dealt a very different fate for they had burned to the ground. The entire village center resembled a ghost town standing as a testament to a battle long passed.

I had forgotten from my experience in Desert Storm how much litter we leave behind in combat. No one is preoccupied with carrying plastic tote trash bags in the limited space we have in our tactical vehicles so we discard everything by the roadside. When vehicles meet their violent demise they explode their insides onto the road for all to trample. When weapons are fired and casings ejected from the sides of rifles, pistols, or heavy machine guns we are not followed by an army of sweepers collecting our discarded deposits. Yet I could not overlook that the greatest evidence revealing the past presence of our forces in this town were the hundreds of small, green plastic bags that carry the main course within our Meals Ready to Eat (MRE). The MRE containers, the wrappers of the beloved CHARMS® candies, and the discarded cardboard boxes that carry the MREs lay on the streets in the way that strips of paper gently blow about following a Times Square ticker tape parade.

We rolled gently by with the small village behind us and I wondered if our trip to Baghdad would be comprised of town after destroyed town. I also noticed the absence of people and wondered where all the people had gone. Our four vehicles pulled onto a major road and it didn't take long for the scenery to change. Small homes began to dot the landscape amidst the open fields. Soon thereafter a few dispersed homes gave way to small pockets of communities. Not unlike many of the other Third World countries I've visited in the past the homes were simple and practical. By US standards they could easily be classified as low income but here this was definitely a major climb on the economic ladder compared to the mud huts we had seen weeks earlier. Some of the homes even had concrete walls fencing them off from the road and their neighbors. With the increase in frequency of homes came an increase in the density of people along with a widening spectrum on the designs of homes. We would pass home after home revealing a lifestyle of deep humility and then suddenly there would be the home with deep vibrant colors, large windows, satellite dish, and the BMW in the driveway guarded by a large concrete fence. Intermixed within the homes were fields of green vegetation, groves of palm trees, and tributaries extending out from the Tigris River.

Emergent vibrancy best described the increase in activity as we drove deeper into the north. Men were dressed in their *dishdasha* — long-sleeved, white cotton shirts that extend down to their ankles — commonly referred to by Marines as "man dresses," and would gather by the road in groups of five or six evidently just socializing. This seemed like a very frequent sight. They would gather by the roadside and in some villages or towns they would erect a little tent cover or set up some chairs and mingle around with one another. Meanwhile it was not uncommon to see the women, covered from head to toe in their *abayahs*, carrying large tubs of water or huge piles of kindling wood on their backs while being tugged at by three or four children. I never once during that trip saw women leisurely hanging around anywhere in one of these small towns or villages. Each woman I saw was gainfully employed in some form of physical labor while burdened with the care of small children.

I can't say that this was a definitive description of life in Iraq because nothing was normal during those days. I surmised that perhaps a rationale for this very blatant inequity in the division of labor was probably due to the fact that the local governments had been beheaded and many of these men had nowhere to go for employment as a result of the war. The war may have freed them from the grips of Saddam Hussein but for many it had also released them of the mutual obligation demanded by employment. Merchants who owned their own shops were seen regularly but, if the vast majority of the community's income had been severed, how busy or how successful could they have possibly been?

The density of the population was quickly increasing. We prepared to enter a town whose center was marked similarly to that of an old town in the Old West. A road would wind itself from the open range into a street that ran down the middle of town flanked by shops on both sides. From one end of town you could see the other end, followed by open country shortly thereafter. The buildings on both sides of the town were no more than two-stories tall, garnered with small shops where women in their *abayahs* leisurely reviewed the merchandise. Just short of the town's limits, preceding the "main drag," there sat the blown-out carcasses of T-55 Soviet tanks evidently caught in the sights of a Hellfire missile. One of the heavy turrets laid upside down about thirty feet behind its tank with a spattered shadow created by intensely burning fuel highlighting its solitude. If there was anyone inside when that missile hit they were surely disintegrated with the explosion and the searing heat. We passed a large field to our left that was littered with about half dozen artillery pieces, a sure sign of the last stand for an Iraqi artillery battery. Hulks of demolished Soviet *Boyevaya Mashina Pekhoty* or commonly referred to as BMPs, an armored personnel carrier utilized by the Iraqis to transport troops, trashed the middle of the road. To the untrained eye, this all seemed like a littered junkyard but in the midst of all this steel garbage stood an abandoned Amphibious Assault Vehicle facing north while all the others faced south. The vehicle was still recognizable but its side had been peeled back and it seemed like a T-55 or some artillery piece got a direct hit on it. It was the first piece of American armor I had seen, both in Desert Storm and OIF that had been destroyed by enemy fire. Uniquely American trash lay in a splash pattern behind it and I wondered if our Marines escaped the deadly blast or if they perished on this fortified road to this dinky little town up ahead.

Chaplains make a very conscientious effort to be a living moral compass in the midst of tragedy such as war. Some people confronted with facing the horrific realities of war are tempted to compartmentalize it and push it down into the caverns of their souls only to deal with it later. The vast majority will conscientiously grant themselves permission to do their jobs in combat because they willingly subject themselves to the authorities over them, predominantly the state or nation undergirded by a conviction that what they're doing is legal. They push forward while attempting to reconcile their actions with the tenets of a higher moral imperative and though uncomfortable they conclude it is a necessary sacrifice

64

that must be executed for the greater good of humanity. It is a very conscientious and intentional process. It is an act of obedience and loyalty to the state where we sacrifice our will for the will of the nation. Such subjugation does not imply an absence of ethics or moral responsibility but it rests on a mutual trust between the soldier and nation to serve one another while not compromising higher ethical values binding them to one another, the world community, and their theological or worldview framework.

Then there is that very small minority who, out of emotional or intellectual immaturity, lazily commit themselves to the rigors of combat with little conviction or thought. This allows the events and emotions of the time to overwhelm them, granting them permission to perform actions fueled by anger or hatred instead of principles, training, and discipline. In theory, if we seek to comprehend the level of intensity, emotion, and grief encountered in the playing fields of war, normally under unimaginable circumstances, we might be tempted to empathize. However, but in the face of justice, a professional ethic, and moral imperative we must still yet conclude that such actions are unjustifiable and inexcusable.

Soldiers stand on moral high ground in combat only when they act accordingly to the standards of moral law, when they are commissioned by a state under the rule of law, and they act professionally in accordance with the rules of war. "The nation expects its Army to adhere to the highest standards of professional conduct and to reflect the ideals of American values. The American people demand a high-quality Army that honors the core values of the Constitution it is sworn to uphold — a strong respect for the rule of law, human dignity, and individual rights."[2] A professional, by definition, is an individual who "conforms to the standards of skill, competence, or character normally expected of a properly qualified and experienced person in a work environment." By this definition, a professional holds a level of competency that informs their actions and character and as such is led to perform these actions intentionally, consciously, and with enough cognizance to anticipate the desired effects of such decisions while subjugated to a level of accountability. In the United States we have enjoyed a professional volunteer military since the end of the Vietnam War.

In the past thirty years, the military has further developed its tactics, doctrines, and even weaponry informed by such standards of professionalism. To serve today is to submit oneself to a certain ethic of conduct and to fully embrace that. Regardless of the circumstances, as professionals, we shall be held accountable for all actions. This becomes one way in which combat soldiers blemished by the violence of combat become redeemed morally, legally, and socially within the context of a civilized society that subjects itself to the rule of law and the pursuance of justice in a moral context where all human life is valuable and equal.

Chaplains are not present in combat to provide religious fervor or to provide justification for acts against human beings through the act of war. In my opinion, chaplains walk in the midst of combat troops to remind personnel of the overriding persistence and presence of a higher moral law represented in our culture through the image of God, while they may find themselves in what appears to be a hopeless and savage adulteration of life. I recall a Chaplain, CAPT Stan Beach, a highly decorated, wounded Vietnam veteran saying something to the effect of, "Chaplains serve to remind people of God's presence amongst them." It is our hope, as chaplains, that in the midst of the vilest of human conditions we not lose touch with the person, character, or understanding of God.

In peacetime, I often find myself walking into a conversation amongst Marines or Sailors, officers and enlisted, and they are engaged in a conversation that might make their own mothers blush. In the spirit of the conversation they engross themselves into the imagery and ridicule of the event but when they become conscious of my presence they are the ones to blush and apologize for their deviancy from general decency standards. In most cases, it's a matter of retelling a sordid joke or allowing an expletive to accentuate their language. But by the very mere presence of me standing there and wearing a cross on my collar I often invoke in them, without a word or nonverbal gesture from my part, an apology or recourse of action. Our very presence is a reminder of the holy — the holy according to their personal standards of faith.

In combat it is no different. In the midst of the wet monsoons, the heavy sandstorms, or the blood pools of our wounded, we find

*Can A person serve if
They believe all war is
Wrong.*

ourselves standing in their midst. Our presence is a silent reminder of the popular metaphor that God is not an absent landlord in the slums of life but an ever-present resource to be leaned upon, invited into relationship, and a reminder of the eminence of the laws that prevail over us. These laws do not exist to confine us or to deny us of free action but to protect us within parameters of reason and consciousness.

As a society, I believe we have come to terms with the fact that if one of our soldiers murders an innocent against the violations of the rules of engagement or the rules of war with intention to murder, then the blood of the murdered individual stains the hand of that soldier and that soldier becomes accountable to God. That soldier becomes accountable to the laws of our society and to the organization of the professional ethics he misrepresented and violated. However, I do believe that as a nation we have failed to come to terms, as a corporate body, with the concept that when a professional soldier acts on behalf of the state and properly kills human beings within the professional and ethical context of the law, then the blood of those combatants killed stains the fabric of our society and it is carried within the national psyche — becoming a shared burden. For this reason, when the legislative body of this country executes a decision that leads to war, such an act establishes the moral and legal framework that corporately accepts the burden of war on ourselves as a society and exculpates individuals unless they act contrary to professional standards. Unfortunately, this is an act of responsibility commonly embraced, rarely in times of victory. Moreover it is an act often used to accuse certain political parties with blame rather than an act of civil and ethical responsibility by our society as a people. Human life, regardless of how evil or threatening it may be, is still a life, and with its extermination comes a price and a burden that must be paid. It is a burden that we as a society can choose to bear under the right justifications. This burden is a right granted to nations in the realm of authority. It is not one that should be taken lightly or executed as a natural extension of public policy but only as a last recourse.

War, by definition, is never a good thing. It may be an honorable or necessary act, especially during those moments when men place themselves on the altar of self-sacrifice on behalf of their friends and their nation. Yet even in the face of such exceptional virtues; war is never good in itself. For this reason it is important to underline that chaplains cannot serve with integrity and be representative of the spiritual kingdom while serving as cheerleaders in the field of combat. It would be morally reprehensible if we used our position, representative of an affirming relationship between humanity and God, and attempted to translate that into a false affirmation of political goals. Some may criticize the reticence of chaplains to associate God's promises and assurances to the acts of this nation but, in my opinion, such reticence is an act of theological and moral responsibility and integrity. We are not here to make people feel good about what they are doing or to provide a stamp of approval on public policy or to establish a pseudo-militaristic religion supportive of government but to provide our troops — our congregation — with a fixed point of moral reference where they may be able to genuinely gauge where they stand morally and ethically in their relationship with God.

Officers on active duty live with a duality. They are expected to defend democratic principles but they cannot always enjoy the benefits of the same. Officers are expected to be non-partisan, to keep their political affiliations and leanings to themselves in order to preserve the integrity and loyalty of their service. Military members, as a corps of professionals, bear "true faith and allegiance" to the Constitution of the United States and not to any particular party. Therefore, as an officer, a chaplain is already bound to this principle. I contend that for chaplains it should go one step further, we are to remain faithful to the tenets of our faith as clergy representing a church and its doctrines. In the execution of these duties I believe that in order for a chaplain to be effective and to integrally serve as a pastor to all the members of their congregation in the ranks, religious and non-religious, chaplains should refrain from, and not be expected to endorse, any political affiliation or political agenda. If a chaplain desires to express such a correlation, there are plenty of venues outside of the uniform services where the chaplain can preach and express their opinions as a private citizen without compromising their role as an officer and a chaplain.

Does such a position then propose that chaplains not take sides or interpret the realities faced by personnel through their theological lenses? No, for this is why we seek the help of the clergy. Thomas Groome's shared praxis approach is a movement toward conscientization through critical reflection.[3] It calls for people of faith to interpret their realities by juxtaposing scripture, interpreted as the authoritative word of God, in their believer's lives, to the circumstances and decisions in their lives. It is a form of very practical theology. Through this process we hold on to what we believe and challenge ourselves to live up to the standards of such faith. Karl Barth asserted that in order to be relevant and effective the clergy should preach with the Bible in one hand and the daily newspaper in the other.[4] Relevancy in this environment is crucial.

In the days leading toward war, while we were still in Kuwait, a brand new chaplain attached to a frontline artillery unit was dispatched to Camp Commando. The Commanding Officer had determined him to be totally ineffective and dangerous to morale. The chaplain, overridden by fear, would not leave his tent. He made his tent a place of refuge for himself and would not engage with any of the Marines preparing to cross into Iraq in a matter of days. In place of being an icon for hope he became one for fear. In an attempt to mentor the junior chaplain I questioned him and he made the remark, "I joined the Navy so I could preach the gospel ... I just want to preach, not go to war." I attempted to pastorally respond and yet remind him of our unusual role so I retorted with, "If you don't walk with them, live with them, and suffer with them, then with what credible authority can you come to share with them?"

Our relevancy as clergy, in uniform and out of uniform, is rooted in that we have walked with the people and having endured with them. In that journey with our people we can then point to places and times where God intersects with us in the journey. We are not present to speak of the unknown distant God but called to walk with the masses so we can model, in our state of imperfection, how to relate to the ever-present God who promised to walk with us until the end of the ages. Chaplains and pastors alike are the leaders of the very visible and present church and as such we are called to serve by example through a life of prayer, a walk

69

inspired in scripture, a countenance of faith, and a commitment to service. Even to those who profess no religious belief chaplains hope to serve as a reminder of that which is moral and ethical in our society. Our desire is to serve as an icon that points toward the spiritual value of humanity.

I reminded myself of this truth as I turned my thoughts to the carcass of the American Amphibious Assault Vehicle and realized how moved I was to sadness over the fate of the dozen or so Marines that might have been in the AAV, yet while I gazed earlier at the mass destruction of the many Iraqi vehicles on the road, not once did I contemplate the worth of their lives. Not once did I consider the possibility that these ill-fated soldiers met their deaths due to compulsory orders by their seniors while yet not desiring to be there nor did I consider the ramification of such loss to their families. As a man who represents God, I sat there convicted in spirit as I realized my own prejudice, the insensitivity in my heart and the lack of compassion. As a representative of God, I have to remind myself that I am a member of the kingdom of God that knows no earth defined borders or nationalities. I serve as a chaplain and I am loyal to the oath I took to my beloved nation, but I have to balance that with my kinship to humanity and my loyalty to God who is God over all of creation.

In our travels north I wondered how others were processing this as they drove by the physical testament to death that was spread around us. I imagine that those who were manning machine guns on the recon vehicles were probably a little more concerned with identifying threatening targets along the sidewalks and in the fields than they were concerned with contemplating the meaning of such devastation. Often the urgency of events overwhelms us and it keeps us from being able to reflect on such matters. By the same token, I don't think it is appropriate to dwell endlessly in the carnage and attempt to philosophically answer the meaning of life while engaged in combat operations. I believe most of us find a healthy balance in the middle where we focus on what needs to be done, execute what needs to be accomplished, and slowly grapple with the issues of the heart and mind little by little each day.

The greatest mistake people often make is to conclude that their experience and impressions represent some definition of objective truth. But the reality is quite different. Two people can be standing side by side during an experience such as this and experience the same stressors, the same hardships, and see the same things but what each one captures in their soul at any given time is determined not by the current course of events but by the eyes of their own heart.

The story is told of a young Marine and his fireteam enduring skirmish after skirmish with the enemy. They were engaging the enemy and stepping over human corpses. Everyone had learned to compartmentalize the events of the day. The team came upon the corpse of a dog and the young Marine was suddenly moved to emotion in an uncontrollable fashion. Everyone else saw the dog as well, but perhaps unlike the others, this Marine had a special bond with his dog back home. Perhaps the cruelty of war can be explained in the corpses of humans because they possessed the free will and understanding to remain in place and stand against a superior firepower, but a dog has no such faculties. A dog can symbolize for some, like a child for others, a symbol of purity and innocence. To see the corpse of that dog may, in fact, have brought that young Marine to tears as his emotions overflowed from within his self-imposed compartmentalized conceptions and brought him face-to-face with the realities of a harsh and violent context. Meanwhile, others treaded on unmoved or unimpressed by the rotting dog in the street.

There were fourteen of us on this convoy headed north into Baghdad. We were all present for the exact same journey but what each of us captured through sight, sounds, smell, and conscious varied very differently. The trek was the same but the experience was unique to each of us.

The further north we trekked, the narrower the streets became, and the feeling of relative safety of an open road that allowed distance between the local Iraqis and us dissipated quickly. With each passing moment, we were moving from small villages and farmlands to small towns, medium towns, and then the outskirts of the

71

city. The streets were becoming narrower and the crowds were closing in on us. I'd scanned the rooftops and alleys attempting to provide another set of eyes to assist in gauging our situational awareness. I would often notice people in houses two and three blocks away on rooftops or balconies and they would wave in our direction — I waved back, conveying two messages: I am friendly and I see you.

The route took us past a large bronze statue of Saddam Hussein that had half of his skull blown off and it dangled to the front of its tall twenty-foot pedestal by a few strands of rebar. There at its base stood a few Marines who stopped their convoy to snap a picture before the Saddam Hussein statue and capture victory for posterity's sake.

We pulled up into a busy street and the cars were backed up half a mile deep and about ten cars across. People were packed into this street like New Year's Eve on Times Square. This street led to a bridge that had been blown out and served as a major corridor across the river into Baghdad. Our vehicles were immediately surrounded by people. This was not good and I sure didn't feel like sitting in a vehicle in the middle of tens of thousands of frustrated Iraqis to provide someone a perfect target. I was getting a little nervous when I noticed the recon vehicle in front of us had begun to climb over the median, onto the sidewalk, pushing the crowds to the side, into the side corridor, back around the median, and forcing its way around the crowd. People saw the aggressive nature of the recon vehicle and got out of its way and we followed in suit. The Army had military police posted at the bridge controlling traffic. What a frustrating assignment that must have been. When they spotted us, they waved us through allowing us to cut ahead of the thousands in line. We sped onto the only lane on the bridge and entered Baghdad.

Once in Baghdad and moving toward the International Airport I was awestruck at how normal everyone seemed to be moving about. Baghdad was a relatively modern Third World city, a cross between Bangkok and Tijuana. It seemed like a normal day in Tijuana traffic with cars blowing their horns frantically while lodged in traffic circles. We worked our way through the city and onto the highway and once elevated on the freeway I noticed the true mark of the "Shock and Awe" campaign. Major government buildings remained as tall charred monuments to cruise missile strikes throughout the city. There were quite a few tall buildings that appeared to have imploded and the four outer walls of the building leaned against one another holding the tall and fragile structures in place.

I witnessed children walking in school uniforms and people dressed primarily in Western clothing who appeared to be on their way to work or moving about busily. Local souks and markets were open and there were old ladies with bags mingling before their stores. People looked at us, but unlike the Shiites in the south who greeted us with anticipation, here the looks were not so welcoming. The residents of Baghdad either stared at us as we drove by or simply refused to make any eye contact. If my memory recalls correctly, there were no smiles in Baghdad offered in return for our presence during that trip. I brought along a few MREs prepared to repeat my experience with the children in need but didn't see the need for any such distribution in the midst of this busy metropolis.

One of the things that I took notice of right away on this particular trip was the lack of US and other coalition military vehicles during those initial days. I expected a checkpoint at every major intersection or heavy patrols of Humvees moving slowly while patrolling the streets but instead what struck me most was the absence of such. There seemed to be no police, no army — theirs or ours. Every now and then we saw other Humvee convoys moving about in groups of three and four vehicles but they seemed to be passing through moving about smartly and quickly on the way to somewhere else — running through town as we were doing.

We arrived at the International Airport and began to look for the terminal where V Corps had located their personnel. We first passed the Very, Very Important People Terminal, then the Very Important People Terminal, and then I guess we were either at the Important People or the regular Joe Blow terminal because I lost track of the big blue signs. What confounded me most about these signs at the terminal was that they were in English. Why would

Saddam Hussein create VVIP and VIP terminals and have them posted in English with bold white lettering on a blue background? We reached V Corps and wandered through the empty airport terminal used for housing. We found Chaplain Carver and we enjoyed a time in church services with V Corps Headquarters' soldiers and then shared an MRE as we ironed out the business of the day while enjoying each other's fellowship. The fellowship with another chaplain was very good, even if he was an Army chaplain (tongue-in-cheek). The return trip a few hours later brought us back through the same route to An Numeniya and we breathed a sigh of relief when we saw the entrance to our camp that provided for us a relative sense of safety and a temporary respite called home.

---

1. Patrick Rogers, Strong Men Armed: The Marine Corps 1st Force Reconnaissance, http://www.forcerecon.com/strongmenarmed.htm.

2. *Field Manual 100-5*, Headquarters Department of the Army, Washington DC, 14 June 1993, pp. 14-22.

3. Thomas H. Groome, *Christian Religious Education: Sharing Our Story and Vision* (San Francisco: Harper and Row, 1980).

4. *Time* magazine published Friday, May 31, 1963.

Chapter Five

Shifting Focus

*Therefore, as God's chosen people, holy and dearly
loved, clothe yourselves with compassion, kindness,
humility, gentleness and patience.*

— Colossians 3:12

The call came for all of the I Marine Expeditionary Force Headquarters Group to muster in a formation. We trekked through the dusty powdered sands and joined the ranks of the other Marine units. Everyone was given clear instructions of where to stand. A little over 200 or so of us packed in close and took our position near a large trailer that was positioned to serve as an ad hoc stage. I was in the third row of the platoon just in front of the trailer when Lieutenant General Conway made his appearance at Camp Numeniya and introduced General Tommy R. Franks, the Commanding General for US Central Command, commonly referred to as CENTCOM. This command is the theater level unified combatant command that reports to the Secretary of Defense and maintains military responsibility for the entire region covering the Middle East, Africa, and Central Asia.

Months earlier, around late February 2003, while we were still at Camp Commando in the northern outskirts of Kuwait City, we were frequently visited by hosts of Generals and other Distinguished Visitors hoping to inspire us in preparation for what might lay ahead. During one of those visits, General Tommy Franks visited and I went to listen to his speech. I was curious to see how he was going to frame this for us. These speeches may seem superfluous to some but to others, including myself, they provided a backdrop toward understanding our role in this war and how we were charging ahead. They were important milestones that fed our understanding and strengthened our moral preparation. To those of us in leadership positions within the command they became talking points for later discussion amongst ourselves or with our troops.

When General Franks first addressed us I was grossly disappointed. We gathered over 1,000 Marines, Sailors, and Soldiers all around a very large Kuwaiti rappelling tower in a corner of the Kuwaiti Army base and encircled him as he addressed the crowd. The context of his speech was lost on me as I recall specifically his reliance on the crass expletive lexicon in his language. What bothered me was that here he stood as the consummate professional leading us into war and yet he talked like a high school dropout who lazily relies on expletives to substitute his ability to pull nouns, adjectives, and verbs to properly compose an effective statement. "We are going to show these M*****F****** who the F*** they are dealing with" and on and on he went. I was embarrassed for him and of him in that a four-star General would stand before his troops and speak in such an unprofessional and vulgar fashion.

It doesn't mean that an occasional expletive may be inexcusable, after all we were not gathered for Sunday school, this is preparation for violent combat. Vulgar words are often part of vulgar activities. I quietly took issue because there seemed to be no point to his delivery except for crass bravado. It is a mistake too many military professionals make in an attempt to connect with the junior enlisted members who often express themselves in this manner. I am not opposed to such foul language because I am some self-righteous prude who is offended by the sound of such language.

Truth be told, prior to the time I felt the calling to ministry, I was known to engage in it profusely while growing up in New York City. It was a great challenge to clean up my vocabulary as I moved into the ministry.

In the Navy I am quite used to hearing Marines and Sailors use foul language in place of nouns or verbs, an act which I gingerly inform them is a reflection of a poor vocabulary. However, when a consummate professional like a four-star General resorts to prolific foul language in such a public forum with such a vulgar intensity it does not reveal a familiarity with the vernacular or portray a resonance with the young warriors; it simply reveals an inability to articulate.

Generals should not be expected to talk or think like a Private and they shouldn't. If anything Generals, Admirals, and senior

officers need to present themselves as the consummate professionals and experienced patriots that they are and this nation expects
them to be. They are to consciously inspire the new generation of
warrior with word and deed thus giving them someone to emulate
and respect. I walked away totally uninspired and embarrassed.

In sharp contrast, when it became evident that we were preparing to cross into Iraq as part of an invasion force, Lieutenant General Conway traveled throughout Kuwait visiting each of our Marine units strewn throughout the desert. He would gather thousands
of Marines and Sailors at a time and bring them together to offer
prepared remarks in an articulate and no-nonsense fashion. His
intent was clear, to inform us that we would be engaged in combat
very soon. In all fairness to General Franks, Lieutenant General
Conway's speech was also peppered with a few vernaculars and
profanities but unlike General Frank they were less gratuitous and
served to accentuate a point as opposed to being the point.

I heard Lieutenant General Conway address a few thousand
Marines on March 17, 2003. He challenged us to have faith in our
training, in ourselves, and in one another. He spoke of facing fears
while still moving forward. He said, "Courage is not the absence
of fear ... It's simply being able to control fear at the appropriate
place and time." He effectively tied our current efforts to the mystical past by proclaiming that we were carrying on the legacy of
Marines centuries before us. He took the time to reassure his Marines. He promised that we would have whatever we needed to get
the mission done. He was intimately real as he promised to wholeheartedly support our wounded, ramming home the reality of casualties in combat. He promised to make available all of the medical resources available to him. He highlighted the importance of
the golden hour insuring us we would receive great care. He went
on to guarantee that Marine Air would be there for the asking and
when he said this the crowd was buzzed by a choreographed flyby
of the incredibly noisy but aggressive Marine Corps AV-8Bs and
Cobra Helicopters eliciting the crowd to break into cheers.

It wasn't an eloquent speech heavy on illustrations but it was
realistic, informative, and poignant. I sat in the audience observing
this new generation preparing to enter war for its first time. My

heart filled with concern for them and I lifted them in a quiet prayer at that moment as I watched them draw on one another for strength as they sought to be filled with a courage and optimism clearly articulated by their Commanding General.

Today we stood before General Franks once again and, unlike the inane brute who stood before us some months earlier, General Franks appeared to be less flamboyant on this cool morning. Gone was his inflamed tone of bravado and crass language that plagued his first speech to us. Instead, he stood on that trailer and genuinely thanked the Marines before him for their great sacrifice, their devotion, and their willingness to do what was asked of them with great professionalism. I stood there rigidly at attention and watched him, impressed with how dramatically different his tone was after the war. I concluded then that he personified the character of a true leader who stood in humble amazement before the "salt of the earth" warriors who served him and made him proud. I wondered how the deaths of those who fell in battle under his leadership shaped his grateful spirit, as he must have read their names and reported their sacrifice to the nation. I can only imagine how the events of the past month and the costs in human lives must have sobered and shaped this man for this moment. I imagined that looking into the dirty faces of these young men standing before him he was awed by their spirit, their confidence, and their character. He spoke to us like a proud father addressing his children and simply ended by saying, "Thank you." He then stepped down and came into our midst and began to pose with young Marines eager to take his picture and shake a few hands.

Over a year later, at Camp Pendleton, I noticed that General Frank's book, *American Soldier*, had been published and was being displayed in a local bookstore. The book immediately caught my eye because on the front cover of his book he had immortalized that moment in An Numeniya. The picture on the front cover was of him with our unit during that genuine speech.

The mood of the war was changing as Marines began to withdraw from Baghdad and assume positions throughout the southern provinces. We, as a force, were no longer engaged in the traditional operations of kinetic warfare where Marines hunted down

78

the enemy's army en masse and closed in for the kill. Operations were now changing in terminology and disposition. As units moved into towns and battalion commanders assumed the role of provincial governors over large regions we were beginning to shift our focus from Combat Operations to Stability and Support Operations commonly referred to as SASO.

According to the _Army Field Manual_ (FM 3-07) SASO consists of two distinctly major efforts: Stability Operations and Support Operations that in execution correlate with one another and can be immediately applicable following major combat operations but not restricted to this timeframe.

> _Stability operations promote and protect US national interests by influencing the threat, political, and information dimensions of the operational environment through a combination of peacetime developmental, cooperative activities, and coercive actions in response to crisis. Army forces accomplish stability goals through engagement and response. The military activities that support stability operations are diverse, continuous, and often long-term. Their purpose is to promote and sustain regional and global stability. To this end, stability missions may require offensive and defensive actions to destroy rogue forces._
>
> _The second element to SASO is Support operations that employ Army forces to assist civil authorities, foreign or domestic, as they prepare for or respond to crisis and relieves suffering. The primary role of support operations is to meet the immediate needs of designated groups, for a limited time, until civil authorities can accomplish these tasks without military assistance. Support operations also have two subordinate types: domestic support operations and foreign humanitarian assistance._[1]

With the shift in focus came major changes. Many of the combatant forces utilized to provide the major punch into Iraq like heavy tanks, jet fighters, and artillery regiments were being allowed to retrograde back to Kuwait to prepare to return to the US, while many of the light infantry battalions, helicopters, and support elements were being repositioned throughout the country to help support the humanitarian and reconstruction effort.

As a Navy chaplain I grew excited about this phase because it allows us, as Americans, to do what I believe we do better than any other nation in the world — reach out and inspire. In the Navy and Marine Corps it is traditional for chaplains to lead teams of Sailors and Marines on humanitarian projects wherever we go in the world. Part of the logic for me is that left to their own devices many Sailors and Marines will take the two or three days afforded them in foreign ports and waste them away inside of bars, girlie joints, and red-light districts. In an effort to further educate our people and expose them to the real conditions in places like the Philippines, Indonesia, and other Third World countries, we facilitate projects that allow our Sailors and Marines opportunities to encounter the local populace in ways that humanize them and their conditions.

This journey of conscientization is an effort to help our Marines "decenter," a Jean Piaget concept crucial to achieving a higher form of operational thinking. To "decenter" is to engage in critical reflection, moral reasoning rooted in the respect of others that calls upon an underlying concept of justice and a move toward intellectual autonomy. To engage in this manner allows us to facilitate the act of humanization. Paulo Freire, in his book, *Pedagogy of the Oppressed*, calls it "humanization as the basic human vocation."

We aim for such humanization by identifying orphanages, hospitals, and schools in the same regions where we are conducting exercises or operations and we determine what support can be provided to assist them. In many cases, it may only require bringing a few Sailors and Marines to play with the orphans. Or perhaps we'll purchase paint and other cleaning supplies from collected donations and touch up a school or hospital. The goal is twofold: It exposes our personnel to the conditions of the host nation and some of the poorest of the poor in order to sensitize them and it prevents them from inadvertently exploiting them. The other goal is to demonstrate to the local populace that we are not here to take advantage of their dire circumstances but to empower and assist those in need.

80

It embarrasses me to no end when drunken Sailors and Marines behave irresponsibly and attack or violate the rights of a host national. As a nation that supports the rule of law and the dignity of humanity, I believe it is our responsibility to convey this in our actions when we travel abroad. As a Chaplain and a Christian I am compelled to be compassionate and to tend to the needs of the poor with a loving spirit and to teach that to our troops. In most cases I don't have to lecture or pressure too hard to make this happen. Many of our troops come from humble beginnings and when they are introduced to the harshness of severe poverty in many of these countries they willingly volunteer and genuinely give of themselves in ways that often surprise me.

In the early years of my career, our Navy ships pulled into Subic Bay in Olongapo, Philippines. Olongapo was an adult fantasyland for many of our Sailors who participated in a vast assortment of debauchery offered by the Filipinos. It was the modern equivalent of Sodom and Gomorrah. I went one evening with a group of officers to witness firsthand what our Sailors were doing. I mistakenly thought I was pretty streetwise from my upbringing in the South Bronx but my past did not prepare me for what I saw on the streets of Olongapo. I was appalled and embarrassed to no end. Not so much because of what the Filipinos were doing but because of the willingness of our Sailors to engage in such exploitation of the poor. In response to this callousness expressed to the locals I began to find schools, hospitals, and villages nearby that needed assistance so that during the day we could expose our Sailors to the realities that the bright lights and dark alleys of Olongapo hid during the night.

Our Sailors began to meet the children born of the bar girls who had been abandoned by promising Sailors. They also met the hungry, poor families who had no choice but give their children over to prostitution and other adult services in order to tap into the fountain of income generated by such an industry. I took them to the local hospital where blood smeared the walls and floors. They witnessed local family members having to come in and tend to their sick because the hospital was understaffed. We traveled into

81

the mountain range and provided medical and dental services to the Negritos[2] who were normally a two-day walk from the village.

I know that in all reality the number of Sailors we as chaplains exposed to these realities was miniscule in comparison to the tens of thousands of Sailors who visited the port over the years but nonetheless we began to make an impact and change lives. Over the years, Sailors donated to schools and paid for children to attend schools. Others purchased school supplies and clothes and donated to the community. Today, some twenty years later, those Sailors are the leaders in our Navy. I am convinced that due to the globalization of our modern world outlook, a growing appreciation for relationship-building stemming from our experiences in Iraq, Afghanistan, Indonesia, and similar experiences like these throughout the Navy and Marine Corps today, our military leadership no longer compartmentalizes humanitarian efforts as a collateral side effect of our mission. Instead it has brought it in as a core element of the multifaceted approach of how we implement and shape our national military strategies.

In October 2007, the Chief of Naval Operations, Commandant of the Marine Corps, and Commandant of the Coast Guard released a new national strategy, "A Cooperative Strategy for 21st Century Seapower," that elevates humanitarian assistance and disaster response to be listed as an expanded core capability of maritime power. The strategy declares, "Building on relationships forged in ties of calm, we will continue to mitigate human suffering as the vanguard of interagency and multinational efforts, both in a deliberate, proactive fashion and in response to crisis. Human suffering moves us to act, and the expeditionary character of maritime forces uniquely positions them to provide assistance."

This strategy was not in place during our time in Iraq in 2003 but its spirit was already at work as we looked at the next phase of operations. To this end, the reconstruction phase of the operations held a great deal of promise and I could envision us doing some very powerful things to help the Iraqis truly understand that we were not here to exploit their circumstances and occupy their land but to catapult them into a new beginning. The quiet reality was that it was a sentiment not often found in the annals of journalism during that time but it was a prevailing sentiment amongst those Marines committed to make this venture work. —

It was time yet again to move to a new location where the I Marine Expeditionary Force would be centrally located and accessible to all of the Marine units dispersed throughout southern Iraq while yet remaining close enough to liaison with the Army in Baghdad. Colonel Cunnings, the Commanding Officer of I Marine Expeditionary Force Headquarters Group or MHG, was one of the lead elements in scouting out a new base for the command. Colonel Cunnings was an intelligence officer by trade. He was a tall, muscular Marine who accented his desert cammies with the scuba silver pin. He had formerly been the Commanding Officer of a reconnaissance unit at Camp Lejeune, North Carolina, before joining us in California. He stood tall and picturesque as a Marine and, similar to the many other warriors in this clan who did not succumb to stereotypical images, he was quiet and had quite the sense of calm about him. It may be incomprehensible but he was a passionate quiet — he had a real fervor for being a Marine and I could tell he loved being in command, not for its authority but for the opportunity to engage side by side with his Marines in this environment. From my observations, the only anxiety I ever saw him express in the two years we served together was when he perceived that somehow he was going to miss out on the action. He was a Marine like so many others, deeply devoted to his calling and completely willing to volunteer to be in the frontlines of wherever his nation called him.

Before this massive headquarters could make any move it was his task to go out with a small team to reconnaissance the route and identify the next location we would settle into. When elements of 1st Marine Division went forward into Iraq on the first day, he and his team were off right behind them traveling the countryside attempting to find the perfect place where we could bed down and employ the Commanding General's operations center.

The search for this new location was not as exciting as previous reconnaissance missions. The bulk of the fighting was essentially over. He went out on a few missions and one day after supper we had a chance meeting when he shed light on his recent trip.

Colonel Cunnings seemed pretty excited about the new location because of its historical context. Rumor had it that Lieutenant General Conway was leaning toward his recommendation and we would be moving west toward Babil province to take over Saddam Hussein's palace grounds off a Euphrates tributary adjacent to the ancient grounds of Nebuchadnezzar's Palace. All military officers are historians by necessity if they wish to be effective artisans of the trade of war. He shared excitedly (as excited as he could be in his usual calm demeanor) what he had seen during his trip and how we were to establish our Headquarters in a compound on ancient Babylonian terrain. Colonel Cunnings didn't wear his faith on his sleeve but he was a deeply committed man to his Christian faith and he understood well the historical context of Babylon. We would bed down where Daniel of the Old Testament lived and where Alexander the Great, one of history's greatest warriors and conquerors met his demise.

The convoy to Babylon was not very long but it was still demanding. It lasted a few hours and as typical convoys that stretch out over the horizon it moved at a snail's pace making it a trying journey in the heat. A Marine during Desert Storm, Captain Denis Muller, had shared with me that in an attempt to help his wife in Hawaii understand what it was like to be in the desert he advised her to pick up a hair blower, set it on hot, set it on high, and have the hot air generated from the hair dryer blow in her face while holding it a few inches away. I laughed at his creativity and his accuracy in depicting what it was like to drive in this terrain.

Once again, we knew cognitively that the majority of the fighting was over but we weren't convinced that the enemy had been totally suppressed. We progressed cautiously. Vehicle-borne attacks had already started and Improvised Explosive Devices, artillery shells, and other explosives that were rigged to explode on command as US vehicles drove by were making their debut during that time. We were not taking any chances as we moved from one location to another. Our presence on the road was aggressive and inflexible. We would climb onto public roads that were four lanes across with a median splitting them but we would not allow anyone to share the road with us.

These behemoth caravans of large military vehicles mulled slowly up the road on the far right lane and we'd have Humvees riding up and down the second lane to the left providing cover fire. Every fifth or so vehicle in the convoy was also equipped with a M2 .50 caliber machine gun or a Mark 19 automatic grenade launcher, not to mention Marines locked and loaded with M16s, M240 G, and M60 machine guns, and an array of other weapons. If an unsuspecting Iraqi failed to heed way to our arrival and they managed to get close to our convoys, it was standard operating procedure at the time to see all of the weapons turn and face the vehicle. Upon seeing this ominous threat of firepower directed at them they would immediately veer off into the median and onto the other side of traffic where the two-lane road normally headed in one direction now by compulsion became a two-way road. It was dangerous for the Iraqis on either side of the road.

Travel in Iraq was dirty and dusty so Marines equipped themselves for the elements. Even when we were on the highways in the midst of the Fertile Crescent the sands of the outer Iraqi desert would ride the wind and pound any exposed flesh. When we traveled we wore our Kevlar helmets and interceptor flak vests weighed down with heavy two-inch thick ceramic plates as inserts to protect us from a screaming bullet. In addition, many of us wore goggles or dark sunglasses, fire retardant gloves, and either a scarf or what we called a neck "gaiter" in order to protect our faces from the wind and the sand. The neck gaiter was like a portable turtleneck that tucked into our shirt collar at our necks and extended upward over our ears, cheeks, and nose. We were armored and protected to our teeth but inadvertently what this did was that it dehumanized us as people and depicted large menacing figures that stood an average of six feet tall in front of the average five-foot-tall Iraqi. Even I, who was not armed, would dress in this fashion to protect my face and often forget that Iraqis could not see me smile or make eye contact. Instead, what they saw was a creature of war passively wave — who knows how that wave was interpreted when it was meant to be a touch of humanity, a mild attempt at connecting while traveling through the same miserable roads of a country torn by war.

In the following year, when most of us returned for a second tour in Iraq, it was evidently clear that our senior leadership at the General officer level had been concerned with inadvertently projecting this "Terminator" image to the local populace. I recall being in a brief at Camp Pendleton where Major General James N. Mattis, the Commanding General of 1st Marine Division, directed us to protect ourselves to the best of our abilities. However, when speaking to Iraqis or attempting to make contact with the local populace, we were encouraged to remove our sunglasses and uncover our faces so we could make contact with our eyes and connect nonverbally with the Iraqis — hoping to convey a gesture of mutual respect and humanity.

Riding east toward Al Hilla, where Babylon was located, we witnessed many Iraqis on the move. It was hard to tell if they were returning to Baghdad, evacuating, or moving on with life as normal. There were many cars that were filled to the brim with Iraqis — a phenomenon classic of all poor societies. I recall as a child, in the era before mandatory seatbelts, that we didn't feel like the car was full unless we had people sitting on the laps of others and children lodged in every nook and cranny when we took those rare journeys from the Bronx to Plainsfield, New Jersey. Life here was no different. There were cattle trucks weighed down with mattresses, personal furnishings, and families all thrown together in the back. Buses were all filled with people crammed into an aluminum frame without air conditioning while traveling for hours on end. At times, the opposite road that had now become a two-way highway for these folks was congested to a standstill and they would all turn to catch a glimpse of us as we rode by. We, in turn, would gaze at them attempting to catch a glimpse of a "normal" Iraqi. The children pressed against the windows innocently waved and smiled at us. We would look across the median at them with the same amazement and disbelief they stared at us with. It was like the past meeting the future, the poor seeing the rich, the West meeting the East.

The convoy finally pulled off the main road and began its circling into a series of what appeared to be switchback roads going around some large domes, bypassing what appeared to be small canals, and onto a small road that began to close in on us. The vegetation grew thicker and greener. The palm trees towered over us and we slowed down to a crawl in their shadows. We passed an abandoned Iraqi artillery piece and two Iraqi armored personnel carriers that had attempted to hide in the thick of the palm grove but were yet discovered and destroyed by someone. As we inched our way up the road, people came to stand by the roadside and watched us as we came to a crawl. I don't imagine until now that they had seen so many of us show up at the same time. More and more of them walked from the nearby villages and came to look at this parade of trucks. It wasn't long before it appeared as if the entire village had mustered the courage or succumbed to curiosity to see the Americans arrive.

We rolled by them very slowly and they stood by the sides of the road coupled in various groups, young men, children, and families all staring at us. Obviously absent were the women. Only handfuls were in the crowd, standing with their children and behind their husbands. I didn't see any standing there on their own or in a group with other women. It was no triumphant entry or boisterous welcome. In fact, it was eerily quiet. They stood there and stared at us as we rolled in with the mundane hum of diesel engines setting the tone in the background and we stared back.

I took off my gaiter, goggles, and helmet and occasionally nodded with a smile. A few young boys clumped together and smiled back at us while holding up their fingers formed liked a "V." I wasn't sure what that meant — peace, victory, or perhaps some other ambiguous message? Even the nonverbal language required interpretation. A few middle-aged gentlemen yelled, "American good!" and we gladly took that to be a vote of confidence and a note of welcome.

We completed a curve in the road and for the first time I noticed Saddam Hussein's palace high above us. It sat regally atop a large hill directly in front of us. The sides of the hill were barren with sand and clay but the road leading to it was sandwiched in between towering palms giving the hill a majestic height from the ground looking up. We drove around the hill and into a small compound that was nestled against the Euphrates. The scenery was amazing as the tall, lush palm trees hugged the winding Euphrates against the bright cloudless blue sky. We passed an ornate building on the right with a great balcony facing the river and then some other administrative buildings.

We were directed to pull alongside the road in front of what appeared to be a large, single-story structure designed to be a reception hall and cafeteria. The Marine directing us pointed to a smaller structure with two door frames directly across the street from the larger reception hall. I was assigned the spaces to the left of the building for the chaplains and the space to the right was given to medical. What a joy it was to discover that our new home was going to be a building.

The first two months we were in Kuwait required us to sleep in large tents on cots. When the sandstorms or any substantive wind for that matter would find their way into our camp, we could not escape the onslaught of dust and sand. The past two months during combat operations we found ourselves sleeping in Humvees while on the move and in small two-man tents when we would stop long enough to establish camp. We brushed our teeth, shaved, and washed up in the open air, guarding our water supplies. We relieved ourselves on small, wooden booths that served as a seat over a hole on the perimeter of the compound. For added privacy, you waited until nightfall and borrowed someone's night vision goggles and trekked over the berms of sand to the perimeter. You lowered your pants and sat facing outwardly so you could see if anyone was coming and you prayed that a mortar, an RPG, or some kind of enemy munitions would not come your way while you relieved yourself in the darkness of night. It was perhaps the most joked about fear encountered by many — the fear of being ultimately humiliated by being killed while sitting on a latrine.

The type of latrine you were obliged to use also became a very clear indicator of where you were in combat. When we were in Kuwait we hated to use the porta-potties that were no different than the ones often found in construction sites around the US. We detested being around when the "honey truck" would come around to suck them clean of their fill because the stagnant, hot air became putrid as well. However, as you moved forward in the geography, the war latrines adapted to the environment and the threat level.

When we moved out of the comfort of a stabilized and thoroughly equipped base like Camp Commando in Kuwait and out into the desert camps near the border of Iraq our facilities went from a private porta-potty with blue water and the customary contractual service of a honey sucker to a small, semi-private booth crudely made of plywood. The grand difference here is that long gone was the blue water and contractual service. Instead, the combat engineers had cut fifty-gallon drums down to about two feet high and they were half filled with diesel fuel. The drums were inserted from the rear of the booth to catch human waste from those perched on the semi-private booths above. Every morning, some poor junior enlisted member who had the misfortune of either being the most junior in rank or who had earned the rancor of his superior would be charged with pulling out the drums filled with human waste, drenching them with more diesel fuel, and then using a metallic four-foot stake to stir the waste until it was completely burned. The heavy, black smoke carried a distinct smell that only further highlighted the fact that it is the simple things in life like a toilet that we most miss when deployed.

The latrine takes a much simpler form when you are deployed inside a combat zone and everyone is at the ready in a small expeditionary compound. As noted before, the latrine is placed outside of the living area close to the perimeter. For your protection it is out in plain sight so that the sentries and patrols can see you and not confuse you with anyone attempting to cross the perimeter. You are well inside the perimeter but are on the inner of the outer rings. Here you have a small wooden slab that serves as a bench and allows you to sit over a hole. In some locations camouflage netting was placed over the stool but rarely. While you sit and relieve yourself you face outwardly toward the perimeter being sure to stay alert. Every morning a crew of junior enlisted men came around and either dropped lye and/or dirt to keep it free from wildlife and in hopes of keeping the stench down.

When engaged in maneuver warfare the designated latrine ceases to exist. By this I mean that it becomes the responsibility of each person to use their E-tool or entrenching tool, a foldable shovel, to dig a hole, relieve oneself, and then cover the hole back up in an expeditious fashion. This is not meant to be a private moment, either. The security of everyone is paramount, so we have to be accountable to one another; therefore privacy is not an option. I recall in Desert Storm we were moving deep into the Al Wafra oil fields and we were moving in at night. We had stopped at one point and encircled the vehicles, akin to pioneers circling the wagons, and we staged ourselves in this posture for a few hours. This gave us the opportunity to be on watch outside of our vehicles. We dug in the dirt and took the chance to catch some sleep. Half of us would sleep while the other half watched and then our roles reversed. In Desert Storm there was a real concern that the Iraqis would be using biological weapons so we were given a series of pills to include the anti-nerve agent, pyridostigmine biomide, and other medications to thwart such an effect. One of the side effects of such an onslaught of medication was that it incited diarrhea. All throughout the night as we sat in that position for those few hours we would hear, "SGT so-and-so leaving the hole" and we'd watch Marines crawl out from their holes and work their way out to a few yards away, dig a hole, take off the MOPP gear and all the stuff they carried and relieve themselves, cover the hole, get dressed, and crawl back. I had my turn and once again, as it was this time around all you could think about as you sat there and did your business in the dark was that you didn't want to get hit with your pants down. It was a relief to be able to sound off, "Chaplain back in the hole."

All of this notes that once you have experienced the more rustic nature of a latrine during combat and you begin your journey back in inverse order to greater levels of security there is an anticipated sense of greater comfort at each level. When you finally returned to the use of the private porta-pottie with blue water and readily available toilet paper, life seemed so good. One felt human again in spite of the fact that the stench was overpowering and in the summer months the temperature in them could easily exceed 120 degrees. One always emerged drenched in sweat — but hey, it was a private creature comfort rarely available in the open road of warfare.

Similar feelings emerged when we discovered that we would be living in a building here at Camp Babylon. The concrete structure before us was a sweet sight. The thick walls would provide protection from those dastardly sandstorms and most importantly it provided relative cover from any mortar or rocket attacks that might occur. The Navy Seabees had arrived with us and they were already at work providing ad hoc plywood doors with counterweights made from water bottles filled with sand. I was convinced these contraptions were lifted off of an episode of *Gilligan's Island*. The promise was that in a few weeks we'd have electricity, screened windows, and even small room air conditioners — hope abounded.

It had been rumored that prior to our arrival, the camp had belonged to the Iraqi Republican Guard. It had supposedly been protected by a small component of soldiers with a few armored personnel carriers outside the gates, whom we had seen destroyed on our way in. It wasn't clear if there was a fight here prior to our arrival or if the Iraqi Army had simply abandoned the camp. However, when it became apparently clear that the Army was no longer in control of the grounds the local villagers outside of the camp engulfed the compound and unashamedly looted it. The small buildings we were in had been stripped clean in the way a carnivore strips a bone of all its flesh. The customary tiles on the floor, the windows and the window frames, the light fixtures and copper wiring, the door and hinges, all had been stripped from this small building. It resembled a carcass of a building with no signs of aesthetic flair. It stood as naked as a building could stand. Yet, in its nakedness we were happy. While it was devoid of all character or flair it still maintained its most rudimentary purpose of providing shelter for those who traveled in the desert. It was our cave.

We unloaded our Humvee and settled into this new abode. We went next door and helped medical with their set up. Once settled, we immediately began to walk about the compound to explore our new home. No one had any real clear idea of how long we would be here so in such times my philosophy is always to presume the stay will be for six months, the average time of a full Navy-Marine

Corps deployment, and if it proved to be sooner it would be a welcomed surprise.

Our curiosity besieged us and we could not wait any longer to climb up to the palace to explore its contents and see its view from up above. Deep in the back of each of our minds was the hope that we might be able to find some small treasure or keepsake. This hope was rationally counterbalanced with the reality that the local Iraqis had left nothing behind during the looting. It sat atop the hill looking down on us in the form of a smaller Mount Olympus, home of the gods, looking over humanity. With the company of a few we climbed up to the palace to see how royalty lived in days past. At first impression, the palace emanated an opulent character about itself as it regally sat so high above all but interestingly enough as we drew closer and closer we were taken in by the massive façade of the whole thing. A closer look at the palace revealed a substandard level of workmanship. While there were some isolated pieces of artisanship it was outweighed by shoddy workmanship and less-than-refined materials. Nonetheless, it called out to be admired more out of curiosity than wonder.

Some of the materials I read and studied prior to making this deployment underscored Saddam Hussein's obsession with King Nebuchadnezzar. This became quite evident as we perused through this palace. The principal doors leading into the main entrance were huge wooden doors with large towering palm trees carefully carved in intrinsic detail known to be the iconic symbol of Nebuchadnezzar. Over the arch of the major doorway there was a montage carved in stone showing the ancient gods Addad and Marduk along with a figure that looked like a Babylonian king, perhaps Nebuchadnezzar. This was flanking a bust of Saddam Hussein to one side depicting a modern scene of a woman carrying something on her head, an Arabian horse, and mosque flanking the other side held together by a spread eagle.

Nebuchadnezzar was the ancient King of Babylon credited with destroying Jerusalem and exiling over 10,000 of its most prominent Jews out of Israel into Babylon while ushering in the age of the Babylonian Diaspora. I can only imagine that Saddam Hussein desired to be seen by the Arab world as the modern incarnation of

Nebuchadnezzar because of his prominence as a regional king during ancient times and his ability to destroy the kingdom of Israel.

The book of Daniel in the Old Testament of Judeo-Christian scriptures tells the account of how Nebuchadnezzar had a dream that represented him as a tall, towering tree symbolizing his great power and reach during his era. Daniel who was a Jewish captor in Nebuchadnezzar's court, renamed Belteshazzar to represent Nebuchadnezzar's deity, interpreted this dream for the king. Daniel notes,

> *The tree you saw, which grew large and strong, with its top touching the sky, visible to the whole earth, with beautiful leaves and abundant fruit, providing food for all, giving shelter to the beasts of the field, and having nesting places in its branches for the birds of the air — you, O king, are that tree! You have become great and strong; your greatness has grown until it reaches the sky, and your dominion extends to distant parts of the earth.* — Daniel 4:20-22

I can clearly see why the imagery of the large and strong tree that touched the sky was incorporated as a public symbol for Saddam Hussein. Such symbolism connected him with Nebuchadnezzar. As a matter of fact, at the bottom of the hill we later discovered one tree that had been cordoned off with concrete as Saddam's tree, a living palm tree that represented him. Evidently someone was charged with insuring the tree was well pruned and cared for. It was marked with a special placard. I find it terribly curious though to ask if anyone who shared this vision with him ever read the rest of the story of that very chapter in the book of Daniel. The vision itself was not a pleasant vision for it prophesied a period of tribulation for the great King Nebuchadnezzar. The text from Daniel actually begins by stating, "Belteshazzar answered, 'My lord, if only the dream applied to your enemies and its meaning to your adversaries!' " (Daniel 4:19b).

The story goes on to depict how Nebuchadnezzar had grown to be haughty and prideful in his kingdom, and this dream served as a vision from God to inform him that he would be humbled before God. The form of humility would come in that Nebuchadnezzar would be turned into some form of a lunatic who would live like an animal. "You will be driven away from people and will live with the wild animals; you will eat grass like cattle and be drenched with the dew of heaven" (Daniel 4:25a).

The vision was dreadful but it contained a promise in Nebuchadnezzar's story assuring him that the state of lunacy would be temporary. In the king's madness he would soon come to realize that true sovereignty and power lay in God's hands and not in any man-made kingdom. The prophecy clearly predicted the resurgence of Nebuchadnezzar in all his glory.

> *Immediately what had been said about Nebuchadnezzar was fulfilled. He was driven away from people and ate grass like cattle. His body was drenched with the dew of heaven until his hair grew like the feathers of an eagle and his nails like the claws of a bird.*
>
> *At the end of that time, I, Nebuchadnezzar, raised my eyes toward heaven, and my sanity was restored. Then I praised the Most High; I honored and glorified him who lives forever.*
>
> *His dominion is an eternal dominion;*
> *his kingdom endures from generation to generation.*
> *All the peoples of the earth*
> *are regarded as nothing.*
> *He does as he pleases*
> *with the powers of heaven*
> *and the peoples of the earth.*
> *No one can hold back his hand*
> *or say to him: "What have you done?"*
>
> *At the same time that my sanity was restored, my honor and splendor were returned to me for the glory of my kingdom. My advisers and nobles sought me out, and I was restored to my throne and became even greater than before.*
>
> *Now I, Nebuchadnezzar, praise and exalt and glorify the King of heaven, because everything he does is*

right and all his ways are just. And those who walk in
pride he is able to humble.   — Daniel 4:33-37

Earlier I had asked if anyone in Saddam's circle had read the rest of the accounts in this prophecy, but perhaps the real story lies in that Saddam Hussein understood it perfectly and maybe he truly believed that he, like Nebuchadnezzar, would experience God restoring him to a place of prominence. Like Nebuchadnezzar he fulfilled the prophecy to the point that he was living away from people and his hair was matted like the feathers of an eagle. None of us can forget the images we saw on global television when he was captured and found to be living in a hole like an animal — just like an animal — just like Nebuchadnezzar. I wondered how many times in the isolation of his hole he raised his eyes up to the sky and wondered when God was going to restore him in the way Nebuchadnezzar was restored. To the very end of his execution he seemed defiant and kept holding on to his title as the ruler of Iraq totally denying the events that had transpired. Unlike Nebuchadnezzar's tree, this tree of Saddam Hussein had been cut all the way to the trunk and the trunk had been pulled from the ground exterminating the rule of tyranny.

Once inside the palace it was difficult to decipher what it must have been like. In its current dilapidated state it was more a testament to the desperation of an impoverished people who resorted to looting than it was the testament of a wealthy king, ruler, dictator, and despot. The grand hall had the remnants of an impressively large chandelier that hung crookedly as someone evidently attempted to pull it down from its high ceiling and like a dying tree in the fall it hung there, stripped of much of its glass, a bit askew. The smaller rooms that followed failed to hold on to their beloved chandeliers for all that remained to bear testament to their existence were a few glass pieces of chandelier on the floor and the stressed electrical strands protruding from the ceiling. I could not help but imagine that somewhere in Iraq, in a small mud hut or poor village abode, there hung an elaborate chandelier that once overshadowed the likes of Saddam Hussein. Perhaps it sat as a piece of decor in the same way a Rolls Royce compliments a doublewide trailer.

We climbed to the top floor and were met by a very large room that could easily be an estate bedroom with tall, wide, open-pane windows leading to a balcony overlooking the Euphrates and the sea of palm trees below. On the ceiling was an intricate and colorful mural surrounding a large chandelier with a montage of Iraq's history depicting the Ishtar Gate and many other snippets of Iraq's ancient past. The room allowed a sea of natural light to enter and it bounced gently off of the wooden floors. It had a large but busy fireplace and I caught myself wondering if Saddam Hussein actually spent any time in this place. I wondered how many young women from this region were violated in this very room as he pursued his bloodthirsty quest for absolute power.

RP2 Stephens found a stairwell that led to the outside and called us to come to him. I left what I thought to be the primary chambers and followed the others as we walked down a darkened hallway and out to a rooftop that faced north by northeast. I couldn't believe I hadn't seen it before. It stood there in defiance of all that was modern and explicitly reminded me of ancient kingdoms of power and culture. I marveled in awe as I looked out at the ruins of Nebuchadnezzar's palace, half of it lay in ruins as discovered hundreds of years ago and the other half had been reconstructed in part by Saddam Hussein. I was looking at biblical history, the history of humanity. We stood there in awe; unsure of exactly what it was that we were looking at but when one encounters such ruins there is a spiritual connection to the ages of the past. We stood face-to-face with ancient history.

From this vantage point we could see how easily Saddam Hussein may have concluded the very thoughts that Nebuchadnezzar exclaimed in self-appreciation that incited madness in each of them,

> [A]s the king was walking on the roof of the royal palace of Babylon, he said, "Is not this the great Babylon I have built as the royal residence, by my mighty power and for the glory of my majesty?" — Daniel 4:29-30

1. Headquarters, Department of the Army, Stability and Support Operations, February 2003.

2. The term "Negrito" refers to several ethnic groups in isolated parts of Southeast Asia. Their current populations include the Aeta, Agta, Ayta, Ati, Dumagat, and at least 25 other tribes of the Philippines, the Semang of the Malay peninsula, the Mani of Thailand, and 12 Andamanese tribes of the Andaman Islands of the Indian Ocean.

Chapter Six

Inside The Ishtar Gate

Enter his gates with thanksgiving and his courts with
praise; give thanks to him and praise his name.
— Psalm 100:4

A high fence tightly enclosed the compound and separated us from the ruins. There were three entrances to our compound, one to the north that led to a road that skirted around the outside of the ancient site, one to the south that let out by the small town of Jumjuma and into the main highway to Al Hilla, and one entrance that headed northeasterly into the grounds of the ancient park.

Regardless of where each road led, the vast majority of us in the compound were prohibited from venturing outside of the wire. Marines heavily guarded each gate that led out of the compound and we were specifically prohibited from venturing out into the ruins. This was as much to protect the ruins as it was meant to protect the Marines.

I couldn't believe that we were so close to Babylon and yet would not have the opportunity to venture out to see it and learn about it. We were discussing this very frustration as we were walking down from the palace when we encountered Lieutenant General Conway. He was a general who implicitly demanded the respect of his Marines by his mere presence and they were quick to give it. He stood tall and distinguished. He spoke with a deep, guttural voice and a subtle Arkansas drawl that carried itself in a stately fashion. He was always the true southern gentleman who carefully enunciated his words clearly with intent and exhibited a dash of grit flavored by his infantry background. He was a three-star general who loved his Marines and Sailors and he showed it unashamedly as he led from the front. He had the rare distinction of being the Commanding General over all US Marine forces in the theater and that included his son and his son-in-law who were serving with frontline Marine combat units. He would often joke that he was more afraid of having to bear bad news to Annette, his wife, over either of these young men than he was of the war. Truth be told, most of these hardened generals were genuinely and deeply moved with the news of any of their young Marines being lost in combat. While it is part of the job it is not one that any of these men takes lightly.

We were hesitant to disturb him, as it appeared he might be enjoying a rare moment alone walking about the compound. As we came upon him we made eye contact and politely greeted him.

"Hello, sir."

"So, chaplains, I see you made it here all right. Good to see you. What do you think?"

"Sir, this place is amazing. It's quite the view from up there." I thought if there was ever the chance to ask, it was now. I asked, "Sir, we'd like to visit the compound next door and see how that's looking. Maybe we can offer some help." I sheepishly asked expecting a negative reply rooted in some security or force protection policy.

"Good idea, chaplain. Go ahead, pay them a visit and let me know how things are over there. See if you can meet some of the leaders and report back. Enjoy the day!" He gave us a warm, faint smile and turned away to continue his walk.

We all proceeded right up the road toward the northeastern gate. It was only about a half-mile hike from where we stood to where the Marines were posted at the end of the road. As we approached their position we noticed a small building to the right where other Marines were resting and standing by to serve as a reactionary force. The asphalt road extended out beyond the Marines and curved to the left and disappeared behind some trees. There was a large, dusty, beige wall that were the outer walls of the rebuilt walls of Nebuchadnezzar's palace running parallel to the road as it extended away from us. There was a large, open, gravel and dirt lot about the length of a football field between the wall and the asphalt road. To the left of the road it opened into a large, open field that looked quite strange. The field was bumpy and irregular. A small foot-traffic path winded its way through it but the palm trees and grass had overtaken whatever was there in the past.

We approached the two Marines at the guard shack. They were manning an M60 machine gun and it pointed down the road with a clear field of fire. One of them turned toward the shack behind them and called for their Corporal of the Guard to come out and meet us.

"Corporal, I'm Chaplain Marrero and this is Chaplain Gwudz. We're with I MEF and we have permission to go down this road and see what's in that courtyard just ahead. I have two RPs with us, a Marine, and a corpsman but we need you to watch our backs from here."

"Okay, sir. There's been some foot traffic on and off. If you go out there be sure to stay on the left hand side of the road so the M60 can do its work if you need it. Try to stay out of our line of fire. I'll call the sentries on the palace and tell them to watch you from up there as well. Once you go past that bend in the road you're on your own since we can't see you."

"Thanks, Corporal. We'll be sure to stay out of your line of fire and if you hear anything while we're out there come after us." I joked nervously and I turned to huddle with our group.

"Okay, were good to go. You guys with weapons be at the ready. We'll walk to the left and slow. Hopefully they can see us from the palace. If anything happens pull to the left and head back here through those trees. Ready?"

"Damn right we are!" said Master Chief Religious Program Specialist Eddie Jernigan. He was a good old boy from North Carolina who was a pioneer in his job as a Religious Program Specialist. He was one of the first Sailors to serve in this new military occupational specialty when it was first created in 1975. Before the RP rating, chaplains were assisted by volunteers or extra bodies, normally the sick or lame, who couldn't perform regular shipboard or combat duties. The RP rating has been a real blessing for the Chaplain Corps because it provides a cadre of professional young men and women who know how to support the chaplain in peacetime or combat. Master Chief Jernigan had served in Desert Storm with the 1st Marine Division and didn't seem to be too afraid of anything. He was a great mentor to the younger RPs in the community. My only point of contention with him was his propensity

101

to resort to foul language, not an attribute I want associated with the chaplain's office, and his desire to play Spades every chance he got. He was a self-proclaimed agnostic who had grown up in a very fundamentalist Christian home and now had moved away from the faith yet he believed in taking care of the troops and was convinced that helping chaplains was a way of taking care of the Marines. He stepped off and led us across the barrier with his hand on his holstered 9mm Berretta.

I stayed close to RP2 Stephens who stood a tall, muscular 6'4" and carried an automatic shotgun — a sure crowd displeaser if ever there was one. We walked carefully down the road attempting to peer around the bend. When we got to the bend we could see straight down the road to an intersection where the road came in from the southeast and stopped at a large, blue-colored gate about forty feet high with yellow and white creatures painted on it. In front of the gate gathered a group of Iraqis who saw us and immediately came toward us in a hurried pace.

"Stay back" shouted RP2 Stephens as he raised his shotgun to plain view.

"Stop" signaled Master Chief with his hand up and palm out.

"Anyone speak English?" I asked.

The crowd of about twelve men and children looked at us with a bewildered look, probably wondering why we were being so cautious. In their eyes, we were probably the threat, not them. One of them signaled yes, and said "English" and waved for us to come. We approached them carefully. One gentleman had an injured boy in a wheelchair and immediately brought him to us.

"America, help." He signaled as he pointed to the boy and pointed back to the road. I took it to mean he wanted us to help the child. Perhaps take him into our camp for the doctors to see. One of the young corpsmen, Doc Smith, who lived next door to us in our new building, had accompanied us and he looked at the injury and assessed that it was an old injury and there was nothing we could do. It looked like a butchered attempt at surgery to the young boy's knees. The scars were old and jagged and the boy's legs were deformed. I looked at him with a sorry look and shook my head hoping to nonverbally signal that there was nothing I could do and I asked again, "English?"

An older gentleman sitting on a crate in front of the blue gate stood up and walked toward us. His face looked leathery with bronzed, sun-dried skin accentuated by a white beard. He was dressed in a white *dishdasha* and held a sickle in his hands. He signaled for us to follow him through the large, brightly painted, blue gate with the yellow and white creatures on it. We followed him through the gates into a courtyard that was filled with people. They were lounging around attempting to find an escape from the sun under the shade of two very large trees in the center of the courtyard. In the middle of the crowd there were a few Marines from our Intelligence group mixed in amongst the crowd and a television crew was interviewing two gentlemen who seemed to speak pretty decent English.

I stepped back to take it all in. The courtyard was surrounded by a series of walls that extended to the left and right of the big, blue gate before us. Inside the courtyard were a couple of small offices that appeared to have been burned to the ground. There appeared to be another small edifice directly in front of the trees that had two large doorways that had been sealed with cinderblocks and cement. To the left of these doorways was a small path that led outside of the courtyard toward the large palace walls we had seen from the palace on the hill.

The courtyard was amassed with people. There were families, old men, and young men just hanging around. Some men had expeditiously displayed wares for sale on makeshift tabletops held up by chairs. There was a man in his early thirties who was selling sodas from a cooler and a little boy and girl played around him as he attempted to conduct his business. On the wall that encircled the courtyard there hung a couple of colorful murals. The first mural portrayed the large, blue, Ishtar gate, a large ziggurat, and Euphrates tributary. Under it in English it read, "Plan of the city of Babylon during the time of Nebuchadnezzar II 600 BC." I also noticed that along the longest stretch of the courtyard wall it was evident that two large paintings had hung there at one time. They were no longer there, only their shadows remained. In front of us was a large mural portraying a map of Iraq and some of its points of interest from Ur in the south to Nineveh in the north. I waited patiently for the gentleman to finish with the camera crew and I walked about the courtyard back toward the entrance of the gate when I noticed that across from me there were people involved in construction. I found this odd. As a matter of fact, above all the noise of conversations and human interaction in the courtyard I was hearing the pinging sounds of hammers and chisels. I looked around and saw people across the street in a building that was formerly a restaurant. They were chipping away at various things in the building and thrusting large sheets of corrugated metal down to the streets below to be placed on small, wooden carts pulled by donkeys.

When the gentleman broke free of the cameras he noticed us in uniform and came to us.

"Do you speak English?" I stupidly asked since he had just finished speaking to an English-speaking film crew.

"As-Salaam-Alaikum" he gently said in a low tone followed by, "Yes, I speak little English."

"Are you in charge of this place?" I inquired.

"Yes, my name is Moussawi." He answered timidly.

"Moussawi, what is here?"

"This is the Babylon Museum. The Palace of Nebuchadnezzar and Hammurabbi. We are part of the State Board of Antiquities and Humanities in Baghdad."

"Moussawi, we are your new neighbors. The US Marines have moved into the base next door and we want to help in any way we can. We represent General Conway. Can we do something for you? Can we help?" I asked in an attempt to make our visit sound official and hopefully invoke a status report of what was happening.

The look on his face was one of consternation. It was evident that he was unsure of whether he should say something or not. He was hesitant to say anything; perhaps he questioned whether we could be trusted or maybe he wondered what it would mean to ask for our help. It was clearly evident on his face that he was troubled and afraid. He hesitated but turned and called the other man who had been by his side earlier when speaking to the film crew.

The other man greeted us, "As-Salaam-Alaikum, I am Abdul." He said a little more assured.

With Abdul by his side, Moussawi turned to us quietly and said, "These people are criminals. They have burned down our offices and shop. They have stolen everything from us. On the day of the war they came in to the courtyard and said, 'Moussawi, take your family and your things and leave or we will kill you.' So I took my things from our home and my wife and left. They came in and destroyed all. We sealed the museum but they broke in sidewall and stole much. Some large things are still inside because they could not take them out through small opening. They have destroyed all — please help us." He pleaded with trembling fear.

Abdul chimed in and said, "These are common thieves. They threaten us every day. There are men here who are stealing from the ruins and taking them away to black market. We are here to watch but we cannot do anything. There are too many of them."

"Moussawi, Abdul show us what belongs to the museum," I said.

They led us into the office spaces located behind the museum wall. The area was being looted by groups of young men who functioned like well-rehearsed construction crews with chisels and hammers. They had strategically placed donkey carts on the side streets to haul off what they chiseled away. Like the building we had just occupied inside the camp, these crews of young men in sandals and man dresses were quite effective as they chiseled away at the concrete to steal the windows and the window frames they were set in. We walked past the stony looks of the chiselers.

Moussawi showed us the living quarters in the back area that had once housed him and his family; it had been vandalized and burned to the ground. He pointed out the remains of the souvenir shop and now it was nothing but ashen remains. We walked past an office that once served as the ticket office and it, too, had been burnt. We followed the men out past the blue gate onto the main street and they pointed out that all of the land to the south of the road leading back to the gate we came from were ancient ruins covered over by grass over the years waiting to be unearthed.

From the blue gate, which I learned was a half-sized replica of the Ishtar Gate in Babylon, they pointed out the Coliseum built during the reign of Alexander the Great, the remnants of a temple to Ishtar, and the grounds of the compound that had housed the offices of the State Board of Antiquities and Humanities along with restaurants. The streets were littered with the remnants of kiosks that once accented the streets designed to assist tourists. We stood there and watched helplessly as this small campus of buildings, facilities, and ancient ruins were being chipped away before our eyes.

We went back into the courtyard and stood before the men selling literature that illustrated the history of the grounds and the area. I purchased a couple of booklets for an American dollar. Abdul whispered into my ear after my purchase that these items had previously belonged to the museum but had been stolen weeks earlier and were now being sold in the courtyard by the very thieves who looted them. I decided to keep the reading materials for later reading in my new home and explained to Moussawi and Abdul that we would return the next day. In return, they promised to give me the grand tour of the ruins and with that we departed from one another. As I walked away from the crowded courtyard accompanied by my entourage of armed men I wondered if Moussawi and Abdul would be there in the morning. I lifted a prayer for their safety and asked God to give me wisdom as I attempted to sort this out and determine what needed to be done on the way back into the compound.

I read with great interest the booklets I had purchased from the looters that afternoon on the history of Babylon. I turned to the Bible and reread chapters in 2 Kings, Jeremiah, and Daniel that spoke of Nebuchadnezzar and the Babylonian Diaspora. I knew little beyond name recognition of Hammurabbi and Alexander the Great and I pulled out a few books on Iraq's history that shed a little light on these subjects. With each passing page I knew I had to go to someone and do something about the looting going on next door. I walked out of my building and crossed the street to Colonel Cunning's makeshift office.

He invited me to sit on a small folding chair by his desk. He had forged a small office out of a corner of what appeared to have been an industrial kitchen's loading dock. His walls were covered in maps and his desk was filled with papers. He had been here a few days prior with the advance party so he had a little more time to settle in but was far from being finished. I sat in the chair by his desk and we began to discuss the situation.

"Sir, I met with two guys who work for the Antiquities Board at the museum. They seem pretty professional and they speak English. I took a short look around and the place has been ransacked and looted. A lot of the looting is still going on. The curators are concerned that the next step will be digging in the ruins with the intent to sell items on the black market. We have to do something before we get blamed for letting it happen. What can we do?" I asked as I sought to gauge his interest level in the subject.

"Well, this place belongs to us now," he stated as he looked for something on his desk. Then he turned his attention to me and said, "We are the law and the ultimate authority so we have to stop it. Put this down in a memo so we can send it up to General Conway and get his support to come up with a plan. In the meantime you have to understand that you have the authority to stop them, so use it."

"Okay, I'll get to work on something. Tomorrow I am going back to get a walk through the ruins with the curators and get a better feel of the layout. I'll take my RP and request a few MHG Marines from the Sergeant Major for backup if it's okay with you."

"Sure, talk to the Sergeant Major and let me see a proposal by midday tomorrow so we can send it up to the Chief of Staff and the CG."

"Will do." I replied excitedly as I was heading out the office with a hundred ideas flashing through my head.

That evening I sat down in a corner of my cot and prayed fervently for direction. I wrote a memo explaining the preponderance of personnel in the courtyard, the level of vandalism that has taken place, and the looting that was currently happening under our watch. I expressed concern for the staff and their safety. I highlighted the concern that the ruins were at risk and we could be targets for black marketers in our own backyard. I noted that this was an important historical site and we needed to do something about this. I proposed that we extend our presence to include the historical site next door and we send patrols in through the campus area and the ruins to stop the looting. With another prayer I hoped it would get serious attention and sent it up the chain of command.

The next morning I dropped off the memo in Colonel Cunning's office and I headed out to the museum area in two Humvees. The first Humvee included me, my RP, the doc, and a corpsman, and in the second Humvee it was Chaplain Gwudz, RPCM Jernigan, and a few Marines on loan to us from MHG's S-4. We headed out to the side gate via the northeasterly road where we had been the day before. We parked the Humvees by the Reaction Force shack and walked out to the gate where the same crowd as the day before continued to loiter.

Abdul was in the inner courtyard by the trees and called out to us. He was dressed plainly in western clothing. He wore a simple, button-down, long-sleeve shirt with a pair of dress slacks. Unlike the others around us he wore dress shoes rather than the slippers we grew accustomed to seeing. He had silky short jet-black hair that complimented his light brown face and of course he had the required mustache of all Arab men but his was on the thin side. He was an average height of about five-feet-seven-inches and the build of an administrator or a person used to doing office work rather than manual labor. He was stout but not very big. He brandished a smile that lit up his face and warmly welcomed those he extended it to. He came over and greeted us cordially, "*As-Salaam-Alaikum*, welcome back."

"Good morning, Abdul," I replied with a reciprocating grin.

As I approached Abdul he extended his right hand out for a wave and crossed his right hand across his chest, as if placing his hand over his heart and gently leaned forward in a bow. It reminded me of the ancient Roman salute. Then he extended his hand out toward me and gave me the limpest handshake I had ever had from a man. He merely placed his hand in my hand while I attempted to catch his hand in mine and shake his limp arm. While we exchanged pleasantries many others began to surround us and continuously repeated, "Hello, hello." I replied "hello" in a general way to all attempting to make contact with the many young men and children that surrounded us.

At that time, Moussawi arrived and worked his way through the crowd and greeted us with the usual, *"As-Salaam-Alaikum"* to which I replied, "Good morning." That's when I discovered that a young man in the crowd knew a little more English than the others and instructed me to respond to the salutation by saying, *"Alaikum-Salaam."* He then proceeded to say, *"As-Salaam-Alaikum"* and I replied *"Alay can Saddam,"* the others snickered and in unison began to chant, *"Alaikum-Salaam."* The young man repeated his salutation, *"As-Salaam-Alaikum"* and in unison with the others in the crowd I replied, *"Alaikum-Salaam"* and they began to smile and chat amongst themselves in reference to me.

Moussawi shooed the crowd away and invited us to accompany him and Abdul into the ruins area. He led us to the edge of the courtyard and up a set of stairs that still had the wrought-iron banister attached to it. Climbing up the stairs I noticed some looters on the rooftop of the museum pulling off some materials from the roof. Abdul whispered, "If they continue like this, they will tear off the top of the museum in a few days and destroy the pieces inside." I ignored them for the time being and followed the two gentlemen on the guided tour. The armed Marines walked behind us creating a buffer between an entourage of curious Iraqis and our group.

We stopped before an elaborate wrought-iron fence that enclosed a long narrow road that ended where we stood and seemed to extend out toward the river. Abdul pointed to a blue sign with white lettering that was written in Arabic along with poorly written English.

"The Procession Street. The street of the main religouse and the new Babylonian year festival. Its length about 1430m, and the width 10m. The northern part (180m) is restored and was decorated element and lion motive of glazed bricks."

Moussawi spoke quite eloquently but in almost a whisper as he informed us that we were standing before the original Procession Street. This street, which resembles a cobblestone path, extended from outside the gates of ancient Babylon in 690 BC and into the main thoroughfare of Babylon proper into the original Ishtar gate. He pointed to the road on the other side of the wrought iron face and stated that the different layers we could see were evidence of the Babylonians unique method for making an earlier form of asphalt, which was used on the roads and in brick laying to avoid cracking in the extreme heat. This road continued through the Babylonian city and out to Babil Tower, a large ziggurat dedicated to Marduk, where religious processions began and wound themselves around the perimeter of the city and then into the city through this very road to where we stood.

He carefully painted a mental picture by explaining that while things looked very plain today we needed to use our imagination to envision the rich, deep blue, and red clay colors that decorated the walls that lined the road on both sides. Moussawi informed us that one of the pieces being preserved inside the Museum of Babylon, behind the cinder-blocked doors, was an original plate of the Babylonian lion that used to drape the sides of the wall. The Babylonians had about 120 lions molded in glaze brick colored with deep blues, browns, and yellows to provide a rich entrance into the city that was culminated by the beautiful Ishtar Gate with its images of Addad and Marduk deities carefully crafted into the brick. I asked him of the original gate today and he replied unabashedly that it had been stolen by the Germans during the latter years of the Ottoman Empire piece by piece and was displayed in the museum in Berlin today.

As a clergyman, I experience nothing that isn't framed by my theology and faith history. I looked out over the road and attempted to envision the beauty of this ancient city and the crowds of people that would have filled the city by the Euphrates. I relished the moment as I realized that I was standing on the very path where King Hammurabi, who was believed to be the first ruler of the written law, the likes of Nebuchadnezzar, Cyrus the Persian, and, in later centuries, Alexander the Great had galloped in victory. My thoughts immediately took me to Daniel, Meshach, Shadrach, and Abednego as they were guided through this very path, along with the remaining members of the tribe of Judah, taken away from their homes and into the service of King Nebuchadnezzar into slavery. My mind raced to think of who else might have been here, and I thought of Ezekiel walking and preaching on these very streets to the crowds of the time.

In comparison to the ancient history that took place in that very spot, American history was akin to a recent text message. The history here is not solely of Iraq and these people but it is the history of humanity. In a very deep and real sense we are all connected biologically, spiritually, and politically to this place. Its significance cannot be ignored. How embarrassed I was to stand there and realize that all of these years to me Iraq was symbolized by the pestering persona of Saddam Hussein while I remained oblivious to its global historic importance.

I was brought back to the present by an invitation from Abdul to catch up with the group as we proceeded down the path to a vantage point where we could study the great wall before us. According to Moussawi, the palace wall we were now looking at was a respectable replica of the original walls of Nebuchadnezzar's palace. If we looked closely at the base of the wall he noted we can differentiate between older segments of the wall and the newer walls. The older segments, he claimed, were the original remains of walls from 597 BC. Moussawi pointed to a southeastern corner of the wall and stated that at one point prior to the reconstruction of the new walls an excavation project had revealed that further down in that corner they believed to have found elements and fragments consistent to Hammurabi's period dating back to 1750 BC. He claimed that below portions of this palace lay the remnants of Hammurabi's Babylon deep in the terrain, too far down now to be of any use because of the rising of the water table.

Ironically, the modern wall is deteriorating faster than the ancient wall sections because of the poor workmanship and materials used by Saddam Hussein's engineers. It is believed, according to Moussawi, that Saddam Hussein desired to rebuild the palace walls of Babylon for all to see and to further connect him to Nebuchadnezzar's glory and kingdom. Close scrutiny of the new walls reveals a splattering of unique bricks mixed in with the common modern bricks. These unique regal bricks were subjected to a press that impressed Saddam's Presidential stamp within the brick to appear as if it was a hand carving. Loosely interpreted, the brick states, "In the era of Saddam Hussein, protector of Iraq, who rebuilt civilization and rebuilt Babylon." The bricks were placed within the new walls to mimic the practice initiated by King Nebuchadnezzar who also had bricks stamped with his regal message and can be occasionally found throughout the remaining parts of the ancient wall.

Saddam Hussein's true intention for rebuilding the regal palace walls has never been satisfactorily explained to me. No one can definitely state what inspired him to do this. There are purists in the field of archaeology who see this replica as an adulterated monstrosity, and they would like to see the entire structure demolished and returned to its state of natural ruins. This was a perspective shared by some on staff within Iraq but who would never dare to counter the desires of this delusional despot. Evidently the erection of this modern construction to depict the southern portion of the palace caused UNESCO to drop Babylon as one of its World Heritage sites. I learned later that many archaeologists from around the world are very interested in returning to Babylon to conduct further excavations around and under this modern section.

Others, like Abdul, have grown to tolerate it. He believes that there are many areas surrounding the site that can be excavated for further study. This monstrosity, as it may be, does provide a very concrete model for many who have little or no background in archaeology. The palace is grand by anyone's standards and though simple it grants the common person a rare opportunity to see what many could not imagine. It can be an educational tool and according to Abdul it could have its economic advantages in the future.

We followed our tour guides into the outer palace ground within the walls that they called the Legislative Hall. Evidently this is where the legislators and administrators conducted the business of the province, perhaps in the format of a City Hall. It was an open area with legislative chambers on each far-reaching corner of the courtyard. The walls were high and it was an open-air courtyard enclosed on all four sides. There were large arches that led from one courtyard to another, and we can picture royal guards posted along these arches determining who may pass into the inner chambers and courtyards.

We passed through the legislative courtyard and into a smaller area that really served more as a passageway that ran parallel to the two outlying courtyards sandwiched in by their high walls. Moussawi explained that these were the soldier's corridors where they placed guards and moved within the palace. If we looked up within the corridors we could observe the parapets that were built into the wall to allow the soldiers to take defensive positions.

The next courtyard that we were led into was huge in comparison to the Legislative Hall. They called it the Royal Hall. It was another courtyard enclosed by high walls on all four sides It was large enough to accommodate an entire Regiment of Marines in formation. To the left was a large wall with a smaller archway and a platform of stone that resembled a stage. In ancient times, according to Moussawi, the royal family would ascend out of the smaller chamber behind it through the arch and greet the official parties of other kingdoms or provinces in this hall. Lacking any real imagery of the time period, I imagined scenes of Rome and its great Caesar's with their royal entourage and soldiers posted throughout this courtyard. Understanding that this was a recreation of the original palace, I inquired how much of what we saw was a remnant of the actual palace and Abdul explained that we were probably about three meters above the actual palace floor. What we saw was not literally at the same vantage point as the original partakers of this hall. I wondered who might have stood here in centuries past.

The group was then led through the smaller archway into the royal chambers. The courtyard here was quite small in comparison to the other halls. It was also a courtyard surrounded on all fours by very high walls and no ceiling. The original chambers, according to our guides, had great cedars from Lebanon laid across the top majestically enclosing this area. Before us was a stage, the royal court area, made of stone about a meter high. What impressed me most about this chamber was that it had very large areas of the original walls that were easily distinguishable from the newer wall. It was here where we were shown one of King Nebuchadnezzar's original royal bricks encrusted in the wall. Our guides explained this to be the royal chambers where the royal family would entertain its official guests. It hit me that I was standing in the very chambers where, in the Old Testament book of Daniel, it states that King Belshazzar, Nebuchadnezzar's son, in the latter years of the Babylonian period, intentionally called for the Jewish treasures captured in Jerusalem to be brought to him so they can drink from them and in doing so defile the name of the Jewish God. It was on one of these walls where scripture states that God revealed a hand to appear and write on the wall, *"Mene, Mene, Tekel, Parsin"* and later to be interpreted to Belshazzar's displeasure by Daniel.

I paused momentarily and stood in total awe. It is a true spiritual experience to stand in the place of such historic events and in particularly historic spiritual events. I attempted to comprehend the reality of such a moment and wondered what these bricks would share with me if they could speak. I worked myself before the royal court and wondered if this is where Daniel spoke as he interpreted the meaning of the events to King Belshazzar on his last night as Darius was to enter the following morning to kill Belshazzar and end the Babylonian period.

Abdul brought the group near me and went on to say that some historians believe that this is also the site where Alexander the Great died. Many have opined on his death, some believe he died of an illness, while others believe that he was wounded in battle in northern India and he returned to nurse his wounds here in Babylon where he succumbed to his wounds. Though the cause of his death may be uncertain it was interesting to note that it was possible that he died here in these very chambers. Military officers over the centuries have looked at Alexander the Great as the great conqueror. It is said that Caesar Augustus attempted to achieve similar fame and grew frustrated in not being able to achieve it as early as Alexander the Great. He is even a background figure in the Christian faith as it is noted that some scholars believe that when Jesus Christ made the statement, "What does it profit a man to conquer the world but to lose his soul?" that he was making an inference to Alexander the Great, whose feats would have been common knowledge during that time. I could not help but reflect on this as we spoke of his death.

We exited the royal court and worked our way back the way we came in to the Legislative Hall and delved into what appeared to be a small alley to the west of the grounds. Here we came into an area that appeared to be shaped like a labyrinth. There were many walls that intersected with one another and led paths into many directions. There were enclosed areas in some and others had no ceilings. Moussawi explained that while we have no real records or factual depictions of where the Gardens of Babylon actually lay, some scholars believed that they may have abundantly decorated this area of the palace. Myth has it that King Nebuchadnezzar married a young woman, Amyitis from Persia who dearly missed the greenery of her home while here in this desert region so he had the gardens constructed to be pleasing to her when she would look out from the residential palace up the hill. The many small rooms created by this labyrinth are actually believed to be the workstations and storage areas that directly supported the palaces. One of the chambers we visited seemed to have walls a meter thick and it lay down below street level thus causing some to believe that it might have even served as an ice or cool storage room for the palaces' use. From within this area one could access both areas of the palace and find oneself out into the main Procession Street. Abdul also commented that another theory often perpetuated about this place was that some of these chambers also may have served as a prison or a jail — a theory that didn't require much imagination based on the design of the rooms.

We entered a room that was cool and dark and Abdul asked to borrow one of our flashlights. He lit up the ceiling that was about four meters or twelve feet over our heads revealing hordes of tiny bats living overhead. All of a sudden, the stench and the white goop on the floor made total sense. Needless to say, this became the favorite area for all of the young Marines accompanying us during this trip as they whistled and harassed the bats inciting them to stir about in the dark chambers causing a few of our troops to excitedly make a mad dash for the exit. The entourage of Iraqis, who had been tailing us this entire time while trying to sell us souvenirs and sodas, laughed curiously as they saw these well-armed men scramble for safety.

Now that we knew who would rather face a horde of angry Iraqis carrying AK-47s versus three-inch bats, we moved out of the labyrinth into an open area teasing one another. When we climbed to the top of the small hill the teasing tempered to a whisper as we stood there and looked directly at the original ruins of what Moussawi called the residential palace. The palace was divided into two major areas, the Legislative or working palace and the residential palace. In between the two palaces stood a tall wall wide enough for chariots to ride side by side along the width of the palace grounds creating a fortified wall between the two palaces and providing a fort-like semblance to the area. We stood atop this wall, which was an original wall from 600 BC, and looked at the large clumps of sections that had been unearthed. The residential palace must have been a large, beautiful structure but all that remains today are sections of square columns and walls that are strewn about an area the size of two football fields filled with ancient bricks and hidden artifacts.

As we admired the archaeological wonder I quickly noticed two groups of Iraqis consisting of two or three men each walking casually amidst the ruins. I turned to Moussawi and asked, "Can we go there and see things closer?" and he responded in his usually polite fashion, "It is recommended that we not go down to the ruins, just walking over them causes much damage." To such I replied, "So what are they doing?" pointing with my face toward the men in the ruins. Abdul whispered back to me, "Ali-Baba ... They are thieves."

The words Colonel Cunnings shared with me the day before rang in my head as he reminded me that we were the law and the authority in the land now. This place was now under our rule. As a chaplain I am both a Naval officer and a clergyman, each with their own authority. Most chaplains prefer to exercise their authority as a clergyperson with greater confidence than that as a Naval Officer. Navy chaplains, unlike the Air Force and Army, wear a rank device on their right collar and a Chaplain Corps device on their left collar. The Army and Air Force chaplains wear a rank device on each collar but they display their Chaplain Corps device, whether it's a cross, Jewish tablet, or Muslim Crescent over the left breast pocket. Chaplains in the Navy and Marine Corps like to operate predominantly from the left collar but the reality is that in order for us to be effective within this institution, we are required to work in balance from both sides of our collars.

There are times when we function predominantly from the left side as a pastor but then there are times where we have to assert ourselves and exercise the authority granted to us on the right side of the collar as well. It's a fine line we walk because most of us, not all, but most of us want to be seen in a different light from the regular officer community in the hopes that we can broaden our level of accessibility to the troops. The authority opens doors for us as we seek to work within the command structure to counsel and support all of our personnel.

As I recalled Colonel Cunning's words, I asked Moussawi to tell the men to leave the ruins area. He looked at me perplexed. I could read his mind. He did not want to be seen as an agent of ours before these people. So I asked him, "Moussawi, do you want those men down there?"

"No, of course not. It is not good." He timidly replied. I knew then that he didn't have the authority to say anything to the same people who had run him out of town just weeks before. I called the two Marines who were with me to come by my side. They held their rifles at port arms, across their chests and I shouted at the men, "Ali-Baba! Stop." Knowing they probably didn't know English but with the tone of my voice I knew that it wouldn't take them long to surmise what I thought of them by referring to them as "Ali-Baba." They stopped and looked at me. Then gave me that universal look that all lawbreakers give as if they were saying, "Who me? We're not doing anything."

I had their attention. I used my arms to point to them and then waved them out to signal the way out of the ruins. They stopped and turned toward Moussawi and directed their comments in Arabic to him. He replied apologetically as if saying, "Hey, I don't know who this crazy American thinks he is but he wants you out of

117

there." I stood there and watched them exchange a few words back and forth in a conversational tone. I figured it was time to show some authority so I delegated the authority to the two young Marines with me, "Go down there and escort them out of the ruins." I don't think I had finished the sentenced before the two Marines were off at a gallop with weapons in hands to enforce the law. The Iraqis saw the Marines coming their way, and they raised their arms in surrender and began to walk away muttering Arabic as if saying, "We're leaving, we're leaving."

I looked over at Moussawi and Abdul and caught them as they glanced at each other and smiled together. Abdul turned to me and in a lower whisper as if hiding it from the Iraqis who were following us said to me, "This is very good, very good. Thank you."

With the ruins cleared of any marauders, we all walked on in our tour. I felt good, and I felt empowered, and I knew we had to do more of this in order to save this place. We moved on and found ourselves before a statue of a lion on a pedestal, the Lion of Babylon that lay in an open cobblestone courtyard all on its own. Moussawi proceeded to tell us how the Germans, during the Ottoman Empire, had attempted to steal the Lion but it was too dense and heavy to sail out of the region. He pointed to the Lion's face and noted that a portion of it had been blown away. He claims that the Germans might have been led to believe that the basalt lion had gold on the inside so they used a small artillery piece to blow a piece of it away only to discover it was solid stone so they left it behind. According to Abdul, the Lion was discovered in 1776 and it is said to be dated back prior to King Nebuchadnezzar and was the oldest relic of its kind in the area.

It occurred to me as I listened to these gentlemen retell their history that for at least the past 3,000 years these people have witnessed armies march into their lives and watched them plunder their lands and walk off with their treasures. Neither Moussawi nor Abdul hid their disdain for the British, Germans, Turks, or others who currently held their relics in their museums under the racist guise according to these gentlemen that the Iraqis were incapable of properly caring for these relics so the world would have to care for them outside of their homeland. They became quite animated and impassioned over this discussion more so than any other time we have had thus far. Ironically, as I listened to them I could not help but to side with them as they desired so much to be respected as caretakers of their own history. At the same time, I thought how fortunate it is that many of these relics are not here now. Initial reports out of Baghdad stated that the museum there had been ransacked and relics all over this country were in dire danger as we had this conversation.

I moved closer to the Babylonian Lion for a picture. I looked at it and made out a large male lion with its mouth opened as it was positioned over the figure of a human being who was on his back and obviously overpowered by the lion. The piece looked unfinished. The lion had more detail carved into it than the human figure. Moussawi shared that the symbolism of the lion represented the power the Kingdom of Babylon had over humanity. The Lion of Babylon, according to him, was an ancient symbol of the powerful Babylonian Empire dating back to the Hammurabi period. I stood there and gazed at this figure that was older than the United States. Looking at this lion led me to think of another lion's story that I've heard since I was a child, the account of Daniel and the lion's den. I wondered where on these grounds King Darius the Mede had kept his lion's pit. The Bible states, "At the first light of dawn, the king got up and hurried to the lions' den. When he came near the den, he called to Daniel in an anguished voice, 'Daniel, servant of the living God, has your God, whom you serve continually, been able to rescue you from the lions?' " This would mean that when King Darius awoke in the residential palace he ran out to check on Daniel. We could then imply that the distance he had to cover was not that far and probably still on the royal grounds, which in turn we could conclude is somewhere near where we stood. Once again we stood in near proximity of a miraculous event and an act of tremendous faith and grace.

We had traveled in a loop, coming out to the beginning of the Procession Street having a much better feel for how it led the crowds toward the city before the majestic Ishtar Gate that originally towered at about sixty feet high. The foundation today is the remains of the original Ishtar Gate that existed prior to the third reconstruction effort by Nebuchadnezzar and it appears as a lower street. The parts of the Ishtar Gate that remain reveal the highly distinguishable workmanship of artisans who knew how to work with bricks and stones. The replica that stands at the entrance of the gate looks like child's artwork in comparison to the actual craftsmanship displayed on the original. The only difference between what lays in the ground in Babylon today and that which is on display in Berlin is that the remaining remnants are not colored, they lay in their original clay format. The Ishtar Gate finished during Nebuchadnezzar's reign was beautifully lacquered in a deep blue color with the figures of Addad and Marduk marvelously colored in yellow and white glaze unlike the plain dusty ones that remain today.

We walked around this area in silence taking it in. Even the most historically challenged person amongst us could not help but be awed or inspired by the sight. We took a few snapshots to portray our visit. We found another brick with an ancient proclamation on it and then we walked back out toward the courtyard where the crowd awaited us.

I thanked Moussawi and Abdul for their hospitality and I assured them that we would be back. I told them we would be speaking to our superiors to see how we can protect the area and make it safe for them and the relics that lay here. We worked our way through all the hands that were trying to sell us some sort of ware or trinket or that clamored for a gift. I learned to look past the crowd for now and we worked our way back onto the road and headed south back to Camp Babylon determined to win some support from the command.

As a Navy Chaplain I have been taught to execute my role through four major functions — to facilitate, to provide, to care, and to advise. I facilitate by ensuring that the command is open to accommodating the religious practices of all its members. Thus as a Protestant, I ensure my Catholics and others have the time and support they need to express their religious faith. In providing, I specifically provide direct services to those of my own faith as a Protestant Christian. I personally lead worship, Bible studies, and prayers. The "care" function is easy because I am here to care intrinsically for all of our people as are the other Chaplains. The last function, however, is the most difficult — to advise. Simply because one has the authority to advise does not imply that one enjoys the rapport and creditability to advise these professionals in matters of religion, morale, morals, and ethics. We should never presume that we possess the only authority in such areas because, in fact, the responsibility and ultimate authority falls on the Commander. As an advisor I am compelled to learn the strategic vision of my Commander and insure that I provide adequate advise from my area of expertise that will allow the Commander to be true to his strategic vision while also being conscious of the need to assist the Commander to be ethically and morally sensitive.

As I walked back along the tree-lined road toward our camp I was determined and challenged to clearly articulate a need to commit resources to the museum so we could do what we all knew intrinsically was the right thing to do.

---

1. Joan Oates, *Babylon* (London: Thames and Hudson, 1980), p. 151.

NOTES:
Chaplain ability here rests on the
Trust & report the CH has with
CDR. When this is damaged
CHop looses much of his ability
to have an impact.
When CDR Trust CHop . . .

121

Chapter Seven

Conquering Babylon

And forgive your people, who have sinned against you;
forgive all the offenses they have committed against you,
and cause their conquerors to show them mercy.
— 1 Kings 8:50

I received word via Colonel Cunnings that General Conway wanted to see me and discuss my memo. I headed out to the Commanding General's office area at a quick pace walking, alongside a path by the Euphrates River tributary that hugged our position. I was excited to see what might become of this but conversely there was a part of me that was very concerned. I underwent a process of rehearsing all of my arguments in the event they would need further convincing. Truth be told, I didn't have a clear picture of what needed to be done. I just knew that something needed to be done and my recommendations were a preliminary jab in the dark at addressing the issues. In the end, however, they were just that, isolated recommendations.   *Staff officer function*

I grew a little uncertain as I'd reasoned within myself that I was not an infantry officer, and I didn't know what was required to secure a location or how to deploy forces to manage the area. On the contrary, even if I must manage, I did not have the authority as a noncombatant officer to attempt such feats. While I wanted to propose action at the same time I did not want to propose that we place such a burden on the command that it would force them to divert forces from other crucial areas in order to meet these recommendations. I wanted something done to insure the security of the ancient site and the people affected by it. I stopped second guessing myself and prayed on the way in, "O Lord, I put this in your hands. Shape hearts accordingly and guide my steps. In Jesus' name. Amen."

I stepped into the building that houses the General's staff to discover that they're living in similar squalor. They had a much bigger facility that once held a greater sense of grandness to it but now it lay equally stripped and naked thanks to the thoroughness of local looters. I was greeted by the young Marine officer in the front office and he went and informed Colonel John Coleman, the Chief of Staff of the 1st Marine Expeditionary Force, of my arrival. Colonel Coleman was a Marine infantryman who stood tall and straight with a typical Marine athletic build and very wide shoulders. He was a gentleman in his late forties into early fifties. His hair was black but thinning. His job was to be the gatekeeper to the Commanding General's access. He had a reputation for being direct and not afraid of confrontations. He had his hands into everything and was abreast of every issue that had to be addressed to the General.

Everyone went through the Chief of Staff for everything every time. He was known to be a real admirer of Civil War era General Thomas Jonathan "Stonewall" Jackson and would occasionally be caught quoting the Civil War General. He didn't appear to be one to frolic in pleasantries and seemed to always have his mind on one or more of the many things pressing on their agendas. I can't say he was stoic because he had his moments of attempted light-hearted humor, but he was a no-nonsense executive weighed with the grim reality of the issues at hand.

I was escorted into his office and I found him standing over his desk looking at a map. He looked up momentarily, "Good afternoon, chaplain. We read your memo and the General wants to move ahead on some of your recommendations." He called me over to his desk and he began to outline the perimeter of the ancient grounds on the map. "Show me the grounds of the museum ... the ancient sites ... the cultural center." We discussed how the entire site belonged to the State Board of Antiquities and Heritage and how they fit into the Ministry of Culture in Baghdad. I showed him where the ancient ruins lay and expressed the concerns of the staff on minimizing foot and vehicle traffic in some of these areas. He asked if some of these paths could support a Humvee patrol, and I confirmed that they could as long as they remained on the path.

124

We discussed the fact that some of the staff had identified the presence of smugglers and their fear of having digging erupt in the area in order to feed artifacts into the black market.

At one point I asked, "How do we secure such a wide and porous perimeter?"

He quickly answered "We'll place barbed wire all around the perimeter and enclose it making it part of our camp."

I responded, to my own surprise with, "Do we have that much barbed wire?"

He flashed a quick glance at me as if to nonverbally question my incredulity but simply replied, "We have plenty and if we need more the engineers can get it."

I nodded in concurrence and disbelief at the same time. I was pleasantly surprised to see us, the Marine Corps, take such an aggressive approach and I couldn't wait to share it with Moussawi and Abdul at the museum. Colonel Coleman went on to explain that we would disperse Marines throughout the perimeter to establish a perimeter guard and have them patrol the areas of concern. We reviewed his recommendations and discussed access to the newly secured site in order to allow the staff to assemble and initiate contact with Baghdad. I asked for permission to ask the museum staff to allow us to lead a few tours for our Marines at the camp in order for them to be exposed to the site in a controlled fashion. Colonel Coleman said he didn't see a problem with that and would bring it up with the Commanding General.

The young officer outside in the main corridor stepped in and advised us that the General was ready to see us so we both stepped in to General Conway's office. General Conway came out from behind his desk and warmly received us as we entered. We were invited to stand around a table he had off to the side and Colonel Coleman briefed the entire plan. The General seemed very enthusiastic and felt it was the right thing to do. At one point, Colonel Coleman noted that once we secure the area we will need to have someone manage the staff, manage access to the site, and serve as a liaison. Without hesitation General Conway looked at me and said, "You got it, chaplain. If you need anything come see us."

"Yes, sir," I replied immediately.

On the way out, I walked out with Colonel Coleman who told me he would task the appropriate people on the staff to take care of what the General had agreed to and I should convey the news to the staff in the museum. In addition, it would be up to me to manage the day-to-day management of the museum so I needed to develop a plan. I thanked him for his support and walked backed to my area to brief Colonel Cunnings of the development.

I could tell Colonel Cunnings was a little concerned that he had lost me to the museum as I excitedly shared with him the way ahead. "Is this something you think you should be doing?" he asked.

"Yes, sir," I retorted. I saw this as an obvious extension of ministry. Besides, I rationalized in my own mind and attempted to convince Colonel Cunnings that I wasn't the only chaplain in the camp, since we did have two outstanding Army Chaplains, Chaplain (Maj) Mark F. Plaushin who was a beloved Roman Catholic priest from Philadelphia and Chaplain (Capt) Terry Callis, an energetic Assembly of God preacher from Texas, located here in Camp Babylon with the Army's 358th Civil Affairs Brigade Headquarters Group. They were assigned to I MEF and we were all co-located so we shared the responsibilities.

Colonel Cunnings reminded me, "Yeah but you're *our* chaplain and I will lean on you for what we need. Go ahead and do what you need to do and let us know what you need ... we do have some Marine Corps Civil Affairs people available to us. Maybe we can get one of those teams to work with you to be sure you're not pulled too far into this."

"I don't foresee a problem but that's a good idea. I'll let you or Paul know," I responded, keeping in mind that Colonel Cunnings might be heading south to Kuwait to return to run Camp Commando and his Executive Officer, Lieutenant Colonel Paul Lebidine would remain in place at Camp Babylon during his absence.

Loyalties to a command are keenly important to Marines and I had to keep this in mind. Technically, I was assigned to the First Marine Expeditionary Force Headquarters Group commonly referred to as MHG. Our primary mission as the Headquarters Group was to support the large staff associated with the Commanding General of the 1st Marine Expeditionary Force logistically and administratively. The Commanding General had his usual staff that consists of his Administration (G1), Intelligence (G2), Operations (G3), Logistics (G4), Future Operations (G5), Communications (G6), and the additional sub-sections and special staff like Force Medical, Force Chaplain, and Force Legal. Each of these staff members works directly for the Commanding General or CG but they are managed by the Chief of Staff. They focus on issues and agendas set forth by the CG as he leads the entire force of the Marine Air Ground Task Force (MAGTF), which is composed of the 1st Marine Division (infantry), the 3rd Marine Aircraft Wing, and the 1st Force Service Support Group. This group, in summary, provides all of the bullets, beans, and Band-Aids needed in the fight while on the go.

The best way to explain the 1st MEF staff is by describing them as a compilation of experienced senior officers who are subject-matter experts that are heavily involved in planning but the people that execute those plans are the subordinate units within the MAGTF. So when this group of experts comes together and congregates in a camp like ours it is up to the MHG to provide the day-to-day support functions for the staff. MHG has the bulk of enlisted Marines with a cadre of officers and non-commissioned officers who are the ones who run the camp and worry about the delivery of services such as electricity, fuel, water, meals, showers, and many other services to include religious services and pastoral care that fall on my shoulders. This is also why Colonel Cunnings expressed some concern over my involvement with this project and thus legitimately worried it would pull me more toward the I MEF staff issues rather than his Marines. Technically, I am his unit chaplain and I don't belong to the Commanding General directly. My billet in MHG is unique in that it does set me aside as the Deputy Force Chaplain in an additional duty capacity meaning that I report to Colonel Cunnings but I also work for the Force Chaplain.

To complicate matters, now that the "invasion" was over, the decision had been made to streamline our forces at the staff level in order to decrease our footprint in Iraq and maintain a presence here in Babylon as well as in California. In our discussions amongst

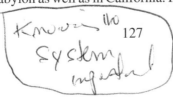

the Force Chaplain, John Gwudz, Rabbi Irving Elson (a dear friend of mine since our days in Chaplain School who served an emergency fill as the chaplain for 11th Marines), and I all agreed that I would remain behind in Iraq and they would both retrograde back to California with the staff that was returning home. I made the discussion easy because I wanted to stay. The majority of my Marines from MHG didn't have a choice and they were staying involuntarily. I volunteered to stay for as long as needed so I could return with them as a group. In doing so I was then dubbed the I MEF Chaplain (Forward) only to complicate matters more.

This now meant that I worked directly for both General Conway and Brigadier General Keith Stalder as well as for the MHG. While this may have seemed administratively confusing I believe it was a real blessing from God because it made it so much easier for me to be engaged in both worlds, the macro-world of I MEF (Forward) with what they were doing throughout the southern regions of Iraq and the micro-world of MHG and their junior Marines right here in Babylon. In my opinion it was the best of both worlds, the opportunity to learn to interact with issues at the MEF level where I interacted with the staff, the foreign forces, and the ministries in Baghdad, while at the same time being a part of a small unit the size of a battalion, which kept me grounded to the needs of the troops. The challenge was to attempt to be effective at both levels.

At heart, my conversation with Colonel Cunnings was not the issue of Command and Control because he understood clearly, as did I, that when everything was said and done I worked for him and he was my Commander. I believe that the real issue at hand was the definition of our theology of ministry or in layman terms the role of the chaplain.

Navy chaplains love to be assigned to Marine Corps units because Marines, officers and enlisted, have no qualms with using their chaplains to invest in their people. Navy chaplains have the very unique opportunity to serve as commissioned officers in the Navy but we are assigned duties with the Sea Services — the Marine Corps, the Navy, the Coast Guard, and we even enjoy a few billets with the Merchant Marines. We get the opportunity to serve on a wide variety of platforms and to minister in a very diverse spectrum of environments as we interact and serve a wide array of specialized communities within the Department of the Navy and Coast Guard.

Each assignment has its own unique demands and peculiarities with it, but there is one commonality that is consistent when serving the Marine Corps and that is that no one invests in their personnel like the Marine Corps. Being a Marine isn't an assignment or a duty, it is an ethos. It is a way of life. I would argue that other specialized units within the Navy and other organizations exemplify similar levels of ethos persona but no one does it like the Marine Corps. In all fairness, I should remind you that I began my career in the military as a young Marine and there may be a hint of prejudice, but nonetheless, I stand by my assertion to go on and state that such an investment in the character and shaping of persona in its personnel allows the Marine Corps to unabashedly use chaplains to care for their people.

Marine Corps history is inculcated within each Marine in boot camp and as such there is a mystical connection between modern Marines and those who have carried the burdens in the past. This mysticism coupled with the realities of war and the confrontation of mortality makes it a fertile environment to discuss matters of spirituality, faith, and existentialism. In such an environment we as chaplains have a place and very distinct role in the face of battle, death, injury, and grief. The spiritual is felt and embraced. It is a part of the quiet reality around us. This doesn't always translate into "religiosity" for that is another matter completely but there is openness to the divine and matters of spirituality.

The inquiries of this reality rarely call into question the existence of God but rather question the relevancy and relationship to God. Marines understand that faith manifested and lived provides for hope and courage during times of tribulation. In my very first duty station as a Chaplain with Marines, my Commanding Officer's instruction were very clear to me upon the conclusion of my incall visit, "Chaplain, I expect you to take care of my Marines. Now go do what Chaplains do." There wasn't a call for metrics or reports in the months that followed but the CO would on occasion ask his

Company Commanders to report back to him on what I was doing. Inherently, they knew if I was being effective or not.

In contrast, when serving for big Navy, we have to make a conscious conceptual shift to serving two masters: the system and its personnel. Navy leaders are wonderful, extremely intelligent professionals in a class of their own, but they're predominantly right-brained engineers who plan everything, measure twice, act, and then measure again for effectiveness. This "business model" approach to leadership is very effective when calculating the costs of providing some force capability or managing the costs to operate one of our multi-million dollar platforms, but it doesn't always translate as passionately or dynamically to the personal care of people within its structures. Navy officers are often charged with the care of the ship or platform and insuring that the platform in their charge is always ready to perform its task. It is understood that the soul of any platform are the Sailors, a reality often grasped best at the highest levels of Navy command but not always embraced well at the lower operational levels, thus unfortunately our focus and efforts are oft more focused on the platform than on the soul.

The Navy has developed a business term for its "people" shifting its emphasis from Sailors to "human capital." Implicitly it is a process that dehumanizes the individual and even disconnects them from the rich traditions and ethos of the Navy past. It is a shift from the soul of the organization to the toys of the organization. With the emphasis on business models, enterprise dynamics, and business rules, the iconic Sailor is sometimes lost in this new sea of processes. This is what happens when the Navy, a service branch steeped in Naval history and proud traditions charged with keeping the sea lanes open for American interests, is treated like a business venture and it is leaned on to do more with less.

What is the quiet reality implicitly communicated in the Navy today? The Navy is given less funds yet asked to do more while attempting to find resources to stay ahead of our foes technologically and strategically. Since the investment into personnel and personnel issues is often the most expensive, it is often the first casualty in the budget process. A consequence of this is that we

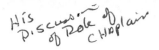

have smaller ships with greater technological capabilities but in order to save costs associated with "human capital" we are equipping our platforms with less people and expecting these fewer people to perform multiple tasks for the same pay as when they were performing one specialized task. Gone are the days of building redundancy into the equation of ship personnel in order to insure that there are sufficient hands available to sail the ship, fight the ship, and save the ship simultaneously during the heat of battle.

This brings me back to the role of the chaplain. In the Navy, chaplains have been systematically eliminated from being assigned as ship's company, a term referring to personnel assigned as crewmembers of a ship, with the exception of very large ships like aircraft carriers. Instead, chaplains have been relegated to providing regional coverage at certain levels of commands. To use a sport analogy: We've moved from man-to-man coverage to zone coverage. Those who are cynical of the Navy's reasoning for this would imply that the role of the chaplain can thus be interpreted in engineering terms to mean that chaplains have very little to contribute to the driving, fighting, or maintenance of the physical ship and as such are not required on ships. The intrinsic role of having the chaplain serve as a functional member of the crew with the intent purpose of caring for the crew seems lost. Chaplains are then placed ashore so they can be accessed by needy family members and dispatched to areas of need on demand in a crisis.

?

Ask GPAS

In order to justify a chaplain's role, the Navy asks, "What does the chaplain contribute?" "Do we need this contribution?" and "How do we measure the effectiveness of this contribution?" Some may say that these are reasonable questions and I would be among them if we could agree upon what is important and what needs to be measured. If we are assessing the need for chaplains based on cost effective models of business or how they contribute directly to the driving of a ship, we will quickly deduce that chaplains are not mission essential and can be outsourced as needed or eliminated. If we deduce that chaplains "do church" and thus in a modern secular society this function is no longer applicable or appropriate then we can also concur that chaplains can be eliminated from the rolls.

If, on the other hand, chaplains are seen as an integral part of honoring the free exercise of religion as a core foundational, constitutional principle, firming the belief that we as a nation do not establish religion but clearly honor the need to facilitate the faithful, contributing toward the development and strengthening of the human spirit and as an organic resource professionally provide a high level of personal care for our personnel then one can hardly argue against the chaplaincy. I note that Title X dictates that Commanding Officers must care for the spiritual and religious well-being of our Sailors. I can also draw from this the implicit tenet to care for the soul and spirit of humanity so as not to lose the value of our people placed in dangerous and arduous conditions. The chaplain is charged with caring for every member of the command, not just those of his or her own faith, but to believers and non-believers alike. I would argue that spiritual health, existential contextualization, and relational dynamics are all services provided by chaplains who contribute positively in the lives of our people. The question lies in whether or not Navy engineer types deem this as a service worth investing in and if so how to measure such a subjective and "squishy" process.

I find it no accident that the communities that deal intimately with the quiet realities of war — death, maiming, destruction, grief, humiliation, hunger, dislocation, finite mortality — are the very communities that embrace the chaplaincy and understand the need for a community of spiritually focused professionals who care for the soul and spirit of its combatants. The further we get from the intimate face of war and sanitize its process by employing weapons remotely, relegating combat to inanimate objects like missiles and never seeing or smelling the consequences of the ground war, the less conscientious we become of the effects of war and the human toll it can have. In contrast, we are seeing a new interest in the personal impact of war in small areas within the Navy as it designates forces toward a more expeditionary ground environment, such as Navy Expeditionary Combat Command, Special Warfare, and Individual Augments, and as a result experience a greater clamor for focus on family, faith, and personal values.

The irony in all of this is that often we believe that the trauma of war lies only in the bloody fields trampled by the infantry and we minimize the traumas that gravely impact the lives of people even in peacetime while affecting the tasks of our nation. Take into consideration the agony of losing a parent or beloved grandparent while in the middle of the Pacific and not having the ability to return home in time for the funeral. Consider the feeling of grief and shame associated with such loss because they feel as if the Navy made them choose loyalties against their kin. There is also the young wife who is new to a geographical area and must endure the difficulties of a complicated birth all by herself while her husband is deployed. Navy culture has normalized or classified this as routine in order to bring people into compliance. How does it deal with the husband when this talented Sailor turns the frustration and anger inwardly because he can't provide effectively for his new wife or feels cheated of a life-defining moment? These are but some of the traumas a chaplain can often help to mitigate and heal by coming alongside a Sailor or Marine and providing confidential pastoral care that eventually may bring about healing and allow that individual to feel invested in by the Navy as an organization and a family.

I further contend that a chaplain or a pastor is most effective during these tragedies when they are part of the community and become integrally invested within the lives of their Sailors. The real value of having a chaplain come alongside to provide pastoral care is deemed valuable only when it is done during a time of needed or perceived crisis. Coming alongside socially or solely for ritualistic purposes like the occasional service provided by a circuit riding chaplain can be categorized at best as opportunistic and fortuitous but it falls short of being profound.

I joined the Navy to bring people to Jesus as a Baptist but I have come to realize that my greatest testimony to what I believe in and what motivates me in life are not my apologetics but my ability to care. I care because I truly believe God cares for me and he demonstrated that care through ordinary people. Today I care because God cared for me first. The love and passion I have for my Sailors and Marines is not of my own making but I believe it has its origin in a spiritual dimension far greater than I. My caring for others is not predicated on whether they accept my message or not. I don't see myself as God's telemarketer or salesman but as a pastor — one who reaches out to touch the soul of others. Over the years I've come to care first, develop relationships, and share my apologetics in that order. I believe that close scrutiny of the ministry model Jesus provided reveals the very same priorities.

The role of a chaplain, in my humblest of opinions, goes far beyond providing a mass or prayer service but in New Testament terms it is a manifestation of God's incarnate presence in the very real and often painful journey in life. Clergy are not God but a reflection of God and the holy in our midst. This may be an imperfect reflection with many smudges but is a reflection of God, nonetheless. This means that the church exists not to isolate itself from the rest of the world and be self-righteous, but it is to be as the swimmer who comes alongside and shares his life jacket in helping others to stay afloat. In the end this means to me that my role as a chaplain extends beyond the care of just "my people" as in those who believe as I do but rather it incorporates all of my Navy or Marines. On a grander scale, it also incorporates caring for those around us to include the Iraqis.

Reaching outside of our support for US forces is a point of contention by many for a variety of reasons. Some people argue that our commission as chaplains is solely to be there to facilitate services to our constituency delineated as Marines and Sailors. Lawyers might argue that if we provide services to people outside of our immediate constituency then it can be argued by some that the state is establishing religion. In order to appear not to establish religion, the services and care of a chaplain are not to be employed outside of the uniformed constituency. I obviously am not a lawyer nor am I well versed in this argument. I am, however, versed in common sense and I believe that if we as chaplains can influence operations, facilitate acts of services, and emulate compassion and care we should not only be supported but streamlined within the mission of the military to do so.

God is not God solely to Americans and for such reasons as a clergy, conscious of political, religious, and cultural ramifications,

I should be empowered to impact the mission by insuring that there is a compassionate and humane dimension to it. I know where my loyalties lie as a Navy officer and an American in uniform. I know where my loyalties lie as an endorsed pastor to the military. I also know where my loyalties lie as a child of God and the responsibility I have to love those innocents impacted by our presence and actions during an act of war.

As a conscientious and ethical being, I choose to be on the side of a conflict by wearing the uniform and supporting the troops and to that degree I therefore must limit my approach. War is complex and with these complexities come hard decisions. However, we should never choose to ethically and morally make these decisions easier on ourselves by making matters black and white and therefore divorcing ourselves of the realities in war. Chaplains of all people have the greatest flexibility and opportunity to highlight decency and compassion in the vilest of environments such as combat. It is not only an opportunity but a duty that requires skillful navigation, self-denial, and a global perspective for compassion.

For this reason I moved forward in this endeavor. It was necessary for me as an American and a Christian to embrace the complexity of Babylon beyond us against them. If we were to aim toward peace in our own little corner of the world then we had to lead by example. To the criticism of some I moved ahead gingerly determined to reach out to the Iraqis as much as we reached out to our own kind.

The Iraqis didn't usually arrive until about nine in the morning at the Ishtar Gate courtyard. I decided to get off the cot and out from hiding under my poncho liners as I attempted to shield myself from the hordes of mosquitoes and flies during the night. It was either suffocate from the heat or be subject to the gnawing of flies and mosquitoes through the hot nights. The Seabees had promised to return and enclose the windows with screens to help us shield against the pestilence. Their return could not be soon enough.

Mornings at Camp Babylon were serene but they tickled the senses in bizarre ways. The sun normally broke through the windowless craters on the wall by five in the morning with the subtleness of a searchlight. The morning air brought in a hint of the ever-present algae smell from the Euphrates with the staleness of sand. On those mornings when the winds traveled our way, we were confronted with the smell of human fecal matter burning in diesel fuel. Morning routines included a walk in shorts, half-laced boots, flak jacket, and helmet while half asleep across the street to the makeshift latrines that reeked of fuel or a pee tube stuck in the sand and covered on three sides by plywood for semi-privacy. It was the Marine's version of an expeditionary urinal. Choosing not to shave was not an option so a cold shave was welcomed in the summer months but loathed during the cold months. The morning included a quick jaunt across the street to the mess hall by the river for a chance at breakfast. In our early days at Babylon, that translated to a hot cup of coffee and some eggs and sausages canned in large containers for large feedings — not exactly Cracker Barrel. About two months into Babylon, we had KBR move in with sub-contractors and provide the usual cafeteria fare found in stateside mess halls. There were no eggs to order but the omelets were pretty good as life improved around the camp. After breakfast, a small stroll by the Euphrates River allowed me some quiet time and a word of prayer and reflection.

On this particular morning, I mustered up RP2 Stephens and SGT Christopher Gowin along with a few Marines from MHG S4 and we headed out to the Ishtar Gate to face the crowds and share the news of how we were going to secure the perimeter. We took two Humvees and pulled right up to the Ishtar Gate entrance and before we could dismount our vehicles we were surrounded by a horde of curious Iraqis. They recognized us from the day before and as a result must have felt comfortable enough to come over and greet us. We had taken the doors off the vehicle to expedite mounting and dismounting of the vehicle so as soon as we came to a stop, they had begun to extend their hands into the vehicle to wave hello and shake my hand.

In the flurry of activity I felt something slipping away from under my seat as it was being pulled out along the back of my legs and I immediately reached down and grabbed it. It was an MRE that I had stashed under my seat and now I was holding on from one end as it was being stolen out from under me. I didn't know any Arabic so I just yelled, "Stop, stop," and pushed everyone back with one hand as I lost the fight for the MRE with the other. Some of them looked at me with a look of confusion but others quickly ran off and then we all realized we had been robbed. So much for the friendly reception. We pushed everyone back away from the vehicles and we looked around to inventory our vehicles. We discovered that in the mad rush, the vehicle fire extinguisher, a few water bottles, and even the roadside reflective triangle that we normally kept in the vehicle were all gone. I shook my head in disbelief and kept everyone at bay as the crowd observed us. I asked one of the Marines to stay with the vehicles and keep everyone back as I proceeded to the courtyard through the Ishtar Gate.

I grew up in New York City and I swear that all of my childhood memories have large crowds associated with them. No matter where you went, to the movies, to school on the IRT subway, or to shop, there were always hordes of people surrounding you. Life here didn't seem much different. As I entered the Ishtar Gate it was a madhouse of people. Some were just leisurely lounging around while others were attempting to sell their wares. The sounds of the chisels and hammers could still be heard over the low growl of the many conversations taking place in the courtyard. I scanned the courtyard and spotted a group of men sitting under the cover of the large trees in the center of the courtyard and there in their midst sat Abdul and Moussawi. We made eye contact and they immediately excused themselves from the group of men and came toward me.

"As-Salaam-Alaikum, Good morning, welcome to you and me," said Abdul as he attempted to greet me in a very formal fashion.

"Alaikum-Salaam," I responded along with the raising of my right hand and placing it over my heart, as if I were getting ready to say the pledge of allegiance, and a slight bow forward to each of them in response to the same action demonstrated toward me.

"Moussawi and Abdul, I have news for you and we need to talk so please come with me."

I knew from our previous encounter that they didn't feel comfortable with the many ears and eyes fixed on them in the courtyard so I walked out toward the vehicles and they followed. I wanted to be sure to keep this conversation between us. I asked RP2

Stephens and SGT Gowin to stand between us and the people behind us to insure no one came within earshot.

"I spoke with our General yesterday and he has agreed to protect the ancient sites," I shared with them.

"Very good, very good," responded Moussawi and Abdul nodded approvingly with his usually big smile.

"What does this mean? When will it happen?" Moussawi went on to ask.

"It means that we, the Marine Corps, are taking over the compound." I paused to gauge a response but none came. "We will include the ancient sites, the palace, the campus, and the Greek stadium as part of our camp and it will be under our control. No one will be allowed to enter or exit without our permission. Marines will defend the position and it will be protected," I explained to them.

They shared concerned looks with one another and exchanged a few words with one another in Arabic and then Abdul turned to me and said, "What will happen to the museum staff?"

"What staff? The two of you?" I asked.

Abdul then explained, "From the beginning of the war, all governmental employees have not been paid. We do not hear from Baghdad and receive no salaries. If they come back we want them to find us here so we can receive our salaries. Will we be allowed to enter?"

"For now I will allow you and a handful of others to enter but it will be a very small number. If you wish to keep working to show good faith and that you are here, we can arrange for it. As a matter of fact I thought we could use you to give our Marines some tours so they can learn more about Iraq and Mesopotamian history. Is that okay with you?"

They both nodded and concurred with me but I didn't note any real level of excitement.

"Soon I will begin to push everyone out of here and only allow your staff to enter the museum. You will have to tell me who they are. If they are to work here I would prefer they speak some English so they can assist with tours of the ruins and palace. Once this takes place then I can get more organized and we'll see what we can do for you and the staff," I explained.

"One more thing, dear sir," Moussawi interjected sheepishly. "This is my home. I lived here for many years with my wife. They destroyed my home. Will you help me build a new place for my family to return?"

I looked at him and with all sincerity said, "Moussawi, I cannot promise you anything like this. I will look into it and see what can be done but I don't know."

"Okay, okay, please let me know if it can be done. I am with no home and live with my family in another town with my wife's brother," he replied trying to accentuate the urgency of his matters.

"Here is what I need from you. Tell the people that we are taking over Babylon. The Marines are here and we will be the law. Tell them no more looting or entering the ruins. Advise them that soon we will close the grounds in order to protect it. Please be sure to tell everyone that we are closing it to protect it and will return it to the people of Iraq. We do not want anything that is in here for ourselves. Do you understand?" I looked them both directly into their eyes and wanted them to see the sincerity of my eyes as I said these words.

Moussawi hesitated and finally replied in a low whisper, "Fine, sir, these people will not listen to me. They are common people. Many are criminal. Some are soldiers and they can kill me or my family."

"Moussawi, you tell them in any way you wish but let them understand that it is coming from me. You will just be the messenger. Will you tell them?"

"I will," he whispered. I lifted a prayer right then and there for these two men. I wanted them to be my mouthpieces to their community but there was something about the dynamics here that didn't seem right. These guys were terrified of the others around them. I hoped that the community would understand that it was coming from me and not from them. I surely didn't want my messengers shot.

Moussawi and Abdul walked back into the courtyard to speak to the men sitting under the courtyard tree intensely looking our way. As I watched them walk away, an Iraqi in his late twenties or early thirties approached me, "Soldier, do not trust them. They work for Saddam Hussein. If you need anything I can help you well."

I turned to find a small statured but muscularly built man with a short, dark, cropped haircut and a prominent Arabic nose with the traditional mustache but he was relatively fair skinned compared to the other Iraqis in the area. He was dressed in simple Western clothing and his English was remarkably good. I looked him up and down and instinctively had a feeling about him. I couldn't tell if he was a villager who was trying to share some truthful information or if he was trying to "play" me against the others but he was savvy. I looked at his hands and saw thick hands similar to farmer's hands. He carried himself like some of the guys back on the block trying to be suave without tipping off his intentions. One of the greatest challenges I had in this role was learning who I should trust. Every single Iraqi had a beef against someone else and you would often find yourself caught between two Iraqis each accusing the other of being an Ali-Baba or a Baathist.

"What's your name?" I asked the Iraqi.

"Ja'far."

"Where did you learn to speak English so well?" I inquired.

"The University in Baghdad."

"Tell me, why shouldn't I trust them? They seem like honorable men."

"Honorable? Moussawi and his wife are not good people. His wife was very cruel to the people of this village. They do not like her. They are bad people who worked for Saddam Hussein."

"So is Moussawi a bad man. A Baathist?"

"I don't know about Baathist. He is not bad man, a weak man, but not bad. His wife was very cruel," Ja'far explained.

"Is this why the village burned his house and stole his things?" I asked.

"No, no. This is not true. When the war began Moussawi and his wife bring their car in here and they put many things in car and they left. When they left the other people came. They have much anger to Saddam Hussein."

"So who threatened to kill Moussawi and his wife?"

He looked at me dismissively, "No one! No one! Some people are Ali-Baba. The people are not bad people."

"Ja'far, so if the people are not bad why did they burn the buildings and steal from the museum?"

"Soldier, the people are very poor. They are hungry. They hate Saddam Hussein. The people are angry." In an almost apologetic tone, he continued, "They take to sell. The people are not bad." I couldn't help but notice the softness in his voice when he spoke of the villagers and the intense drama expressed in his face as he made reference to them, more than likely he was attempting to portray his own tribe in a very positive light while protecting them at the same time.

"Ja'far, you speak good English and I believe you. We want to help the people."

"That is very good soldier."

He had gotten closer to me during the discourse and I noticed him focus in on my flak jacket. Most Marines wear their ranks on the front of their flak jackets but as a chaplain I chose to wear my cross. Out here my rank isn't really that relevant but I do want all who see me to know I'm a chaplain.

"You Christian, soldier?"

"I am, Ja'far. I am a Christian holy man, like an imam."

He nodded his head as with faint approval but didn't say much more. I wasn't quite sure how to take this.

"You can call me Chaplain Marrero. Chaplain is holy man and Marrero is my family name."

He looked at me and asked, "You Arab?"

"No," I replied with a smile.

I was used to being asked. I have a darker complexion, a mixture of sorts. Puerto Ricans are a mixture of Spanish, Indian, Moors, and/or Africans. While my parents hold a more European complexion, I, like my uncles, hold a more mixed look. In my career I've been mistaken for Pakistani, Indian, and Arabian many times.

"My family is from a small island in the Caribbean called Puerto Rico. They speak Spanish. I'm from New York."

"Ah, yes. But you look Iraqi." He smiled as he circled his face with his hands.

"I may look Iraqi but I don't sound Iraqi," I joked and he laughed with me.

"What did you call holy man?" he asked.

"Chaplain," I responded.

"Chaplain," he repeated.

"Ja'far, the Marines are taking over the museum. We want to stop Ali-Babas and protect the area. We will be closing the area in a few days. Please tell the people that we are doing this to protect the treasure of Hammurabi and to give it back to the Iraqi people when peace comes. Do you understand what I am saying?"

"Chaplain, what about the people? There is no work and no salaries. With war there is no business. We need to do business."

"Ja'far, I will think about that and see what we can do. Will you tell the people no more stealing?"

"Okay, okay, but you help us."

"I will try, Ja'far."

I watched him walk away and immediately draw a crowd as soon as he entered the Ishtar Gate. This guy had a following. He was connected to this community in some form or fashion unlike Abdul and Moussawi and I could not let that get away. I made a mental note to stay close to this guy and be sure that we would keep him on our side. As I watched him interact from a distance and without understanding a word of Arabic I couldn't help but think that this guy was functioning like an NCO or junior grade officer with his troops. He was probably a former soldier, hopefully a reformed one.

I wanted the word to filter out. I now had two conduits whereby I was pushing out the same message. I gathered our people after this short visit and promised to return to clean out the looters. Tomorrow I would return to see if they stayed away or if we would have to push them away.

Evenings for me were a mixed bag of activities. We had a daily evening briefing where the I MEF staff sat around the table to update the CG so I usually opted for an early dinner. A few times a week we would hold a Bible study in my office/sleeping quarters followed by prayer. Other times I would walk about the camp occasionally visiting the guards on duty, people standing watch at the

Operations Center, or visit with other officers and Marines as I walked about the camp nonchalantly. This was an opportunity to visit or an opportunity to counsel and minister. Some evenings it was an opportunity to walk along the Euphrates quietly and take time to pray.

The big draw on some evenings was when I allowed the docs and some of the Marines to come into my space and use our bare wall as a screen to catch up on movies. Some of these movies were CDs or DVDs sent from home. Others were acquired by Marines or docs who, while on a convoy, would purchase bootleg movies from Iraqis for as little as a US dollar. These were funny and annoying to see. In most cases the movie was of someone watching a movie in a movie theater. You could see people walking in and out of the theater or coughing during the dialogue. Once normal movies began to flow in regularly we kept the bootleg movies down to a minimum out of mere frustration.

The following day after our usual Babylon morning routine we headed into the Ishtar Gate. I was hoping to find fewer Iraqis assuming that they didn't want a confrontation. The word had been put out so now I figured we could reasonably enforce the law. When we pulled up on this particular morning no one came out to greet us so I had hoped that the crowds had dissipated. As soon as we turned off the Humvee engine, we could hear the chisels and hammers pinging away around us. Some came from behind the palace walls, others from where the museum was located, and more from the buildings just across the street from the Ishtar Gate. Maybe it was my imagination but it sounded louder and more frantic to me. Maybe they were trying to get their last bids in.

I sent RP2 Stephens and SGT Gowin to investigate the sounds we heard coming from behind the palace walls. I told them if someone was back there looting, they were to confiscate their tools and chase them away. They took off on a trot, quite enthusiastically, to clear the grounds of any would-be looters. I had a corpsman, HM3 Smith, and a Marine from S-4 with me and we walked into the courtyard. I walked directly to the crowd of men under the courtyard tree and exchanged salutations with them. As I stood there in the shade, Abdul appeared to be returning from the ancient sites with a group of Marines. The Marines were a small squad of Marines from 1st Battalion Fourth Marines who had control of Al Hilla, the city right outside of the museum area. Their chaplain, Tom Webber, was a fine Christian pastor who had also worked his way to Babylon a few days earlier and encouraged his people to come by and see it if they had a few hours off.

I greeted the Marines and Abdul as they concluded their tour. In front of the Marines I asked Abdul, "Did you speak to the villagers to stop stealing?"

"Moussawi spoke with the villagers yesterday and told them your words. They said they will not stop and so they are here today."

"I have to find a way of stopping this until we can get this area secured," I said out loud, not knowing when we were going to officially take action on securing the area.

"We can take care of it, sir. What do you need?" asked the Corporal who had just finished the tour.

"I told him that we wanted to clear the area of the looters. I wanted them to know that this area was off limits to looters and their donkey carts."

"What area do you want us to clear?" he asked more specifically.

I pointed out the buildings across the street, the museum in particular, and anything inside of the ruins area. The young Marine turned away and gave directions to his nine or ten Marines. He broke them off into groups of three or four and they just walked off with rifles ready and began to confront the looters.

RP2 Stephens and SGT Gowin had returned and I asked them to go through the tour route and clear it of all possible looters, loiterers, and anyone selling anything inside of the ancient route. Once again they enthusiastically took off. Little by little the pinging from the chisels and hammers was stopping. I walked out to the front of the Ishtar Gate to look down the road and the Marines were going building by building shooing them away and in some cases grabbing the tools out of their hands, throwing them onto the donkey carts, and signaling them to go. I was so overwhelmed with the response that I didn't notice that I was standing in front of the Ishtar Gate all by myself with no protection.

I had violated a very important rule, go nowhere alone, stay with your battle buddy at all times. Chaplains and RPs understand that they are to be inseparable under combat conditions but when I dispatched RP2 to go on patrol I was then surrounded with Marines. He was sure I was taken care of and I tasked everyone away without thinking of my own protection. It was stupid on my part. I felt quite vulnerable as I stood there in the courtyard watching Iraqis being shuffled along by the Marines. Lots of angry Iraqis walked by going home feeling like they've been robbed of a chance to get their cut of the pie. If looks could kill I would have died 100 deaths.

The men in the courtyard just sat there and watched me as I kept my distance from them and stood alone at the front of the Ishtar Gate. I worked my way away from the crowds and closer to the vehicles hoping that the sentry on top of the palace could see me. I had no communications with anyone so it was just wishful thinking. The only communication access I had that morning was with God and so I prayed. I prayed that the Lord would watch over the Marines and RP2 so that this little operation would not turn into a shooting match, and I prayed a prayer for protection over me asking God to help me in this moment of vulnerability and stupidity. I was there a good twenty minutes standing by the road watching as the various Marines disappeared into buildings and side roads but it felt like an eternity.

What hit me right away as I stood there was how quiet everything had become. I could hear the birds and the wind rustling the leaves of the tall trees. Gone were the pinging hammers of the looters. The silence only made the minutes tick slower.

Little by little the Marines returned laughing and sharing accounts of the bizarre things they had encountered that morning — construction crews with sandals, no hard hats, and yet they had managed to strip copper and aluminum off every concrete structure they encountered. I thanked the Marines and they headed home.

The next morning I returned, prepared to begin to convince the loiterers in the courtyard to stop selling their stolen wares and to move out of the courtyard. This time we rode in one vehicle and I was once again accompanied by RP2 Stephens and SGT Gowin. I could not believe my eyes as soon as we completed the curve that

145

led to the Ishtar Gate. There they were again. The donkey carts were parked in front of the buildings and our looters were brazenly back at work. RP2 Stephens and SGT Gowin walked right into the courtyard while I remained outside for a few more minutes. I walked up to the sidewalk area and yelled at the top of my voice, "Ali-baba!"

Curiously enough, the Iraqis who were chipping away at the building closest to me stopped and looked at me. I looked sternly at them and signaled nonverbally with my hands for them to come down. Of the three I was confronting one lowered his hammer and began to come down. The other two, however, looked at me and returned a hard stare and then shook their heads letting me know that they were not coming down. One continued to look at me and the other one defiantly returned to work.

"Lord, what am I going to do? How can I stop these people?" I thought to myself filling with frustration.

I took two steps forward and then the guy on the roof suddenly changed his facial demeanor. He turned quickly to his partner and pointed back at me. The other guy looked, picked up his tools, and the two of them began to descend to collect their donkey cart.

I was amazed. "Lord, thank you!" I muttered under my breath, unsure of what had changed. Then I heard the chatter of a radio. I turned around and on the road behind me was an entire platoon of Marines coming in armed to the teeth flanking both sides of the street. The lead Marine gave them the halt sign and they all paused on the road. A Humvee came up the middle and stopped where I was at. "You the chaplain?" the occupant on the passenger side asked.

"I'm Chaplain Marrero from MHG," I replied to a Marine Lieutenant, or so I thought.

"Sir, we're here to secure the area."

"God bless you. You know where to go?"

"We have our instructions."

"Thanks," I replied with a wide grin from ear to ear.

The Marines moved in and headed right for the looters. These Marines had experience doing this. They emptied out the donkey carts, confiscated their tools, and sent the Iraqis on their way.

As the Iraqis left the compound, the Marines established machine gun posts at various intervals throughout the perimeter. The primary road to come into the Ishtar Gate from out in town was blocked and the gate secured. The Marines took over an old shack and used it as a new security shack and thus a formal Entry Control Point (ECP) was established. They initiated a roving patrol through the ancient grounds to insure no one sneaked in and attempted to smuggle out any items. They established radio contact with the Marines atop the palace and coordinated their efforts with the help of a set of eyes high above them.

The people in the courtyard were corralled and escorted onto the main road with no exceptions. Everyone stared at me as they were herded out. Moussawi and Abdul looked toward me and I asked them to leave with the crowd but I would see them in the morning. I turned around and the courtyard was deserted. Nothing was left but the blowing trash left behind by the crowd. It had grown quiet once again and now it could be surely said that Babylon had been conquered.

Chapter Eight

The Souk

The chief business of the American people is business.
— Calvin Coolidge
30th president of US (1872-1933)
speech in Washington, January 17, 1925

It was a hazy morning and everything appeared to be filtered through a sepia lens as fine sand blew all around us and painted reality in shades of brown. The routine was the same this morning as any other except that after having concluded breakfast I was met by a Marine who informed me that I was needed at the new ECP.

"What's going on?" I asked him as we walked back toward my building.

"We've got a crapload of Iraqis asking to come in and a few of them keep asking for you by name, sir."

"Hmmm!" I said with interest.

"You can go. I'll get my RP and I'll meet your guys there in a few minutes."

"Roger that, sir," replied the young Marine and he hopped into his waiting Hummer and went on his way.

I found RP2 Stephens and SGT Gowin inside the building. We put on our 782 gear, flak jackets, and helmets and hopped into our Hummer. We drove out toward the Ishtar Gate. When we came around the bend we slowed down enough to peek inside the courtyard without leaving our vehicle. It was empty. The sounds of pinging chisels were gone and things were quite calm. RP2 Stephens stepped on the gas and pushed on up the road toward the new ECP. The road from the Ishtar Gate to the ECP was wide enough for three cars to travel abreast of each other. It was flanked on both sides by very large mature trees that extended out over the road almost creating a canopy. We passed the Greek Coliseum to our left. It was believed to have been originally built during the time

Alexander the Great resided in Babylon and was recently rebuilt by Saddam Hussein.

We arrived to the end of the road where we found an abandoned looted structure to the left that had been commandeered by the Marine security detail. Twenty feet to the west of this building, directly facing the road, was a small shack that the Marines used as their guard shack. Conspicuously sticking out of the shack was the muzzle of a M240G machine gun. In front of the shack was an entry gate with a counterweight that allowed you to lower or raise a long metal pole across the road to inhibit vehicle traffic. It was light enough that any of our large vehicles could easily crush it but it provided a clear signal that this was a restricted area. The Marines had also artfully place barbed wire and concrete blocks between the vehicle gate and the intersection to force vehicles or people to zigzag slowly on their way in for about 200 feet. No one was going to barrel their way in without getting entangled, shot, or both.

At the end of the street where our road intersected with the main road, the Marines also laid out a long strand of barbed wire all the way across the street to keep anyone from entering into the labyrinth without permission. They placed a handle on the barbed wire and the Marine sentry on post would pull it back and allow pedestrians or vehicles access. Here at this point, just adjacent to the barbed wire entry point, was another small shack capable of holding a Marine inside. This Marine kept his weapon at the ready always providing coverage for the Marine exposed at the entry point. Dependent on the heat of the day or the level of activity, these two Marines would change places alternately during their watch. The M240G machine gun was about 200 feet behind them but juxtaposed to them so that from their vantage point they could provide covering fire without hitting the forward shack.

On the other side of this labyrinth, on this particular morning, were about 100 Iraqis all desirous of coming into the grounds. Some of these people even had their donkey carts as if to so brazenly believe that we would allow them to enter so they may continue with their looting chores. When we approached the gate, many who had recognized me from before began to call out in Arabic but all I heard was an increase in the deal of chatter. I understood none of it. Wrestling through the crowd I spotted Abdul and Moussawi. Abdul waved shyly almost as if to hide his attempts of catching my attention. I informed the Marine on watch that I wanted to allow access to a few people and they moved toward the barbed wire fence. The crowd grew excited and began to push forward as if anticipating an opportunity to run in. In their excitement, they began to entrap some people in the front against the sharp barbed wire. I began to yell, "Stop, stop!" and signaled them to move back.

RP2 Stephens and SGT Gowin came alongside me and began to wave their hands, motioning them to move back. The two young Marines saw a little girl crying as she was being pushed forward into the barbed wire. They reached across the barbed wire and began to furiously push anyone they could reach. They pushed back hard while yelling a few expletives that the Iraqis didn't understand. Their faces and the force they projected, however, required no interpretation and the Iraqis fell back. The others retreated waiting to see what would happen. One of the Marines reached down and comforted the little girl as her father scooped her up. The other Marine raised his rifle up for all to see. The butt of his rifle rested on his waist and the muzzle was facing straight up with his fingers on the trigger and he sent a very clear signal. I grabbed Abdul and asked him to tell the people to move back. He reluctantly raised his voice a few decibels. He always seemed to speak in a whisper, but he addressed the crowd. The crowd began to mutter amongst themselves and then young Ja'far worked his way through the crowd toward the front.

"Chaplain, chaplain," he called out.

"Ja'far, what can I do for you?"

"We want to come in. We want to work. We want to sell our things to your soldiers to make money. We have no work. Please let us in."

"Ja'far, tell the people that only the museum staff will be allowed to come into the grounds. We want to protect the area from further damage."

He looked at me disapprovingly and disappointedly as he said, "Ya, ya, I will tell them."

I realized his frustration so I told him, "There is nothing that stops your people from selling things on the road before our Marines come into the camp. Just don't block the traffic."

He smiled at me as if content that he had managed to negotiate with me to some degree. He turned to the crowd and very authoritatively addressed them, quite different from Abdul's quiet words. The crowd discussed amongst themselves but moved away from the gate. I am sure the prospective looters were very disappointed as they gathered their donkey carts and headed down the dusty covered asphalt road. Others chose to loiter around the ECP, probably hoping to beg for a little charity while others attempted to sell what trinkets they had stolen from the museum along with a few flasks of whiskey. As they dispersed and dealt with the new rule of the day I turned to Moussawi and Abdul and waved them in.

The Marines waved one in at a time then had them stand spread-eagled with their hands extended out from their shoulders and palms up. The Marines proceeded to frisk them and search for contraband on each one. I thought Abdul was going to blow a gasket. He looked like he was at a cross between infuriation and crying. While he was being searched, the Iraqis on the other side of the wire began to make some comments and yelling barbs our way but I had no way of comprehending what they were saying. Abdul's golden tan face seemed to turn red or as red as a brown face can get. He was cleared and allowed to walk on when Moussawi was called by the Marine to endure the same routine. The remarks from the Iraqi crowd continued.

I came up alongside Abdul and initiated the usual salutation, "As-Salaam-Alaikum" with the posturing of my hands and he replied courteously. He looked at me with hurt and anger and asked, "Is this humiliation necessary?"

"Excuse me? What humiliation? The search?"

"Yes. I am not a common criminal to be treated like one in front of the entire village."

"I am sorry, Abdul, but this is a security issue and I cannot excuse you from this. If we begin to allow some in without a search and others in with a search it will not be fair. In order to be fair to all everyone will be searched. It is the only way we can protect the grounds and ourselves. Do you understand? Without it you will not be able to come in."

"I understand. Maybe next time they can allow me to stand behind the guardhouse and they can search me away from the villagers?" he stated and asked at the same time.

"I think we can do this to protect your honor, Abdul."

"Thank you," he said as he regained his composure.

When Moussawi had endured his search he humbly came alongside us and we placed them in the vehicle and escorted them down the road to the Ishtar Gate. SGT Gowin remained at the front gate since we can only carry three people plus the driver in our vehicle. RP2 Stephens dropped us off and headed back to pick up SGT Gowin. Moussawi, Abdul, and I migrated toward the big tree in the center of the courtyard and took some seats in the respite of its shade. They immediately noticed that the courtyard had been cleaned. LtCol Lebidine had walked through the area after it had been secured and noted how dirty it was. He assigned a working party to sweep the area out and make it presentable since it was now under the care of the Marines. The debris, loose papers, and soda cans were all gone.

"Chaplain Marrero, what you have done is very good. Thank you to you, your General, and your Marines. This is very good for Babil," declared Moussawi.

"I think this is very important. Many armies have marched through here in history to conquer your land. We are not interested in conquering. We wish very much to return this to the Iraqi people someday in the near future. Please believe me when I say we want to usher you into a new age for the Iraqi people."

Abdul then leaned toward me and said, "Chaplain, we believe you. We have great hopes. You Americans put man on the moon and now you can do good things here. We Iraqis are coming out of cave where we have been blinded by darkness for many years under the rule of terrible man, Saddam Hussein. Now we exit the cave and the light is very bright. We are blinded by its brilliance and it will take time to become accustomed to the light but eventually we will. Thank you for bringing us out of the cave and now I ask you to be patient with us as we grow familiar with light."

His poetic words struck me as deeply genuine and revealed to me that the Iraqis were attempting to interpret their place in this new reality we had thrust upon them. They truly had no idea of what the future held for them and their families, let alone what it meant for them as a people or a nation. I can't imagine how fearful most of these folks were as they realized that their government — one that denounced any sense of entrepreneurial or individual spirit, the same government that had forced them to unanimously conform — was now in ruins. The future lay uncharted. Yet, in the midst of this fear and uncertainty, these people seem to hang on to some semblance of hope, a hope tethered to us as Americans.

We went on to speak of many things that morning, much of which was nothing more than an exploration in curiosities of one another. I learned that Abdul loved American movies but he was quite outdated. He expressed a great deal of excitement for Jean-Claude Van Damme's earlier martial arts films like *Blood Sport* and *Universal Soldier*. He looked at RP2 Stephens and dubbed him Jean-Claude Van Damme because of his muscular physique and threatening presence behind those sunglasses while holding on to an automatic shotgun. He also went on about Clint Eastwood's *Dirty Harry* episodes. A thing of the past in our culture. It was just the beginning of many conversations that would capture our attention and hearts in the months to come. In the midst of this I caught myself hoping that we could develop a friendship where I could truly come to understand these people. I found that as I came to know them, I grew more passionate in my prayer life and often raised them up to God for mutual wisdom and understanding. The more familiarized I became with them, the more I would pray for peace. I knew that as I stood before them I was not only the incarnation of America but also of Christianity. I prayed deeply that God would give me the words to build bridges and help toward deconstructing whatever prejudice they may have had of both of these realities I represent.

Our conversation shifted to what this place looked like in the past and how Saddam Hussein had visited it on numerous occasions. Saddam had commissioned that the area be reconstructed to resemble the ancient originals based on some old German reconstruction plans created before World War I. It took over seven years to complete the southern palace project from 1982 to 1989. Abdul shared that on one of those visits he was down in the museum grounds and he had seen an official party up at the palace. He assumed it was Saddam Hussein because of the entourage surrounding him. He happened to have his camera so he pointed it up and zoomed in hoping to get a photograph of the entourage. It wasn't an expensive camera so he didn't expect to capture much but at least he would have a famous image he could point to as Saddam's. He took his photograph and continued to go about his business in the museum area.

A few minutes later, two of Saddam's Republican Guard soldiers cornered him and asked for the camera. He knew better than to refuse so he handed it over. They opened the back of the camera and pulled out the film onto the floor. He watched nervously. They handed the camera back to him and asked him who he was and where he worked. He identified himself as an employee of the museum. They assured him that he would be punished for his disrespectful act of taking a photo of Saddam Hussein without permission. As they walked away, Abdul breathed a sigh of relief realizing that fortunately there was no physical punishment to accompany the destruction of the film but soon afterward Abdul learned that he would be docked two months pay for his act.

We eventually returned to the matters of business at hand and I explained to them that the only way I would allow them to continue to enter the grounds every day was if they could be reasonably employed. I shared with them the desires I had to contact the Coalition Provisional Authority and other resources to attempt and identify funds to help us restore the facility. We spoke of the areas that needed immediate attention and what could wait for future resources. I shared with them my desire to travel to Baghdad and liaison with the people up there to insure the staff is not forgotten. I also informed them that our Marines in intelligence were going to be investigating what happened at the museum and looking into their pasts. They looked at me quietly as I went on to let them know that I would be taking on all leadership responsibilities for the museum in the interim and Moussawi was no longer in charge. I carefully explained that my role was as temporary as the investigation would allow and soon we would either reinstate Moussawi or appoint some less controversial figure. Moussawi sheepishly looked at the floor as I spoke, nonverbally acquiescing to the fact that his reign was over.

I shared with Moussawi and Abdul that I truly appreciated the historical value of this site and how important it was to human history. I openly expressed my own excitement for being here as a Christian because my faith history is rooted in this region with Abraham, Daniel, and so many others. I went on to say that I'd like to provide a formal means where I could introduce it to our Marines. They expressed concern in having US personnel walk independently throughout the sites and therefore enacting the same level of damages on the site as the Iraqis had been doing until now. I assured them that my vision was to have controlled tours through the grounds led by each one of them. No one would be allowed into the ruins area without a proper authorized escort. I promised that our people would be very well controlled and no further damage would come to the site because of American personnel.

Our conversations with the Iraqis never progressed very far without them reminding us that they were without salaries and were in need of funds. I then proposed to them that they bring back with them some of the other curators who could speak good English and were well informed on the history and we could arrange to run tours through the sites. I also informed them that I would encourage some donations from the Marines so we could offer them a few dollars each day for their tours. When I discussed this with Colonel Cunnings he had informed me that on average a professional Iraqi such as a doctor made the equivalent of five US dollars a day. The staff was used to making about two to three dollars a day as semi-professional white-collar workers. That's roughly $60 per month. Colonel Cunnings had warned me not to be too generous in my plans to pay the Iraqis and thus inflate their salaries to a point where it would be painful for them when things normalized. This seemed like a very legitimate and wise concern so I promised them a few dollars a day depending on the size of the crowds we would receive. They agreed to this informal arrangement and agreed to bring back at least three more curators who spoke English.

We enjoyed the rest of the day exchanging information on one another and growing in trust as we walked throughout the campus identifying the extensive damage. Moussawi shared how this site and the buildings where the Marines were living were all part of a curious festival that Saddam Hussein sponsored once a year in honor of Mesopotamia. They recounted how Saddam had completed the southern palace walls and how he would hold an annual festival where he invited people from all over the world to celebrate the Babylonian period. Abdul believed that Saddam resonated with the image of Nebuchadnezzar and how these festivals were lavishly tended to in order to celebrate Saddam's connection to the Babylonian King.

The quiet grounds were turned into a festival ground resembling an amusement park and people would stroll around campus and visit restaurants, shops, and the museum. Iraqi employees would wear costumes to depict the clothing of the Babylonian time period. In the evenings, large scale celebrations with music and dancers from around the world put on exquisite performances to entertain the guests. The staff spoke of these events in such romantic terms full of nostalgia as if recalling wonderful times. It was a celebration of history and it brought this place alive, they recalled. Moussawi looked at me and said, "One day we will enjoy such wonderful celebrations again and you will have to come back to see for yourself."

The next morning we pulled up to the ECP to find another restless crowd. In the midst of it all was Ja'far. I walked up to the very front of the ECP and was immediately greeted with salutations but also with questions. First I had Moussawi standing by sheepishly with an entourage of people whom I had never met before.

In the meantime, Ja'far was yelling out "Chaplain, chaplain!" vying for my attention. RP2 Stephens and SGT Gowin went to assist the Marine sentries with the searches as Moussawi brought in his entourage. I walked over to Ja'far to greet him.

157

"Good morning, my friend," I said very loudly, "Alaikum-Salaam."

He returned my greeting and seemed impressed that I called him friend.

"My friend, my friend," he began after his greetings, "Why are they going in? She is the cruel woman of Moussawi. Are you bringing things back the same to before?"

"No, no, my friend. Things have changed. Only the museum staff will be allowed in but they now work for me."

"Chaplain, my friend says they will make money giving tours. I can give tours I speak good English. What about me and them?" He pointed to the people in the crowd.

"Ja'far, only official museum staff who have worked for the museum in the past will be allowed to enter and work in the museum."

"Chaplain, we want to make money. Selling things on the side of the road is no good. Soldiers do not stop. They drive by too fast and no one buys anything. This is not good. I want to work like them."

"Ja'far, I want to help you but I don't know what I can do. I can't allow everyone who wants to make a few dollars into the museum. I'll have to think about it. I will get back to you."

"You know many of these people worked in the museum selling things in kiosks and in shops. We want to return to sell to a few."

"I understand, Ja'far, but I will have to think this through. Please trust me I will not forget you."

"Chaplain, you know those people are bad. That man is Saddam Baathist. Moussawi's wife, bad. You cannot trust those people."

"I will look into it, Ja'far. Stay close and we will talk more later."

"I will be here, chaplain, there is no place to go," he chided me.

I turned my attention to the crowd being searched and approached Moussawi. I noticed peripherally that Abdul was being searched but privately off to the side behind the guard shack. The villagers could still see him but it made him feel better.

158

"Moussawi, who are these people?"

"Chaplain Marrero, these are staff that worked in Babil museum." He proceeded to introduce a handful of people to me. One was a tall Iraqi who carried himself quite confidently and almost pretentiously. He was introduced as the director of the local State Board of Antiquities and Heritage office in Babil, which was the equivalent to some county office. He introduced me to his wife who would not look up at me but simply nodded from under her head covering. He then introduced me to three other curators, an older gentleman by the name of Mahmoud, and two middle-aged women who were dressed with wide smiles and bowed politely, Amira and Farah.

"Moussawi, I asked you to bring only people who have worked or can work in the museum. Do they all speak English?"

"Uh, my wife does not speak English and she is coming only to see damage. She will not work for us. The gentleman from SBAH is also here to look. The others speak English very well. They are archaeologists here for long time."

I pulled Moussawi to the side in order not to embarrass him.

"Moussawi, I can't, cannot allow you to bring your wife back here. She is not liked by the people. She has been accused as were you of stealing treasures from the museum. The people say you are Baathist. You know I have reported your names to our Intelligence people and Civil Affairs and they will investigate. I don't know what happened here in the past but I cannot guarantee her safety. It is best after today that you leave her home. Also know that until you are cleared through an investigation I will not allow you to function as the senior curator. I want to be fair to you so I will allow you to work here and make a few dollars. This will keep you close to me where the investigators can ask you questions and I can use your knowledge. You understand?"

"Yes, yes. Thank you very much. I will cooperate."

I looked at him and wondered, is this man a pawn in all of this? Is he just henpecked? Or is he a good actor? I couldn't figure it out yet, but I figured I had better play all the sides of this before I got into a situation I couldn't handle. I decided to allow the gentleman who's name I never really got from the county office and

So How is a chaplain trained for This?

Moussawi's wife to enter for an hour or so walking through the spaces and witnessing the damage but they left together soon after their assessment.

Over the next few days we had dozens of Marines stopping by to see the ruins. It was amazing. I had shared the word with the chaplains and the command passed the word through the Commanders. Our growth was increasing exponentially as trucks loaded with Marines would stop by just to see the ruins and attempt a little rest and relaxation. It wasn't uncommon to find some of them just parking themselves under a tree and taking a nap after they had walked the tour. Every Marine that walked the tour, regardless of their interest in history, was greatly impressed.

I would often start them off by highlighting the historical relevance of this place and what the Bible said of Iraq and Babylon. I would then pass them on to a tour guide who would walk with them for about 45 minutes to an hour. Many of the chaplains who were sending these Marines out to the tour were giving briefs and classes back at their base camp explaining the biblical relevance of Babylon in order to excite them before they got here. The vast majority of these Marines were coming in from infantry battalions in the immediate area to include Al Hilla, Karbala, and as far away as Al Kut. These young Marines had led the assault on the war and were still engaged locally in operations. When they came to Babylon they came to unwind and get a change of scenery. This was meant to be their day of rest and relaxation — a break that came along only once every month or so.

I noticed that about two weeks into the tours each of the tour guides were establishing their own ad hoc souvenir shops in differing corners of the courtyard. I confronted Abdul who happened to be the one selling at the time of my arrival. He explained that the villagers had learned of their earning opportunities and they were jealous. In order not to make enemies, the curators had all agreed to sell trinkets belonging to some of the people who claimed to have been vendors before the war and share the profits. I didn't see any harm in this but I remembered my words to Ja'far and I didn't want him or the villagers thinking that we were going to cut a deal with a handful of people — especially the old regime.

160

"Abdul, I promised each of you a few dollars a day. I also know that the Marines are giving you tips on top of the money we collect for you. You are doing better now than you ever have — is it not so?"

He broke eye contact with me and looked at the floor. "Yes, this is true." He momentarily agreed but immediately followed with justification, "We had no salaries for over two months. My family is very ill. My wife needs surgery."

"Abdul, I understand how difficult all of this is on you and your family. I am sorry to hear about your wife. Maybe we can help in another way but we have to be fair.[1] I can't have you earning so much money under my protection while excluding others from the opportunity. The way I see it you are making a fair salary that is better than what you made before. I need all of the selling to stop immediately. Do you understand?"

"Yes, yes."

Over the course of past two weeks, I kept running into Ja'far at the front gate when we would escort the curators into the museum. Ja'far and his friends were very persistent and they continued to attempt to sell wares outside the gate to make a few dollars. They had discovered that Marines would easily pay fifty cents for a cold soda and selling a six pack of Pepsi generated more money in a day than they were used to making in a week. The primary complaint from Ja'far was that the Marines would purchase items on the run. They'd slow down enough to have the vendors run alongside or as they were waiting to enter through the barbed-wire gates but they would not stop or dismount, thus frustrating their efforts. It had been clear that the people outside the wire were aware of what was happening inside the wire and ill feelings were rising. I grew concerned that the villagers would grow impatient and even violent against our curators.

One evening Abdul had even asked that we give him a ride in our Humvee to the taxi stand about a quarter mile up the road because he was afraid of the villagers. I couldn't decipher if the curators had cut a deal with the vendors voluntarily to make a few dollars or perhaps they were strong armed to do so as a means of making the peace.

161

The flip side to Ja'far's complaint was the very real fact that while Ja'far was willing to supply the Marines with goods the Marines were just as interested in purchasing items. Before me lay a perfect scenario — match the Marine's willingness to purchase a few items with the Iraqis' desire to sell some. The greatest challenge was how to do it safely. I couldn't allow vendors to enter the compound, the danger of losing track of them and having them wander off was too easy. I wasn't going to propose a plan to weaken our security posture so I needed to explore the possibilities.

I was intent on trying to find a solution to this. We had the perfect setting to encourage a good exchange between our Marines and the local populace. The small village nearby, Jumjuma, was just outside our wired boundaries. The village was named after a religious story that stated that a prophet had been lost in the area and encountered a skull that spoke to him and enlightened his path. Jumjuma means "the skull" and thus the name of the village. Some of the villagers had already been employed by our base on a day-to-day basis to perform a variety of tasks in the base. These workers functioned as contractors in that they would perform basic functions like trash collection, chow hall services, or street maintenance while always escorted by an armed Marine or two. I was convinced that if we fostered a free-market economic opportunity it would have tremendous impact on the local villagers and our relationship. It would certainly be an empowering experience for the villagers.

Intent on finding a solution, I surveyed the camp and came up with a couple of ideas. The challenge was always the same — security. How could I guarantee mutual security? We didn't have extra Marines standing around to serve as babysitters especially for Iraqis to make a few dollars while providing no real tangible service to the infrastructure of the command. I even discussed a few of my ideas with Abdul, Moussawi, and the other curators. They recommended that we renovate the museum shop and place the original vendor in there but that would serve one person, and I had a more encompassing vision. It was recommended that we allow them to enter the base and they could set up shop in a small parking lot directly across the street from the Ishtar Gate. This idea was feasible in that we could contain everyone. However, once again it meant access into the confines of our base and it would require more security personnel. I discussed this with Colonel Cunnings and while he was supportive of the concept, he didn't care to have a large group of Iraqis inside of our fence line without the proper security measures especially lacking Marines. I couldn't help but concur with his concerns.

One morning I worked my way to the ECP to visit the Marines and encountered Ja'far. I shared with him my dilemma. I wanted him to know that I was addressing his concerns and that we were invested in attempting to find a resolution that would benefit the local area. He looked at me and pointed at an adjacent parking lot behind me. Like a prospector eyeing a claim it appears that as Ja'far sat on the other side of the wire he was dreaming of the possibilities. I turned to look at his recommendation and it was the perfect solution. It had been before my eyes the entire time and I had not seen it.

A wall extended from the Marine security shack all the way across this huge lot. The wall hugged a side of the Greek Coliseum establishing a perfect barrier between the road and our perimeter. With the coliseum enclosing the western and northern edge of the parking lot a tall fence enclosed the remaining eastern and southern perimeter of the lot. The entrance to the lot lay between the two Marine shacks. This would allow for us to permit the Iraqis to enter into our space but not inside the compound. It would also mean that we could search them, control access, and contain them. As I looked at the lot I also figured if we used the far western portion of the lot closest to the Coliseum wall and kept a healthy distance away from the fence closest to the adjacent road, it would make it more difficult for someone to lob a grenade into the area without the Marines responding immediately. I knew that the Marines had a react team inside the primary shack and I could ask them to assist with some security, perhaps a roving patrol.

I returned to the main camp and was able to discuss this with Colonel Cunnings. He hesitantly agreed but we both agreed that we would attempt to establish it on a tentative basis to see how it works. The key to this would be security. If there was any hint of a threat, it would be closed down immediately.

I returned to the ECP that same afternoon and discussed the plan with Ja'far. I told him that we would allow ten vendors to come in and establish a place to sell their wares. My intention was to allow the Marines to visit the vendors' parking lot following their tours on the ancient grounds. This would add to the Marine's experience and help out the vendors. I explained to Ja'far that it would have to be on a first come, first serve basis. If it worked well for a week or so we would consider expanding it. I explained my concern for security and he quickly volunteered to patrol it with his own people.

"We can control our own people," he assured me.

At that thought I said, "Okay, Ja'far you will be my chief at the market. I will turn to you to help me manage the market."

"I will do this. There will be no problems. My brother, Yousef, can help."

"That's fine. You will work with me. Here are the rules, Ja'far. There will be no exceptions, no 'sorrys.' If anyone is caught selling whiskey, artifacts or stolen items from the museum, or hashish, they will be out permanently. No coming back. Understood?"

"No whiskey?"

"Marines are not allowed to drink whiskey or beer. They have weapons and we don't want them drunk with rifles. So get the word out, no alcohol. Also, no food. We don't want anyone getting sick. You can sell fruits or things that are wrapped like bubble gum or candy but no food. Okay? Do you understand the rules?"

"I will talk to the people and help them understand," he said assuredly.

"Good, bring the first people tomorrow. I'll see you in the morning around eight."

"Tomorrow, yes tomorrow." He left excitedly and I walked away equally excited.

Curiously enough, I shared this conversation with the curators that afternoon. Farah, who lived in the village, was very encouraged and smiled profusely but Moussawi and Abdul were not so thrilled with the ideas. Moussawi warned, "Chaplain Marrero, this

164

not good idea. These men are trouble. They are simple people and they will create problems."

"Moussawi, it is important to be fair. You want the people to know that everyone will be treated equally. It is not fair for you to be the only one to earn a few dollars. For this reason we will not sell anything inside the museum. All selling will take place in the vending area. All the Marines will be encouraged to go to the market and shop there. If you think you can make more money than what I am offering you, then feel free to join the vendors and you can compete with them there. In this new age it is important to be fair and equal."

They all quieted down and looked at each other. The rules were clear-cut and now they had to choose their own fates. I explained that we would begin in the morning and I would see them then. They gathered their things and began to walk out the Ishtar Gate toward the ECP when Farah pulled me to the side and said, "Chaplain, you have white heart, a good heart to care for the people. This will be good. Thank you." She bowed slightly and smiled warmly as she walked away. The alliances were being drawn and I was slowly learning who stood where.

The next morning we headed over to the ECP a little early, anticipating a large influx of people at the gate and our hunch proved correct. It was a circus. I specifically told Ja'far that we would only begin with ten vendors and there must have been sixty people out there. I wanted to be fair but I also had to be reasonable. How was I going to discern who got in? I did say first come, first serve but I also knew that Ja'far would accommodate his friends. While I wanted to be true to my word, I also wanted to adamantly convey the message of equal opportunity. These were the times when I would send God flash messages in prayer and ask for wisdom. I needed a plan fast because I knew if I went with the flow here it was not going to be pretty. The people are going to feel like someone won out over them because of connections and no one likes feeling like they lost out unfairly. "Lord, grant me Solomon's wisdom," I fervently prayed under my breath.

Ja'far was waiting patiently on the other side of the barbed wire by the ECP entrance surrounded by all of his prospective vendors. I went right for him and instructed the Marines at the ECP to allow the museum staff through before we begin to determine who is coming in to be a vendor.

"As-Salaam-Alaikum, chaplain. We are ready," he proudly smiled.

"Alaikum-Salaam, my friend. Who are all these people?"

"They come to sell as you promised."

"Ja'far, I said we would begin with ten vendors. We will begin slowly but there are too many people here. I can't let everyone in."

"I will pick ten sellers ..." Ja'far stated, but I didn't let him finish his sentence.

"Here's how we're going to do this. Get everyone to line up one after another. I will have one vendor at a time step forward and we will search them and see what they have to sell. In order to be fair to the vendors and the Marines, I will allow the first ten original vendors. In other words, I don't want ten people selling sodas or selling the same museum trinkets. I will search them on a first come, first serve basis and I will select what items get sold. You understand my plan?"

"Yes, yes, I will tell them."

"Okay, Ja'far, let's begin and we'll start with you so I know what you have but then you will stay with me and help me to speak to everyone, okay?"

Under my breath I thanked God for the last minute inspiration I thought to be fair and evenhanded.

The minute that RP2 Stephens, SGT Gowin, and I stepped forward, they began to crowd the fence once again. Ja'far addressed them and asked them to get in line but the concept was foreign to them. They just pushed forward and tried to weave themselves into the front of the line while holding on to their wares. I asked Ja'far once again to tell them to get in a straight line, one behind the other. I stressed to him that I wasn't going to begin until they were in a straight line. He turned to them and yelled at them. His face was red with frustration but the other Iraqis barely moved. I stood next to Ja'far and pointed my arm straight out trying to nonverbally show them where I wanted the line.

After a good ten minutes of trying to push them back into a single line I soon realized it wasn't going to work. The concept of lining up patiently behind one another was not part of their reality. It was an issue I had discussed at other times with our Marines who often grew frustrated with the Iraqis' impatience and apparent lack of cooperation. It seemed that even when we had the best of intentions like giving out toys, candies, or soccer balls it didn't matter how organized we try to be, we always ended up with chaos. It always turned into a shouting and pushing match trying to get them to cooperate in an organized fashion.

On one occasion, a Marine cursed under his breath and said, "Why are these f****** people so impatient, don't they know how to get in a damn line?"

I realized that there was a dynamic here that we had failed to understand and while I had no hard data on this I attempted to explain to the Marine.

"You know why we know how to wait in line in the US? We'll wait patiently for hours as long as there is a line and it's because we have faith that eventually we will get our fair share. We believe and understand that the people who are handing things out or offering a service will attempt to give all that they have. We have faith in our systems. These people are afraid that they will not get their fair share. They're afraid of missing out and not having another opportunity. There are no guarantees and when you think of it they have no hope. So if you didn't trust the system or the people would you wait patiently?"

The Marine looked at me curiously pondering on what I offered forward. I'm sure he was surprised to hear my dissertation but I think I connected with him and helped him to understand the psychology of this while at the same time impressing myself while recognizing inspiration at work in my ministry.

I finally succumbed to their impatience and we opened the barbed wire to allow Ja'far to come in. Right behind Ja'far another gentleman attempted to walk in nonchalantly. I stopped him and Ja'far immediately grabbed the man and began to explain, "This is my brother, Yousef. He will help me to sell. I need my brother, okay, chaplain?" Suddenly I realized that if I allowed Yousef in I was going to have to allow others the flexibility of having family members accompany them. This meant that my idea of having ten vendors at ten stations could triple. It seemed like an eternity but I mulled it over in seconds and decided to allow him to enter.

I looked at Ja'far's wares and noticed that he had a hodge-podge of postcards, some military insignias, and a few small plates with pictures of Iraq. I allowed Yousef to proceed into the parking lot after being thoroughly searched to pick his choice spot. He proceeded to lay down a rug on the floor and placed all of his trinkets on top. Ja'far stayed by my side as I reviewed each vendor's wares and RP2 Stephens and SGT Gowin searched them thoroughly.

The vendors were trying to sell Iraqi things to the Marines but what they offered were simply trinkets or "five and dime" store inventory. The most valuable commodities available were cold sodas and ice. I searched to find variety but there was little scope in choices. The vast majority grabbed trinkets from the museum or prayer beads from home and attempted to sell them for a quick profit. Over the next hour, Ja'far and I reviewed the wares of each vendor and by the end we let about thirteen vendors take their place in the parking lot. The candidates that were turned away were not many and it was because of their wares. In spite of the warnings we still had people show up with liquor, drug paraphernalia, and some museum souvenirs that looked too real and we were concerned might be real artifacts.

I stepped over to the lot at the end or our inspection period and looked out to see well over fifty people milling about setting their shops out in the open parking lot. Each vendor had a minimum of two people assisting them along with some children in the lot. I turned to Ja'far and asked him to insure that everyone stayed in their own areas. Already I could see tensions rising as I witnessed the vendors' accomplices immediately rushing to meet the few Marines who had already found their way to the lot that morning and attempted to lure them to their impromptu shop. I instructed Ja'far to go and inform the vendors that they were not to walk in and out of the site during the day. If they needed food or water they could send one person out once a day but I didn't want them overburdening the Marines at the gate. With each exit and return it meant another full body search and we didn't need that. I also told him to that we wanted an orderly process, so when the Marines arrived, I wanted the Marines to come to each station and leisurely choose if they wish to conduct business. I wanted no luring or attempting to steal business through aggressive tactics. Ja'far nodded but I could tell he was not happy.

"Ja'far, if you want to make good business you must sell what people want. Good business is not attacking people or harassing them to buy. The Marines won't put up with it."

Ja'far nodded and asked, "What do you think they want? What will be good to sell?"

"Ja'far, if it was me and I was in their shoes I would be looking for souvenirs that said Iraq. Nice souvenirs like plates, glasses, or pottery to take home to my wife or mother. The Marines are professional soldiers and they like military things from Iraqi uniforms. Iraqi flags, prayer rugs, and other nice things to take home. Do you understand?"

He looked at me and asked, "Why military things? To show conquest and show military strength?" He spoke with a defensive tone, almost insulted so I proceeded slowly and carefully.

"Ja'far, soldiers respect other soldiers. It is a contest of heart and strength. We do not collect things to dishonor others but to show respect. No one honors a weak enemy. We remember the strong because it makes our victory stronger. It is mutual respect. Marines want to collect the things of uniforms because through it they learn about their strong enemies. This is not a fight against the people of Iraq it is a fight against Saddam and his regime."

"What kind of military things you think they like?" he asked me.

"Things like badges that proud soldiers wear on their uniform to show they are part of Special Forces, parachute awards, commando units, or the symbols of rank. If you bring things you can explain, they will show interest. Don't worry about it I know these things are hard to get. Some of your friends had some and that will be enough."

"Chaplain, I can get uniforms and many things. I know where to get. You think they will like?"

169

"Ja'far, were you a soldier in Saddam's Army?"

"I was a soldier in Iraq's Army but not Saddam," he responded quietly and seriously.

"I understand, Ja'far, but will I be able to trust you?"

"Yes, yes. I want to feed my family and make some money. You help me do this, you can trust Ja'far."

"Ja'far, you are my chief at the market. I will trust you to keep order and make sure everyone follows the rules. If any rules are broken, I will have the Marines throw the lawbreakers out. If this gets out of hand we will close it. I need your help to make this work."

"Yes, yes, we will follow the rules."

"Oh, by the way Ja'far, we want to be respectful of your customs. If you wish, we can close the market on Fridays to make time for prayer."

In a whispered tone, pulling me back from the earshot of others he replied, "Not necessary to close the markets on Fridays. We can pray at our own times but we do not want the market closed. We need money for food and this will help."

"Okay, okay. If that's what you want that's fine with me. We will open the market early morning around 8 a.m. every day and we will close at 4 p.m. in the afternoon. Good?"

"Yes, good, very good" he nodded in approval.

I turned to leave when a vendor excitedly walked by Ja'far and flashed a handful of bills in excitement, laughing as he spoke with Ja'far. I later learned that a Marine approached the vendor with the sodas and asked him how much for the sodas. The vendor had replied that it would be fifty cents a soda, knowingly marking his price up 400 percent. The Marine leaned over, counted the sodas inside, picked up the cooler with the ice, handed him a handful of singles, and paid him for the sodas, the ice, and the cooler handsomely. They each thought they hit the jackpot. Ja'far said the vendor was on his way to buy a donkey-cart load of sodas to sell.

Over the next few weeks it was exhilarating to see how our efforts grew way beyond our wildest expectations. Marines and soldiers learned of the museum and they would use their R&R days to come down in large groups to visit for the day. Following

170

their day through the ruins they would walk the half mile up to the souk by the ECP and shop. The vendors were wise marketers who listened carefully to what their customers desired to purchase. Over the next few weeks, the trinkets were replaced by more sophisticated wares. Initially, homemade products abounded along with prayer beads and simple items from the local market. In time, I learned that Ja'far and many others would travel to Baghdad to purchase bona fide souvenirs like picture plates, various rugs, clothing, lighters, and we had one guy who set up his own version of Blockbuster videos — probably at the behest of some Marine.

The Iraqis were very proud and innovative people. The parking lot sectionals began with the setting of a rug and trinkets upon it. They evolved to wooden frames big enough to drape rugs and linen over the top to keep the summer sun at bay while they conducted their business. This gave way to actual booths and tables where the vendors offered tea and conversation along with their wares. The conversion from flea market to souk was amazing. Every single Iraqi saw themselves as a serious merchants conducting business in the most serious of fashion. One of the collateral byproducts of this venture was the interaction between the merchants, their assistants, and our Marines and soldiers who would visit.

I found myself visiting the market at least twice a day to insure there were no issues and to have Ja'far report on the affairs of the day. I so enjoyed walking through the market and discovering Marines and soldiers huddled inside the booths or behind the tables enjoying a cup of sweet tea and discussing a wide range of topics from comparative religions to economics, politics to family life and values, on to democracy and dictatorships. The wide range of subjects and their high level of interest in an open exchange of ideas astounded me. The conversations never lacked passion or depth. I often found myself walking by a conversation here and there and being compelled to stop to listen and observe. I was as impressed with our Marines as I was with the merchants. I was surprised to discover that some of the Marines had even contracted with some of the merchants to teach them Arabic and to expound on cultural mores and ideas.

The museum and its tour through the ruins connected us with world history and ancient Iraq while the souk connected us with the people of modern-day Iraq. Each event, on its own accord, was an intensely spiritual experience. Joining together both events in the same day made the experience surreal in the face of the many other experiences these young Marines, Soldiers, and Sailors would often encounter during their workdays. In the souk, Iraq bore a face, a name, and a history that responded back in kind and allowed us to interact with it in a way that we could not do while on patrol or on a convoy. I saw Marines exchanging email addresses for continued contact in the days to come, perhaps in the age of peace desired yet far from reality.

The souk allowed us to interact with another population uniquely adored by US Marines, Soldiers, and Sailors in Babylon — the Iraqi children. I am always amazed at how tenderly our service members can be with children. It was not uncommon to see our troops purchasing candy and toys from vendors to turn around and give them to the children of the very vendors who sold them the items. I, myself, would receive packages from my wife, Wanda, and from my family in Arizona. I made it a habit to always have candy or little trinkets in my cargo pockets. The children of the souk grew accustomed to my gifting and when they saw me early in the day, they would always run to me for a hug or handshake and a gift. I was often greeted with the words, "Hadia, hadia" which meant "gift, gift" by the crowds of my adoring child fans.

The warmth I felt in engaging with such smiling faces in the morning was probably the very reasons why so many of our Marines and Sailors would go out of their way to kneel to the ground or sit cross legged on the dirt to engage the children. Many engaged with the children so they could vicariously interact with their children whom they dearly missed during this long separation. The quiet reality was that in doing so, whether they were seeking selfish satisfaction or selfless expressions of benevolence these merchants and children learned something about Marines, Soldiers, and Sailors normally lost on the many whose only experience with them was on a checkpoint or during a patrol, they met real men with hearts filled with compassion and generosity. It is my hope that this image will prevail in the years to come as they reflect on what is an American. It is my hope that as we Americans look at Iraq that we move away from the visions of terrorists or despots like Saddam Hussein but that we may recall the smiles, open hearts, and free exchange of ideas afforded in a spirit of hospitality as was engaged in that souk.

I can't help but recall a conversation I had with a young Lance Corporal who served in one of our infantry battalions and was involved in the heavy fighting during the onset of the war. He confessed to me that he had no love for Iraqis. They had tried to kill him and his buddies. In his opinion, this land was so void of beauty or worth that he couldn't understand why we were bothering with the Iraqis. In his own words he confessed, "I then began to talk to some of them and got to know them. Some of them even know English. They reminded me of my parents who were hard workers. They were nice to me and I learned that these were different from the others. They were decent people like us." A realization that comes as a direct result of interaction with the common Iraqi that in turn makes way for the humanization of a people. I hope we all remember that they, too, are, in fact, like us, struggling to survive day by day worried for their children's future, the safety of their family, and were concerned over the provisions for tomorrow with a deeper sense of intensity than they did about the politics of their time. The politics of war are by no means the reality of war.

---

1. Chaplain Tom Weber, the chaplain of 1st Battalion 4th Marines, was able to get a church from the US to send some funds and pay for Abdul's wife's surgery in Baghdad. Her surgery went well and she recovered from the growth on her neck.

Chapter Nine

Mayor Of Babylon

And the Lord's servant must not quarrel; instead, he
must be kind to everyone, able to teach, not resentful.
                                               — 2 Timothy 2:24

I was initially dubbed the "Mayor of Babylon" in jest by General Conway during one of our evening staff meetings when he reminded the staff that we had a distinguished visitor, or a "DV," scheduled to visit the next day. One of the collateral effects of leading this project, in addition to my regular duties as pastor and chaplain to our Marines, was that I now had the unique task of being the official Babylonian tour guide to our distinguished visitors.

My first assignment as tour guide was to escort Mr. Paul Bremer, the US Presidential Envoy who was later named the Director of Reconstruction and Humanitarian Assistance and eventually the Head of the Coalition Provisional Authority (CPA). Colonel Coleman had informed me that he wanted to make sure I highlighted our efforts in the compound and helped him envision what we had done thus far on our own initiative.

I decided I would invite Moussawi to stay with me and serve as my subject matter expert and contextual reference. Everyone else had been asked to leave earlier in the day to insure the area was tightly secured. The courtyard was cleaned thoroughly by Marines from MHG and it looked as pristine as a looted area could look. I chatted with Moussawi prior to their arrival so that we would understand one another's roles. I was to address issues of security and protection, and he was to provide any answers that related to the history, the nature of the museum, and the events that took place prior to our arrival. Moussawi normally spoke very lowly and I asked him to make an effort to speak up clearly so everyone in the entourage could hear him well. This was not intended to be a tour but an orientation visit to outline the actions we had taken independently as a force. It was intended to highlight the need for his support in acquiring some funds to begin a symbolic rebuilding of the compound.

The gentle quietness of the courtyard was broken by a convoy of vehicles that pulled up just outside of the blue Ishtar Gate where we waited patiently to greet Mr. Bremer. I was taken aback to see the entourage that followed. There were a series of SUV vehicles in addition to our Humvees and from them out poured droves of private security personnel. They were all dressed similarly; it was like the invasion of *Men in Black* except these were Men in Tan. The security guys were draped with flak jackets, stylishly cut hair, cool sunglasses, unlike the ones issued to the Marines, and small machine guns that appeared to be affixed to their chests. I'm no security expert but to me it was total overkill since we were inside a US Marine Corps compound surrounded by over 2,500 well-armed Marines and Sailors. Nonetheless, they needed security to get here and back to Baghdad so I assumed this is how the state department travels about.

My preference would have been to blend in and be less conspicuous but I'm no diplomat. Prior to this event I had never seen Mr. Bremer, so he wasn't someone I recognized when he emerged from his vehicle. However, I picked him out of the crowd right away due to his blue suit and tie and brown combat boots — his trademark appearance already was known through the region. Right behind him I spotted the familiar face of Lieutenant General Conway who directed the Ambassador in our direction through the gaggle of people admiring the reproduction of the Ishtar Gate. Lieutenant General Conway introduced me to Mr. Bremer and in turn I introduced Moussawi to both Lieutenant General Conway and the Ambassador. We turned into the courtyard and I immediately began to outline to Mr. Bremer the level of damage that had taken place in the spaces surrounding the courtyard.

I spoke of the looting and the burned office spaces. He asked about the museum and the looting. Moussawi replied that many of the antiquities in the museum were reproductions and those were stolen. There are a few large pieces that were originals and they remained inside the museum. He went on to explain that many of the original artifacts once held in Babylon had been moved to the

Baghdad National Museum after the war in 1991. Mr. Bremer asked about damage to the other areas around the museum. Moussawi explained that there were some accounts of damage within the ruins, such as attempts to carve out some of the bricks from the original Ishtar Gate area but he believed we had stopped it in its early stages and prevented any of the heavier excavations feared to supply the black market. He nodded and looked about curiously but continued to set the pace for the tour. He didn't ask a lot of further questions. He took out a small camera and snapped a few personal pictures of the ancient site.

When Moussawi attempted to share his standard historical information we were both surprised when a representative from the local CPA office in Al Hilla, who seemed very well versed in the history of Babylon, stepped in and took over most of the tour. They appeared to know each other well enough for the Ambassador to ask questions while referring to him on a first name basis. Moussawi managed the opportunity to get in a few words but for the most part we ended up being part of the tour and followed them around. He allowed himself to be handled during the tour for about thirty minutes. He then cut the tour short and noted that he had to leave so we headed back toward the Ishtar Gate to marry up with his convoy of oversized shiny and spotless American SUVs.

A large crowd of international and Iraqi reporters were anxiously waiting for his return to the Ishtar Gate to greet Mr. Bremer and get him to make a statement. He paused like a well-seasoned politician and provided what appeared to be a brief off-the-cuff speech before the cameras where he promised to return the Museum of Babylon back to the people of Iraq and pledged $20,000 and future support to jumpstart the reconstruction effort. I turned toward Moussawi to catch his gleeful smile and nodding approval as this surprise unfolded before us. He completed his statement and turned toward his vehicle with his crew in tow. Lieutenant General Conway slapped me on the back in a congratulatory fashion along with a grin as he passed me by to say his good-byes to the Ambassador.

I later read his book, *My Year in Iraq: The Struggle to Build a Future of Hope*, and learned of the great distaste he had for the

177

experience. Of notice to me was the brevity of his reference to this visit. In the grand scheme of things, I can clearly understand why this visit translated to one paragraph in his book. In sharp contrast to my small team and me, the quiet reality was that it proved to be a pivotal point that empowered us to embrace a vision and begin to move forward. This was not because of anything Mr. Bremer said to us but because by at least publicly stating his commitment to Babylon before the media, we now had a point of reference that we later used to articulate and support our vision. In fact, this visit facilitated my efforts to meet some key personnel at the Al Hilla CPA regional office who later provided over $120,000 to begin the serious steps toward rebuilding the museum and the grounds of Babylon.

The tours and interaction with the Marines and DVs made time pass a little faster. A few months into this new assignment our venture had grown significantly. My tour staff had increased to seven curators so I became less involved with the tours. I was, however, further challenged with balancing my responsibilities as a chaplain and the needs of the staff and the reconstruction of the site. I continued to do the occasional DV tour and for the grand majority of the time they proved to be very pleasant experiences allowing me to share our efforts with Generals, politicians, and the media who recognized the very unique nature of this opportunity. If I were to highlight the one DV who seemed most engaging and excited to be at the site it was Dr. Paul Wolfowitz.

When he arrived, he didn't wait to be handled or escorted but instead he immediately began to fire off questions right after we were introduced by Lieutenant General Conway. He almost appeared giddy to be there. So was I when I first arrived. I figured that being from a Jewish family this was not only world history to him but it was personal history coming alive before him as he stood in the birthplace of the Babylonian Talmud. We walked through the entire tour route taking well over an hour and it seemed like fifteen minutes. He was pleasant and engaging. His presence was not rushed but conveyed a real desire to be there with us. He not only asked about history but we even began to delve a little bit into the whole Nebuchadnezzar imagery that Saddam might have been trying to capture with these efforts.

When we concluded our tour he grabbed my hands with both of his and was genuinely appreciative of the time I spent with him. He gave me an unexpected gift, a Deputy Secretary of Defense coin, a tangible way of expressing gratitude within military tradition. It sits with my memorabilia in my office today. It was memorable if for no other reason than that it lacked any pretension and he honored our time.

In sharp contrast, the worst experience I had in giving a tour was to representatives of the Senate Armed Services Committee. Our command had planned for weeks for their arrival. No one wants to have a dead senator on his or her watch so the command threw every available Marine to this event for insurance. Part of the plan was to receive them at the Babylon airfield located within the campus area of the Babylonia mall or restaurant village that now lay abandoned within our compound. They arrived by helicopter and were ushered into a bus. A large convoy of armed Marines escorted this one bus out of the base and into the region of Al Hilla to expose them to a recently discovered mass grave outside of town. Every intersection between our camp and the mass gravesite had Marines blocking access roads. We surrounded that bus with Marine vehicles and followed them closely — ready to react. In addition, gunships flew ahead of us to insure the path was clear. Colonel Coleman was in a command helicopter, a UH-1N Huey, flying directly overhead orchestrating leap frog movements with vehicles and personnel to insure that the safety bubble moved along with the senators.

The day was a clear and hot summer Iraqi day. We were all in our full combat gear, in vehicles lacking air conditioning, sweating up a storm enroute to this site. They sat in an air-conditioned charter bus. I am sure that all of the Iraqis who saw us on that afternoon either thought we were initiating the second phase of an invasion or they must have guessed that we were protecting the President of the United States himself. Even for having been in the military for over twenty years, this display of coordination and firepower impressed me thoroughly.

The plan called for me to ride in my Humvee to the mass gravesite and once the senators spent thirty minutes or so with the Marines who discovered and processed the site we would return. On the way back I was to hop onto the bus to share with the members of the committee our efforts in Babylon. We arrived at the mass gravesite where they stepped out of the bus, walked about for a few minutes, and hopped back into the bus. Not more than ten minutes had passed. We headed back toward the camp in the same fashion we arrived with massive helicopter flybys and reinforced leap frogs. The safety bubble was on the move.

On the bus I discovered the internal microphone didn't work, so I began to brief without the aid of sound equipment. One look at them and you could tell they were jet-lagged, irritated, uncomfortably hot, and occupied with their own thoughts. I began my account and one of the senior senators closest to me asked me to speak louder. As instructed I began to yell, attempting to compensate for the undergirding hum of the bus, the sideline conversations at normal speaking tones, and their deafness. I yelled louder and the senior senator only heard portions of what I said.

He would reply, "What did you say? Speak up louder, son." It was like a bad comedy routine. Fortunately, I had my flak jacket on and it covered my name on my uniform so I reasoned that I would escape this storytelling fiasco in anonymity. The ride back to the camp was not nearly as long in the bus as it felt in the hot Humvee so I was pleasantly surprised when we began to pull off the road into the base and we passed the souk to our right. I shared our success with the souk and how it had grown exponentially in the last two months. They seemed to take some interest in that development and asked a few questions. I continued to direct some of my remarks to those that asked the questions while others continued to carry on their own conversations.

Following the short trip to the mass gravesite, we pulled up by the Ishtar Gate and escorted the senators onto the ancient grounds to provide them with some further background on what we had accomplished by this time. That included having acquired contractors to clean out the looted and burned office spaces. On average, it takes forty minutes to walk through the Babylonian grounds at a comfortable Marine pace. DVs normally took an entire hour or a little longer. This group of senators, those who chose to leave the bus, got as far as the Procession Street, which is the first relic one encounters as we begin the tours, and they were overwhelmed by the heat. Take into consideration that these gentlemen were older, overweight, and probably exhausted, so some grace must be allowed.

They interrupted me as I attempted to guide them further into the grounds and they exclaimed that they would prefer to return to the air conditioning in the bus. I granted their wish and escorted them back to the bus and set a record for the shortest tour ever led in Babylon. I grew a little frustrated more for them than at them. Here they were on the cusp of encountering a moment with ancient history, the history of humanity, and they sought the comfort of the tepid, air-conditioned bus while I and many others stood there with flak jackets, helmets, and long-sleeved camouflaged uniforms in the midst of a hot summer day in Iraq.

When we got to the bus they blissfully climbed on board and went on their merry way. They were so consumed with their own discomfort that they didn't even realize how lofty and unpleasant they appeared. I would dare to presume that they had no intent to be unpleasant. Yet, they were unpleasant in that they were dismissive. A group of general officers later arrived, probably assuming that they were still on the tour, and they were very warmly received by the delegation once they had had the opportunity to refresh a little in the bus. However, it did feel like the rest of us were invisible in the grand scheme of their agenda. It was a matter that had little impact on me but the three junior enlisted Marines and Sailors who were providing security on our excursion were very vocal to me about how disappointed they were.

I won't list their names because it is not my intent to embarrass them and I hope you don't presume that this is behavior consistent with any particular political party over another because half of the group was Republican and the other was Democrat. Perhaps what is best said of this is that when people with celebrity status, political or otherwise, make the gesture to show others that they wish to visit and support the troops during these combat tourism jaunts, they may wish to consider the grand impact they make with their presence. Simply showing up is half the battle and the troops really don't mind at all doing a little extra work to insure safety and security for a celebrity when they truly feel the visit is about them — them being the troops.

I saw troops stand in line for hours to get a picture or exchange a handshake with people like Bruce Willis, R. Lee Ermey, and Oliver North. When celebrities came, they usually made the effort to up-lift and connect with our young troops. In one of these visits I had the privilege of enjoying lunch in Babylon with Senator John McCain and a handful of other Marines who lived in Arizona. As a Navy Commander at the time, I was the senior officer at his table. I was very conscious of not monopolizing his time and being sure everyone participated. The fact was that the concern proved to be unfounded because Senator McCain made every conscientious ef-fort to bring everyone into the conversation and allow everyone to be equally addressed. He spoke of neighborhoods in Arizona, sports, and thanked us for our service. It was the way it should have been and as a result it proved to be an enjoyable experience full of im-pact for all of us.

After all, it is reasonable to expect these visiting politicians to spend a great deal of time with the General officers in order to consult on the status of affairs, but if you want a little credibility with the troops, be prepared to sacrifice some of your personal creature comforts and take time to notice the young enlisted troop in the background carrying the weapon. They are the ones who carry the lion's share of the physical burden and the one's making the greatest sacrifices.

After having expulsed this frustration, I realize that it needs to be put into perspective. If this was my worst experience with a DV delegation in Iraq then in the grand scheme of things this was noth-ing more than a minor inconvenience. The quiet reality is that the vast majority of times our encounters were quite pleasant, and we always felt a sense of pride and honor being able to represent our organization before such dignitaries. In addition, as a chaplain I had the very unique opportunity to speak as a person of faith and interpret history in light of the Old Testament and share it with

Could the Note handed too off to Andan staff off it - ?

some very senior delegations. Our Marines and Sailors who were picked to work these delegation events had a great disposition and they made us proud every single time. Besides, it made for great emails back home.

Serving as the Mayor of Babylon wasn't all about tours and DVs. The better portion of my time after getting the tours and the souk well established was dedicated to attempting to prepare the site for turnover back to the Iraqis. This meant that we had to establish contact with the Culture of Ministry, get official support for our goals and visions, appoint people into official positions, and troubleshoot the issues surrounding the lack of salaries for government employees at the State Board of Antiquities and Heritage (SBAH) who far outnumbered the handful who worked directly for us as curators. It meant hours of coordination with CPA and the Civil Affairs teams who would liaison with agencies in the Green Zone on our behalf. It also demanded my time in continued coordinated efforts between I Marine Expeditionary Force and their requirements to establish a base while at the same time being sensitive to the archaeological concerns of the staff.

The local State Board of Antiquities and Heritage office was located just outside of our compound. The many members who used to work inside the compound in Babylon were no longer allowed access because there was no place for them to work. Their offices were completely looted. These were the archaeologists, specialists, support staff, and other professionals. These were the ones who were most hurt by the looting. While the majority of the relics in Babylon were certified replicas, we can argue that the museum itself lost little when it came to relics. Of greater consequence was the loss of their work in cataloguing, the recording of their life's studies, and findings that were all destroyed. They were dedicated professionals at all levels of support who simply wanted to return to their duties. They would gather together at this small office building weekly attempting to gather further information on the progress of matters at the Ministry of Culture in Baghdad. They had organized themselves enough to select a spokesperson, Dr. Raneen, for their cause and launched her along with some of our curators to Baghdad to plea for support from people like Dr. Donny

George and those at the Ministry of Culture. These efforts proved to be frustrating for them. They often were not allowed access since the area was cordoned off by American troops.

The impact of the looting had greatly affected the National Museum of Baghdad and along with this there were thousands of others sites. The Ministry of Culture had fervently sought to identify and find ways in which they could mitigate future looting at some of these other locations. To a degree, Babylon was off the scope because the Ministry of Culture knew that the Marines had secured it and it was no longer threatened. The fact that we had secured the site actually helped to lower our visibility on their priority list. Baghdad was only about fifty miles away, yet it felt as far away as another country, another world, or another dimension for that matter.

In my short time in Babylon I personally made three trips to the Imperial Palace in Baghdad to visit the Ministry of Culture and attempted to advocate for the needs in Babylon. Identifying the office spaces inside the behemoth of a structure was easy enough compared to traversing the bureaucracy that was woven between the Iraqi Ministry of Culture and the Coalition Provisional Authority. In one of my short trips I had the privilege of meeting Dr. Pietro Cordone who served as the Ambassador for the Ministry of Culture and his military liaison officer, Colonel William Keller, US Army. The majority of my encounters and exchanges were with a series of young CPA staffers who served as the gatekeepers to both the CPA and Iraqi subject matter experts.

Placing faces with names helped since the lion's portion of my contact with these people was done through emails, which interestingly enough were all public accounts with yahoo or hotmail. This perhaps provides some insight to reveal how poorly organized or ill prepared they were to develop an infrastructure that would support their efforts. The other factor that made it difficult to follow through on issues effectively was the lack of consistency with some of their people. In the realm of people I dealt with it was not uncommon to be introduced to someone who ended up in Iraq for a matter of weeks and then they would just disappear. Rumors abounded of people showing up and being disillusioned or unhappy with present circumstances and they would turn around and return home.

In Babylon we had a young woman, Helen MacDonald, who held some association with the British Museum. I can't recall if she represented them as an employee or if she was some kind of consultant for them but nonetheless she was appointed to work with the CPA in the Ministry of Culture. She brought a great deal of experience in the field of archaeology and seemed quite friendly and at ease with the Iraqis. She was a mild-mannered academic with large glasses and always wore her hair pulled back and covered by a hat. She had a very quiet demeanor but was incredibly ardent in her own way when she was addressing issues related to artifacts and ruins. CPA in Baghdad assigned her to the CPA office in Al Hilla as the Cultural Affairs coordinator in the region south of Baghdad, and she was charged with overseeing issues in Babylon. Her chain of command did not intersect with mine in any way except that we were both physically located in the same place and concerned, in general terms, over the same area. She was driven from the Al Hilla offices every morning and dropped off at Babylon and then picked up hours later.

Though her assignment called for her to assess the region south of Baghdad she had no staff, no vehicle, and no real support. She went about doing what she could by asking to ride along on other missions and requesting transportation through CPA for occasional carpool support. She received most of her Intel from our guys at I MEF whom she met through our own Civil Affairs team and various encounters with the Civil Military Operations Center (CMOC) Marines stationed at the Al Hilla CPA inside of the Babel Tourist Hotel.

In the midst of her arrival I had recently identified someone to serve as the interim director of the museum. We were unsuccessful in determining Moussawi's culpability, or lack of, at the time of the museum's looting. Since he and his wife had become such controversial figures with the villagers I decided to appoint another director, who came very well recommended by the members of the State Board of Antiquities and Heritage (SBAH) in Al Hilla while managing to keep Moussawi gainfully employed. She was declared interim director. I had the authority to effect operational changes in the museum but to effect any real administrative changes I still had to enter into dialogue with CPA and the SBAH in Baghdad. They weren't too happy with our efforts to appoint Dr. Raneen and at times I don't know if they were administratively challenged or simply evading the entire issue hoping to avoid the issue until after our departure.

In Al Hilla I had worked with the local CPA to remove Moussawi and his immediate supervisor in the Babil Directorate. The local CPA and our Intelligence people had concluded that the Babil Director was a well-connected Baathist, unlike Moussawi and the other staff members, and they advocated for his relief. This was an effort generated by our Intelligence personnel in conjunction with the CPA and I simply followed their lead by identifying a replacement. Everyone seemed to be comfortable with the arrangement to have Dr. Raneen step in and assume leadership of the museum staff and Babil Directorate.

Dr. Raneen and Helen MacDonald got along superbly and they spent a great deal of time together attempting to identify the other ruins and archaeological sites in the Babil District that needed protection. At times, Helen and I conflicted philosophically because in her short time she grew very impatient with the fact that we were not dedicating more forces or resources to protecting the other sites. I understood her frustration and I shared it. On the other hand, I attempted to reason that we were making good progress in that we were attempting to preserve and protect what we could. We can't always frame our success on what we can't accomplish but rather we need to build on the successes we have.

Babylon was a perfect example in that it was not the Marines' primary mission to enclose Babylon, however, good judgment prevailed and we took advantage of an unprecedented opportunity. I felt that it was unrealistic to expect the limited number of forces stretched thin throughout the southern regions of Iraq with policing historical sites. It should be understood that the Marine Corps released a large number of forces to return home immediately after the cessation of combat operations. We had a limited amount of Marines strategically located throughout the southern provinces in order to provide security. When the missions were assigned no one in our chain of command was ever told to explicitly prepare to guard over historic relics. The efforts that were made were spontaneously done due to the rise of opportunities.

We had Marine battalion commanders functioning like regional governors charged with maintaining the peace and security. As much as we respect and honor historical sites and their value to society and culture at large, the protection of human life took priority and in my mind, rightly so. Helen, like a few journalists during that summer, continued to criticize that we should be able to dedicate helicopters and troops to protect these world treasures. In an ideal world with unconstrained resources this may be true but in Iraq it proved to be a massive challenge and grossly unrealistic.

Part of the problem lies in the fact that Iraq has around 10,000 historically valued sites strewn throughout the country and about 1,200 in our immediate area. To divert forces in protection of such sites would be to take forces away from heavily populated areas that depended on our presence to remain stabilized. It would mean moving forces from protecting heavily used local markets and school areas to watch wide-open spaces with soon-to-be-discovered treasures. In the pyramid of priorities and in a world of limited resources I still contend it was the right thing to do.

The requests for support of these areas were made regardless of a pay grade much higher than mine. The response was to comply with the spirit of the request where circumstances allowed us. If a helicopter was returning from a mission they would fly low and take note of activity on the ground. If a patrol was in the area they would swing by and sweep the looters away. Our responses were limited and unacceptable to some but it was all we could do as we also maintained the peace. Not one Marine during this time was lost in combat, and it allowed the Iraqis to begin to take ownership of their own civic responsibilities.

The reality often eluded was that in many areas the looters were well organized and well armed. They were also smart enough to avoid contact with US military patrols. Media reports indicated that they were not shy about intimidating other groups. Local groups that had traditionally guarded the sites were normally outnumbered and outgunned. In response to this frustration the CPA even developed a plan to train Iraqis into a force that would serve as armed security designed to protect government buildings and patrol remote areas. Unfortunately, it fell short of its intended purposes. In the latter months of the summer of 2003, I recruited over forty men to go through the training. They understood that the Marines would be leaving by the close of the summer and the great rewards of the souk may not be available after their departure so many volunteered to receive the training with the hopes of future employment. They received two hours of training, were registered, and were sent home with the promise that they would be contacted in the weeks to follow. Months later, at the time of my departure, they had not been contacted.

I didn't think that the idealists who called for many of these interim solutions grasped the stark reality of the situation. In order to effectively combat the bandits that were looting these historical ruins, it would not be enough to post a few security guards armed with AK-47s and a radio in remote areas. What would they be expected to do if they encountered a gang of bandits? Were they expected to get into a firefight with well-armed thieves with no hope of receiving backup or additional support? It was unrealistic and if we moved in that direction it would be irresponsible to place these people into such a circumstance over relics. Civil Affairs officers engaged in some of these discussions shared with me that even some of the tribes that were hired to protect the sites were simply bought out by the bandits.

I understood Helen's concerns, passion, and impatience but the facts were that we just didn't have the forces to deploy to these areas. The other element of truth in all of this was simply that it wasn't our job; it was the job of CPA. My comrades in uniform also tasked with serving as liaisons to other CPA ministries would complain in similar ways over the CPA in Baghdad. These diplomats or subject matter experts were brought in to manage these various problems but their structures were usually two or three people deep. They were an army of assessors and surveyors but were ill equipped to effect much change. To a degree they simply frustrated the efforts of rebuilding because many locals grew tired of teams coming through to assess but no one would show up to do anything.

We had all these tremendously smart and motivated experts but no soldiers within the CPA infrastructure to make anything happen. They had no real reach or teeth to get into the weeds to effect change. In many cases they leaned on us, the military, to provide the manpower to make things happen. In short, the Ministry of Culture at the urging of outside organizations called on us to protect the sites but they also wanted the Marines to keep the streets safe, hunt down the criminals, maintain the electricity, and insure gasoline and LP gas was flowing. At the same time there were rumblings that the CPA wanted to keep the military footprint to a minimum so the Iraqis didn't feel like they are under an occupation. The expectations were magnificently unreasonable.

Helen made her assessments, shared her findings with the people in Baghdad, and in a matter of weeks she was gone. Through no fault of her own she appeared to leave in frustration. Her real legacy in Babylon, perhaps unbeknownst to her, was not tethered to her failed attempts to expand security at remote archaeological sites but to the influence and encouragement she gave the new interim director, Dr. Raneen. Dr. Raneen is a very short, petite Iraqi woman. She was a fundamentalist Shiite who enjoyed a great rapport among her fellow professionals but was standoffish with us. She was trusted and deemed very capable and that was good enough for me. In her own way, she was a very determined and strong woman as indicated when she chose to make her opinions known. She was no pushover, yet when assigned as the interim director she seemed hesitant. This could have been cultural or perhaps circumstantial because she was predominantly interacting with foreign military men. It could have also been because she didn't want to be drawn into a conflict with the Ministry of Culture, CPA, and I MEF as they hesitantly moved to support her in her new position at my behest.

Baghdad spoke well of her yet they dragged their feet and placed many barriers in officially appointing her as the director. The Iraqi team in Baghdad made it clear that they had some real problems with dismissing her predecessor, who had been accused of being embedded with the Baathist, and in turn resisted her appointment. Through this process I saw Dr. Raneen lean on her friendship with Helen MacDonald and I believe that Helen's assertiveness, self-confidence, and encouragement played a big part in strengthening Dr. Raneen in her emerging leadership position.

One of the greatest challenges I faced along with Dr. Raneen and her appointment was attempting to understand how government employees were paid. There was a convoluted process where we had to identify each member of the local State Board of Antiquities and Heritage and place their name on a roster. Just identifying the process and receiving direction on how to properly initiate this request took a month of email exchanges and a visit to Baghdad. When we were finally able to outline the process we initiated efforts to produce a roster of employees. This roster was compiled on a large pad of duplicate carbon copy paper where each name was recorded and their official position listed.

Once the list was generated I had the staff translate it and RP2 Maria Hernandez, my new RP from California, entered it into an Excel spreadsheet in English so that we could attempt to cross-reference it when the list returned to us. The list was signed, stamped, and hand-carried by Dr. Raneen and her assistant, Amira, to Baghdad via public taxi to be verified and approved. Of all the people I interacted with in this large group of professionals, not one owned their own car. Travel to Baghdad fifty miles away usually meant an all-day event by taxi or bus. The list would be received in Baghdad and then stamped. A copy of the list with the stamp would be returned to the Babil district office and then we waited. The first time we did this, which reflected about four months of back pay, nothing happened.

I took a trip to Baghdad to follow up on the process. The second time around, the CPA authorized the pay and we were able to identify the problem. This meant that when approved we received a telephone call at the SBAH office that held the only telephone with connections to the Iraqi telephone system, informing us that the funds had been authorized. It now meant that we had to travel to Al Hilla and speak to someone in city hall who in turn would speak to the bank manager to review our papers and allow us to withdraw the funds from his account. I grew concerned with the amount of money in question so I received permission to escort Dr. Raneen and her assistant, Amira, with some of our Marines.

We took two Humvees with armed Marines and the two ladies. We posted three Marines outside with the vehicles and the rest of us went in to find the appropriate office within the Al Hilla city hall government building. We climbed up the darken stairs and shuffled past crowds of Iraqis populating the wide hallway. Upstairs we were led to a small office in the back by a security guard. Here, a gentleman in Western clothing and shaped like the many bureaucrats in the US joined us and chatted with the ladies in Arabic. While we waited, an assistant came in with a tray of glasses that looked like oversized shot glasses that were half filled with sugar and black tea. We each received a glass and the bureaucrat offered us a smile and we enjoyed our tea.

Following the small talk and drinks he inspected the paperwork and provided us with some instructions and further papers with a stamp. I took time to look around the building and notice its dilapidated state. This had nothing to do with the war; the signs of aging and inattention were clearly showing in this old government building. The gentleman escorted the ladies out of the building and we followed in tow.

We drove only a few blocks within Al Hilla as we wrestled with congested commuter traffic and the occasional donkey carts. We were directed to stop in front of what looked like a store front. When we walked in I realized we were at the local community bank. There were no teller windows, booths, or bulletproof glass. It was a large open room with a concrete half-wall coming up about four feet off the floor, dividing the room and also serving as a counter. On the one side of the half-wall were the bank workers and opposite them on the other side of the wall were the customers. We were asked to wait in the large room for a few seconds while someone knocked on the bank manager's door to fetch permission for our entrance. In the meantime, I looked around curiously at the customers and bank employees. I often caught the ladies glancing at us but pulling their eyes away when we made eye contact. They seemed as curious of us as we were of them. In general due to cultural traditions we met very few women in our daily functions. The few men in the room seemed unimpressed with our presence. I looked around and could not help but think of the old banks depicted in childhood cowboy movies. I envisioned myself being in the wild, wild west of Iraq.

The manager's door opened and revealed a short, dark-skinned, thin man sitting behind a very large desk cluttered with papers. He looked to be in his forties but it was really hard to tell. Equally cluttered was his office with other men sitting on lounge chairs along the wall enjoying tea and a smoke. When the manager learned of our presence he asked everyone to step out while we stepped in. The traditional greetings were exchanged between the exiting and entering groups as we passed one another and exchanged places. He immediately called on us to sit down in broken English and no sooner had we taken our places than someone appeared with a tray of sweet tea. This drink was like sweet syrup. In order not to offend the manager we each slowly sipped another cup of the sugary black tea. Dr. Raneen shared her paperwork with the bank manager and he reviewed it carefully. After close scrutiny he nodded his head and stepped out of his office via a back door. A few minutes later he returned with a bag and handed it over to us with a smile. Dr. Raneen signed a receipt and after almost five months of no salary for our SBAH employees we left the bank assured that we would have some people who were going to be really happy to see us. It was a great feeling to finally see this to closure after such a long time.

Payday at the SBAH was fashioned after my first payday in the Marine Corps. I was a recruit in boot camp and payday had sneaked up on us. A table was set up with two people sitting at the table; one recorded who got what and the other counting out cash and handing it out while an armed Marine stood behind them. In order to insure an orderly process we did the same thing at the local SBAH office. Dr. Raneen had called ahead and asked the employees to be present. When we arrived outside of the small, worn building that was housing the SBAH staff there was a crowd of employees standing about inside and out of the building. I posted two of our Marines by the door to control the flow of people coming in and out of the building and to send a clear signal that we were present. I was compelled to do this just in case anyone else who had heard of the arriving cash had any crazy ideas of intercepting it.

We had all of the employees enter the building into a large, open room and wait to be called into a side office. In the side office we had one Marine stand behind the staff while Dr. Raneen, Amira, and a gentleman whom I did not know very well but was identified as the SBAH accountant reviewed the list and called employees in one at a time. Everyone was very cooperative and waited patiently as names were called and multicolored Iraqi dinars were distributed. I stood by the doorframe leading into the small room and kept an eye on the staff while also checking on the two Marines posted outside the door.

It was a long, tedious afternoon but it was well worth the effort after seeing the smiles on their faces and the deep gratitude they expressed. I was profusely thanked by every person who left the building. On several occasions, I was once again called "white heart" by a few of the English-speaking staff because of my faithful efforts. I could only smile and share their glee on this day. There were, however, a few who were either underpaid or not paid at all but now that we had a system and a structure, Dr. Raneen took on the responsibility to follow through with these issues.

From day one it has been about meeting one challenge after another. I've never received any formal training in any of this and in light of the issues there was no way to formally be prepared for such a position. It was about thinking on your feet, building relationships, and navigating systems and resources to make them work for us. As a person of faith it provided many opportunities for prayer and requests for wisdom. It was also about love. We endure personal hardships out of hope because we love ourselves, and we desire to reach a better place. However, when hardships emerge in our quests to help others that have no real bearing on ourselves, we have to realize that the only real motivation is love. I grew to love these people in a *philos* way, a brotherly way. It was not paternalistic or self-serving but it was rooted in my faith. My faith gave me the context that allowed me to give of myself to desire to serve them. I loved them as a pastor loves his congregation and as I loved my Marines and Sailors.

One of the challenges I faced in my relationship with the Iraqis was attempting to meet the needs of the Marines to develop an efficiently designed camp while also keeping to my word to Moussawi, Abdul, Dr. Raneen, and the SBAH that I would protect their desires to avoid unnecessary expansion into areas not already developed. Colonel Cunnings had agreed and now his successor and Executive Officer, LtCol Paul Lebidine, agreed that no one would dig or expand any construction project without speaking to me first. In the first few weeks of our relationship with Moussawi and Abdul, I gained permission to bring them into the Marine Corps compound so we could conduct an initial survey and they could inform me of what areas were off limits.

A few weeks later when Helen MacDonald and Dr. Raneen became available we consulted them whenever we were considering a construction expansion. This became a little more difficult because Dr. Raneen was much more restrictive than the initial guidance we had received from Moussawi and Abdul. They allowed us to build two trash fire pits that required some shallow digging by the river in an area very close to our camp in order to be rid of our trash. Dr. Raneen forced us to burn our trash but we could not bury any of it and we complied. I recall Helen thinking of bringing in a specialist who would be able to analyze the dirt near the riverbed to inform us if the soil revealed any traces of past historical development or if it was merely river soot. The study never took place but the dialogue was there.

The quiet reality was that not only I but the entire command element was very conscientious of the fact that we were guests on an ancient site, and we did not desire to have our legacy associated with looting or the defacing of ancient history. I can attest to the fact that sometimes Marines charge ahead with pure bullheaded determination and they force an outcome out of pure brute will and determination. This was not one of those times. I was very impressed with the level of conscientiousness and commitment to responsible stewardship that was exercised around these ruins at every level of leadership from Lieutenant General Conway to the Lance Corporals in charge of our working parties.

Following our departure in August 2003, there were those who accused the 1st Marine Expeditionary Force with damaging Babylon and building on top of archaeologically rich terrain. An article by Jim Krane in June 2004 that was released by the Associated Press reported,

> *The expansion of a military base may have damaged the remains of the ancient city of Babylon, and the US-led coalition's leaders said Friday they have halted construction and ordered an investigation.*
>
> *US occupation chief L. Paul Bremer and top military commander Lieutenant General Ricardo Sanchez dispatched a team of archaeologists May 27 to examine construction at the Polish military's Camp Alpha, which was set up last year to secure the ruins from looters, a coalition statement said.*
>
> *The remains of Babylon, one of the world's most important archaeological sites, were occupied since the early days of the invasion by US Marines and, since September, soldiers from Poland and other countries. Babylon is 50 miles south of Baghdad.[1]*

In an article by Rupert Cornwell from the Independent UK on April 15, 2006, he specifically attributes damages to the site by listing the following,

- *US Marines from the First Expeditionary Force first set up camp in Babylon in April 2003.*
- *Soldiers filled protective sandbags with sand containing ancient artifacts.*
- *2,600-year-old pavements were crushed by heavy military vehicles.*
- *Landing helicopters caused structural damage to some of the city's ancient buildings and sandblasted fragile bricks in the palace of Nebuchadnezzar.*
- *Archaeologists say gravel brought in to build car parks and helipads has contaminated key sites.[2]*

Similarly a report on the "War and Occupation in Iraq" prepared by the Global Policy Forum and co-signed by a federation of multiple organizations published in June 2007 claimed,

> *In some cases, Coalition forces have caused serious, irreversible damage to important archeological sites. The US military built bases on the sites of ancient Babylon and Ur. At Babylon, construction crews used heavy earth-moving equipment as they built a helicopter landing pad, installed fuel tanks and concrete walls, and dug a dozen deep trenches. They brought in tons of gravel to make parking lots for military vehicles, next to a Greek theatre built for Alexander of Macedon. Polish troops camped at Babylon (known as Camp Alpha) from September 2003 to January 2005.*[3]

The underlying premise expressed by the Global Policy Forum is that the coalition, primarily the US and UK, are responsible for all of the looting and damage incited immediately following the war. Global Policy Forum places this responsibility squarely on our national shoulders because we initiated the war and were incapable of preventing the chaos that followed suit. This is an argument, I personally believe, difficult to counter and thus a responsibility we can't shirk at a national level in the realm of international policy. It is a failure reflective of our national psyche, which is marred with the failure to live in a world of concrete realities rather than in the superfluous notional world of political correctness.

We invaded Iraq with the intent of overthrowing the regime, yet we as a society refused to treat it or approach it as an invasion. We took a business approach to it and softened the language. We called it liberation rather than occupation and hoped for existing infrastructure to hold Iraq together. With these softening terms we failed to comprehend the dirty business of war and in turn failed to anticipate as a society the real ramifications of combat.

In part, the hypocrisy of our national and international soul is betrayed in these acts as now in years to follow we have people who wish to place blame *ex post facto* on going to war as if though the decision was sneaked by them. The quiet reality is that both the

196

international community through a 15-0 vote agreed to pass the United Nations' Resolution 1441 that led toward the pursuit of action against Iraq unanimously and we as a nation passed the Iraq Liberation Act (Public Law 105-338) which reads in part,

> *Whereas the Iraq Liberation Act (Public Law 105-338) expressed the sense of Congress that it should be the policy of the United States to support efforts to remove from power the current Iraqi regime and promote the emergence of a democratic government to replace that regime.*[4]

This law postured us as a nation to wholly pursue war with Iraq as a unified body. In those days we pursued our quest to war with Iraq with the same passion the Roman citizenry called for the death of its gladiators in a stadium. Some will continue to argue today that we were misled. I don't want to entertain conspiracy theories but as I recall, the grand majority of us believed the intelligence and agreed to react in light of it. It appeared then that the left and the right along with everyone in between concurred with the notion that we needed to posture ourselves for war.

In the days following the invasion it became apparent that the consequences of this war could not be so tidily packaged or concluded. It was then, after the fact, that it became fashionable to begin to point fingers at organizations and people for their failures in the same way that local communities often fight to lower taxes and underfund public services but then balk at the actions of police officers for being incapable of preventing crime. In this light I do admit, even in this book, to voicing criticisms for the failures of the Coalition Provisional Authority. However, the CPA as an arm of the government needs to be separated from the army of CPA workers who dedicated and risked their lives to attempt to realize a reality that was underfunded, undermanned, and ill-prepared to equip its people at the tactical levels to do what their conscious led to them to attempt.

The reality that the looting can be ultimately linked back to a failure in policy is not lost on me yet to conclude that our forces

197

are at fault for these shortcomings is faulty. When we begin to tunnel down to making broad-brush accusations on the conduct of our forces to attempt to show a link between poor policy and the conduct of our troops in order to attempt to demonstrate an intentional disregard for life and property is irresponsible and immoral.

In all three accounts shared above, these organizations are grossly misinformed. One accusation does not necessarily correlate to justify the next. How is it possible that an archaeologist from any outside organization can claim to be able to assess the damage incurred onto Babylon when they have no context to see what was there before, what happened during the looting stage, and what damage currently exists? The only true witnesses to such acts were Moussawi and Abdul and even they could not tell you with certainty what was damaged at what times.

The reports claim that the Marines built a helicopter airfield on an archaeological site. The truth of the matter is that Camp Babylon had two airfields. The first airfield was within the grounds of the developed Babylon village center that was fully developed by Saddam Hussein. The entire area when the camp existed that lay adjacent to the archaeological site was bulldozed, paved, and asphalted by Saddam Hussein's regime in order to develop a fully functional support base to the royal palace in 1989. In the center of this compound there were two large open areas that served as a garden of flowers. Our Marines did, in fact, grate over these two fields and pack them down in order to create our first expeditionary airfield. In time we placed gravel over this area to also use it to park vehicles inside the camp. The fact remains that these lots were inside the compound and had been developed long before we arrived. Our tampering was superficial in that we handled the topsoil to support our helicopters but refrained from digging or concreting the area.

I MEF needed a larger area to land three or four helicopters at the same time about two months after we had settled into the area. It should be understood that the Babylonian camp consisted of three distinct areas, the palace grounds with its own self-sustaining camp (Saddam Hussein's grounds), the archaeological site which sat directly east of the camp bordered on one side along the Euphrates and on the southeastern corner by the Alexandrian coliseum, then there was the Babylonian campus — a developed area on the far eastern corner of the plot that was just south of the original Ishtar Gate and Nebuchadnezzar's palace and just northeast of the coliseum. This area was fully developed with asphalt roads leading from Al Hilla into the compound and through it. This site had a series of small man-made ponds, walking paths, and many small structures which once served as shops, restaurants, and museum kiosks.

What is of key importance here is to note that while it may be true that there might have existed areas of archaeological interest in this area the grounds had already been bulldozed, cleared, and leveled by Saddam Hussein's work crews in 1982, long before we arrived in April 2003. This is the very reason that the staff agreed to allow us to build the secondary airfield in a large open field adjacent to one of the ponds and just south of the Ishtar Gate. The field had been overtaken by tall grass but it had already been leveled and worked long before our arrival. It is true that I MEF cut the grass down, stripped all grass off of it, grated the top layers, and then packed it in.

In both instances, which are the primary focus of some of these accusations, I can say with all clarity of conscience that we consulted with our Iraqi staff and both sites had been developed far before our arrival. The very fact that these areas had been previously developed became the primary reason for legitimizing their use. If we had been as insensitive or brute stupid as the accusations have implied we would have concreted over the sites with no regard but in fact we proceeded with the intent to make as little an environmental impact as possible. Therefore, to declare that Marine forces in Babylon built on an archaeological site is at best misinformed and at worst outright disingenuous.

One of the organizations accused us of destroying a 2,600-year-old road with heavy military equipment. I'd have to first qualify and state that we did not have any heavy tanks with us during our stay. I do know that US tanks from the 1st Marine Division had come through the area but while there I was never shown any evidence that they tracked through an area identified as an ancient site. There were no tracks or reports from the staff that the American tanks had violated the ancient site. The water table in this area is very high and the terrain is soft. If a heavy tank would have traversed through any of this area the evidence would have remained far into the future. I did not see any evidence of such. I will state that when we first arrived to Babylon, we saw Iraqi tanks and light armored vehicles that had been abandoned just outside the ancient site. The evidence for such charges is weak and appears to be an attempt to exaggerate the damage in order to rationalize the charge.

Other charges reporting in 2006 claim that the area was littered with shell casings and sandbags loaded with archeological fragments is also questionable at best and suspect with ulterior motives behind such inflammatory remarks. We arrived weeks after the fighting into the Babylon area and found little to no debris from firefights. What we did find we cleaned up extensively under the guidance of the workers. A few "foxholes" were, in fact, dug in the area but they were there when we arrived. No one could ascertain whether these holes were dug by Iraqi troops preparing for a clash or by passing American troops prior to our arrival. Once in Babylon we were well fortified and did not need to dig any foxholes because we were well in control of the area.

With regard to the charge that our helicopters were so close to the ancient sites that their rotor blades caused sandblast damage to the ancient walls, this is simply preposterous. The new helicopter expeditionary airfield that was located toward the eastern border of the campus was the only one near any ancient site. The distance from the closest ancient wall to the northern edge of the airfield was almost two football fields long. While it is true that the rotor blast of US helicopters can deliver a heavy blast upon touchdown and takeoff, it is highly improbable that these helicopters were ever close enough to the lower walls to be able to directly cause any sandblast effect.

I stood in the area nearest to the airfield on many occasions while helicopters were taking off and while their noise was loud there was no blown effect as they passed overhead. In most cases they had gained enough lift that they were well overhead to affect us. I can believe that the vibrations might have had some subtle effects but in this section of the overflight pattern if it were to affect anything it would be the taller newer wall created by Saddam Hussein and not the ancient shorter, sturdier walls closer to the ground.

In fairness to these concerns, I cannot speak with absolute certainty or authority on what took place in Babylon after I MEF turned control over to the Polish forces under the Multi-National International Force following our tenure in August 2003, but I can definitively speak with authority not only on what we did but we as Marines intended to do with this responsibility. By the same token, I can also state that the Polish and Italian Forces that took over the southern provinces once under Marine Corps control were thoroughly briefed by me on what needed to be addressed and what the concerns were in the area of archaeological sites. I can also state that there is plenty of evidence that the Polish brought in archaeological experts of their own to address many of these issues and interface with local experts.

In our time in Babylon from April through August 2003 I believe that instead of being chastised for causing irreversible damage, which could not be proven, instead we should have been lifted up as the model of faithful stewardship and conscientiousness. It can be said that the invasion catapulted a period of chaos and such chaos gave way to uncontrolled looting. This chaos also provided thieves with an opportunity to flourish. Such opportunistic vandalism cannot simply be seen as a direct result of our policy but as a reflection of the poverty and lawlessness of Iraqi society coupled with the state of hopelessness so characteristically imbedded in their politics. In the big picture, we must bear some responsibility for bringing on such violence and chaos but once again we must separate the effects of policy with the manifestation of actions by our troops.

In the midst of war, armies calculate each step forward intending to destroy their enemy. Marines define their mission simply as "closing in and killing the enemy." Destruction, annihilation, and chaos are tools in the shed that allow these warriors to flush out the enemy and suppress them to surrender or die. In ages past, militaries would leave behind a path of total devastation of biblical proportions in order to insure the subjection of nations. One has to understand that in order for warriors of the past to be able to achieve this task, they sought to compartmentalize themselves into a monolithic bloodthirsty mindset that fueled itself with anger, hate, and the spirit of destruction.

The modern American warrior is no such one-dimensional creature. We reflect a society that respects the law of rule, the sanctity of life, and the value of democracy. These characteristics are as much a part of our woven ethos as it is to be a faithful warrior. The modern American warrior is expected to be ruthless in the face of combat, fearless, and selfless but also compassionate, lawful, and honoring in the midst of chaos and hatred. The demands placed on our warriors are complex, and they force the blending of a multidimensional conscious human being who is forced to function responsibly and with discipline in varying dimensions of warfare. This is the quiet reality of the modern American warrior.

For this reason I believe that our nation owes our warriors a great debt. For though we are given permission on behalf of the state to inflict chaos and destruction we manage to do so in a controlled, professional, and intentional fashion that insists on protecting the personification of our values, ideals, and faith. In the midst of war, I find it amazingly hopeful that men and women who have had their very existence threatened by physical actions against them can still find it in their hearts to be compassionate and mindful of their responsibilities as stewards of greater values.

The I Marine Expeditionary Force has been openly charged with being an agent of destruction in Babylon. On April 15, 2006, the British Broadcasting Company (BBC) demanded an apology from Colonel Coleman for damaging the ancient site of Babylon. Colonel Coleman replied,

> *"If it wasn't for our presence," he told the BBC, "what would the state of those archeological ruins be ... Is there a price for the presence? Sure there is," he declared. "I'll just say that the price, had the presence not been there, would have been far greater."*[5]

It is interesting that many media outlets immediately defined his comments as an apology or as an admission of guilt. I interpreted this as a gentlemen's effort to not argue but to provide a noncommittal response. True, had we not shown up there at all we would not be guilty of having made a few guided incursions into the soil but by the same token we would have clearly been blamed for the dismantling to ruins of the Babylon museum and the looting and trampling of the ancient site beyond recognition. I suppose the US could be held accountable by the French for having vastly littered their beaches during the invasion of Normandy but unlike these idealistic and politically motivated critics the French are a little more grounded in reality and its consequences than these accusers.

It is ironic that in this modern age of mass media and global outreach the very message that we had hoped to demonstrate to the world through our actions, that we acted responsibly and cared enough of Iraq's treasures to preserve it, the very opposite has happened and our message has been lost and in some cases intentionally buried.

1. Associated Press, Jim Krane, June 11, 2004; fair usage applies.

2. Rupert Cornwell, Independent UK, April 15, 2006; fair usage applies

3. "War and Occupation in Iraq," Global Policy Forum, June 2007; fair usage applies.

4. Congressional Resolution on Iraq (passed by House and Senate in October 2002), http://hnn.us/articles/1282.html.

5. British Broadcasting Company, April 15, 2006.

Chapter Ten

By The Rivers Of Babylon

By the rivers of Babylon we sat and wept.
— Psalm 137:1

I was standing outside of the Ishtar Gate preparing to head back to Camp Babylon after having spent a few hours with the museum staff in the courtyard on May 19. I was walking toward the Humvee when I noticed the CH-46 helicopter fly down toward the tree line and disappear behind the green horizon. It looked like it was descending kind of fast but under these circumstances it wasn't uncommon to see helicopters banking hard and flying low. We decided to drive up to the market area to insure everything was going well before I headed back to the camp to address some of my other duties. When we arrived at the checkpoint by the souk one of the Marines on duty asked, "Sir, did you hear of the helo that went down?"

"No, what helo? Where did it happen?" I asked quickly thinking of the helicopter I had just seen.

"It just came over the net, sir. It went down by the south gate," he said with a saddened voice.

"Thanks, we'll head over there right now."

RP2 Stephens turned the Humvee around and sped down the road to get me to the other side of the camp as soon as possible. We arrived at the southern gate and asked the Marines at the ECP, and they pointed us toward the town of Jumjuma just outside of our wire. "Sir, they're reporting it went down in the river over by the road that leads to the trash-burning site."

We turned off the main road and onto a dirt road that led us to an adjacent path along the river. When we turned onto the river road I could see the tail section of the helicopter sticking out of the river. We pulled up as far forward as possible to be directly adjacent to the helicopter. I stepped out to find that Colonel Cunnings had jumped into the heavy current in the river and swam out to the helicopter. He was sitting atop a portion of the emerging helicopter catching his breath from having attempted to go under and find the crew. A few Marines along the riverbed informed me that the call was out for more troops to come to attempt a search and rescue. Behind me a few Iraqi men from Jumjuma were discarding their slippers and jumping into the canal swimming out to help Colonel Cunnings. It was then when Colonel Cunnings asked us to hold the Iraqis back because we didn't want any more casualties.

I learned at that moment that a Marine from 1st Battalion 4th Marines had been on patrol along the canal when he witnessed the helicopter crash into the canal. All reports indicated that he immediately discarded his gear and jumped into the water to assist the crew but sadly drowned under the very heavy current of the green river. SGT Kirk Allen Straseskie's body was pulled out of the canal by other Marines who came to his rescue but unfortunately were unable to revive him.

I looked back behind me and realized that a crowd of Iraqis were coming out from the village of Jumjuma and racing toward the river path. There seemed to be over a hundred of them gathering along the riverbank. That afternoon I was accompanied by RP3 Nelson Correa, from Brooklyn, New York, who had converted to Islam and was fluent in Arabic. I asked him to control the crowds and push them back away from the river so our teams of incoming Marines could get their equipment into this narrow road. He immediately turned around and began to ask them to step back. They politely obliged as they continued to look on. Many of the men atop the grass mounds above us were either employed in Camp Babylon or were vendors at our market.

RP3 Correa soon returned to me and stated that there was an unconfirmed report that a body had been seen floating down river immediately after the crash. Colonel Cunnings had swam back to our location and was orchestrating the initial efforts of the rescue when I shared the unconfirmed report with him. He asked the other officers within earshot if anyone had a Humvee available to go investigate. I knew that it would take a few more minutes for the other teams to arrive and they should be investing all of their resources to find the crew. It was late afternoon and we only had a few hours of sunlight before us. I volunteered to take my Humvee and RPs down the road to see if there was any truth to these claims.

We ran back to our vehicle. The road was too narrow to turn the Humvee around so RP2 Stephens rolled it back in reverse to the turn. We then turned onto the main road and into Al Hilla and attempted to find an access road to the canal. As we got closer, we kept dismounting the vehicle and looking along the canal to see if we could spot our missing crewmember floating down river. We'd hoped that if he were conscious he would grab onto the overgrown grass along the riverbank. On the other hand, if he happened to be unconscious there were spots along the river where the flow turned, and we hoped he would get caught along with debris on one of its winding banks where we could spot him.

In order to get further downstream we needed to cross an overpass where we discovered a Marine from 1st Battalion 4th Marines was on post with a radio. We pulled up alongside him and informed him of what was happening. We asked him if he had seen anything floating down river and he answered negatively. He asked us if we'd heard anything on SGT Straseskie. I told him that I heard reports that he had been recovered but unfortunately he didn't make it. But, I had not seen him yet. He cursed under his breath and was shaken by the news, having hoped that the report of his death was wrong but I dashed that hope. He openly grieved for his friend and said he would remain on watch on the overpass as we jumped back into the vehicle. We drove as fast and as far down the canal as the road allowed us. We then drove back slowly with ongoing intermittent stops to walk around and look along the banks. We spent a good part of an hour doing this without any additional security, no radios, and we were alone in our quest. We grew frustrated in not finding anyone. What seemed equally strange was that we had not seen any debris float by either. The current was obviously very strong.

We rolled back to the site to find both banks of the canal filled with people. Small Iraqi boats had been acquired and there were ropes strewn across the canal as teams of Marines kept going under fervently attempting to find their peers in the murky waters. I stood there in the midst of all this activity feeling quite helpless. How does one pray at a time such as this? I hoped we would recover them but by now over an hour had passed, and we knew that the crew didn't have enough time to get out. I looked around and I could see and feel the angst everyone had as they desperately hoped for a good result in a hopeless situation. I took a step back and quietly prayed for the families of these brave souls. Our angst would pale in comparison to the wrenching pain they were to feel in the hours ahead.

The hours passed and it was explicitly clear that we had moved from a rescue to a recovery operation. The current in the canal proved too fierce even for our strongest swimmers in the group. I was standing quietly along the banks when RP3 Correa approached me and introduced me to one of our vendors whose face I recognized but didn't know very well. He spoke only Arabic and so RP3 Correa translated while informing me that the current was so strong because the dam had been recently opened. If we drove up the road to the dam we could convince them to close the dam. This would stop the fast current and facilitate the recovery operation.

I asked through RP3 Correa, "How far is the dam?"

He turned to the Iraqi man who replied, "Just up the road."

I found Colonel Cunnings in a huddle with other officers still soaking wet from his multiple dives into the river. I pulled him aside and shared the information on the dam. He concluded that it wouldn't hurt to make the attempt and asked me to drive up in my Humvee with the Iraqi and get it done. I asked the Iraqi to follow us to the vehicle. RP2 Stephens jumped behind the wheel, RP3 Correa sat behind me on the passenger's side and the Iraqi gentleman sat behind the driver. We headed north on the road out of Al Hilla and RP2 Stephens pushed the Humvee forward as fast as it could go. We'd been on the road for ten minutes when I turned back to face RP3 Correa and over the rumbling of the Humvee I yelled back, "How much further? I thought he said it was up the road?"

He turned to the Iraqi and asked but the reply was the same, "Up the road."

We were now committed to this road trip but I was uneasy. I really didn't know this guy that well. If it had been someone recommended by Ja'far or Abdul it might have been different but the info on this guy was pretty thin. In addition, we were one Humvee and two of us were unarmed, the Iraqi and I. We were driving deeper and deeper into inhospitable surroundings and we were driving blind.

The Iraqi led us through a few turns and past a series of villages. At each village we slowed down through the main road and were greeted by dozens of emotionless stares. We crossed through one town where it looked like all the men were gathered in front of a shop by the road. It seemed like all conversations ceased and all eyes were quietly following us as we cruised by.

I felt like a child continuously turning around and screaming to be heard over the whirring sound of large Humvee tires on an asphalt road and would ask, "Are we there yet?"

The Iraqi would casually look at RP3 Correa and reply in Arabic, "Just up the road."

Forty minutes later and after a winding path and a great deal of anxiety on my part we were pulling into the facilities of a large dam. It's not what I expected. I imagined a small dam handled by a local Iraqi but I didn't expect a full-blown dam system with locks and generators. It was a major compound with an elderly guard and a few engineers at the controls. The guard hesitantly let us in as the Iraqi pleaded our case. We pulled up a ramp road to the locks and were met by two Iraqi gentlemen.

"As-Salaam-Alaikum," I greeted.

They both replied, "Alaikum-Salaam."

I turned to RP3 Correa and asked him to explain the situation to them and see if we could get them to close the dam in support of our quest. They exchanged words back and forth in Arabic and the engineer seemed concerned. Finally RP3 Correa turned to me and said the chief engineer would agree to our requests with one condition.

"What would that be?" I asked assuming we were heading toward a request for a bribe or something of that nature.

"He's saying that if he closes the dam it will reduce water flow for everyone from this point on. This will affect fishermen, farmers, and many others along the banks. He is willing to do it during the night hours to assist us but we need to post soldiers for protection. Otherwise some of the villagers will come with grenades or rifles to force them to open the dam."

I didn't have the authority to promise him anything so I told him that if my commander agreed to this we would be back in two hours with Marines for his protection. He agreed and we jumped back in the vehicles and headed south back to the site.

It was still light on our way back but I knew that if we did return we would be caught by darkness. I wasn't sure if Colonel Cunnings would buy shutting off the dam once he knew the consequences and the cost. I devoted the remaining forty minutes to prayer as we drove back to camp and I attempted to remember the path so I could lead the next team back.

We returned to the crash site to discover that they were still having difficulties locating the portion of the helicopter that housed the crew members. Divers were called in but they wouldn't arrive until the next day. We couldn't drive onto the canal banks any longer due to all of the support gear and lights being utilized. I found Colonel Cunnings amidst the crowd and pulled him to the side. I explained our situation and without hesitation he approved the mission. He asked me to go speak to the Commanding Officer of our guard detachment at Camp Babylon from 2nd Battalion 6th Marines Fox Company and ask him to send a team out to the dam for the night.

On my walk back toward the Humvee I was stopped at least six times by the residents of Jumjuma, most of them associated with the market, each to express their condolences in their own way for the loss of our Marines. In the midst of so much activity, I found it heartwarming to have them express what appeared to be genuine concern and empathy.

It was dark by the time I arrived to the guard shack to speak to the CO of Fox Company. I explained the situation to the CO and

XO and showed them on a map where the team needed to be located. They called a team of Marines together and equipped them with heavy weapons and radio communications. In less than twenty minutes we were all on the way back to the dam up the road in a three-vehicle convoy. The trip to the dam took almost an hour as we attempted to make our way through the same road that looked so different under the cover of darkness and the occasional streetlights. We passed through the same towns as before, and they didn't seem any happier to see us the third time around.

Upon arrival, the senior Marine assessed the position and proceeded to station his Marines to provide coverage through the night. I said my good-byes after their radio check, and we headed back on our own. It seemed to take an eternity and the night seemed blacker than any I recalled in recent past. We weren't moving too fast because we didn't want to get lost but we were on hyper alert. Once again it was one of those times when I asked myself, "Emilio what in the world are you doing here?"

We had passed our first town on the way back to the camp and now we were flanked by agricultural fields on both sides of the road when we spotted the first flare going up to our right. I had no idea if it was friend or foe but someone just signaled someone else. It was less than a quarter mile up the road I noticed the next flare on the left side of the road. This happened at least three more times during the trip and each time I prayed the same prayer, "Lord, if someone is planning something against us blind the enemy. Bring us through safely, Lord, the way Jesus walked passed those who wanted to stone him."

Twenty minutes later we reached the well-lit, hard-top road that led us back south to Al Hilla and we let out a sigh of relief.

We returned to the crash site that evening to support the many teams so hard at work through the night. We were exhausted but no more than the many Marines by the canal and that kept us going. Lights were set up along the banks casting rays of white candescent light onto the canal revealing the tail of the helicopter as it protruded out of the water. The water looked dark, heavy, and continued to move fast. There were many who were hard at work in the water and by the shore while others just wanted to be there to show support. I walked along the bank and greeted many of our Marines who looked so intently at the water continuing to hope for progress.

As I worked my way deeper into the road I noticed that even at this time of the night there were many Iraqi men squatted along the banks behind our lines of operation continuing to watch and desirous to provide support. A few saw me and reminded me that they were used to the waters. They grew up swimming in the canal and it would not be a threat for them. The fact was that some had already been allowed to assist the recovery and it proved fruitless. I thanked them for their concern and willingness to help us, but we had enough qualified people in the water and we needed to let them do their work. I found an exhausted Colonel Cunnings and let him know that we were back safely and the security team was in place at the dam.

I stayed along the banks for a few hours and then retreated to our quarters at Camp Babylon. I returned in the early morning to the crash site and milled about with those at work. The river's water height was significantly lower due to the dam closure and the current appeared to slow down some but I was disappointed to note that it didn't slow as much as I had hoped.

The recovery effort was frustrating but no resource was left untapped to recover the crew. A special Navy salvage recovery crew with special gear and equipment was called in for the search to relieve the current divers. These guys had the ability to literally walk along the floor of the canal and map it out systematically. The green river flowed fast and allowed for zero visibility in its depth, making it impossible to see anything. They discovered that the heavy currents had carried the forward section of the helicopter further down river than expected. Each crew member was equipped with a dye release packet designed to let out a large yellow dye patch upon hitting the water.

It dumbfounded us that after being on the scene so quickly we failed to see the yellow dye. It was concluded that the current was so strong that the dye was carried downstream so quickly that it never had the opportunity to rise to the top of the water where it could be seen. The special team worked through the night and early morning. They recovered every crewmember, relieving our fear of having lost a crewmember downstream when they accounted for everyone.

The mood in the camp was solemn for days following the recovery operation. So many people had been so invested in the recovery process that the loss was taken very personally at many levels regardless of the fact that most of us didn't know the crew. The crew flew in and out of Camp Babylon but like so many crews they were so busy and on the go that they rarely interacted with the residents of the camp with the exception of the flight line support crew and our operations people. In my ministry about the camp one would have thought otherwise due to the great loss that was being expressed by so many. It was no surprise that when we held *So important* a memorial service a few days later, we had people packed into the largest hall in the camp filled to capacity and beyond.

That day we lifted in prayer and honored Captain Andrew David LaMont from Eureka, California; 1st Lieutenant Timothy Louis Ryan from Aurora, Illinois; Staff Sergeant Aaron Dean White from Shawnee, Oklahoma; Lance Corporal Jason William Moore from San Marcos, California; and Sergeant Kirk Allen Straseskie from Beaver Dam, Wisconsin. Friends from their squadron, The Purple Foxes, were in attendance along with representatives from 1st Battalion 4th Marines and many from our camp.[1] We had volunteers come forward to share a few words honoring their comrades and another volunteer offered up a beautiful rendition of the Star Spangled Banner. The only thing missing was the opportunity to convey to the family how truly sorry we were that we couldn't save them. We leaned on one another and shared our loss as a corporate body. Chaplain Gwudz shared a few words of reflection and I led them in a few prayers. I've had more than my fair share of memorial services during my career and to this day I still find them incredibly difficult and gut wrenching.

The rivers of Babylon proved not only to be a symbol of loss to us but one of goodwill as well. In the days of the recovery efforts we could not help but notice the many gestures of empathy and camaraderie that were expressed by the local Iraqis. I believed most of us were touched by their willingness to assist and risk their own lives in order to help us search for the crew.

The rivers of Babylon came to be a sign of faith for me as well. With no intent to stay in Babylon for a long period of time it was determined that we would not build any new facilities. When I queried for a place for church, we settled on erecting a camouflage net over fifty chairs and made it our chapel. It was nice to see with frequency that we often exceeded our seating capacity. It sat along the river just to the north end of the chow hall. At first it would go up every Sunday for services and then it was dismantled so the chairs could be used in the chow hall. About two months into our stay we were able to get more chairs and make it a semi-permanent fixture. The Seabees provided a wooden floor base so we wouldn't sink into the soft dirt. For the five months we were in Babylon we prayed, worshiped, shared the scriptures, and enjoyed God's presence along the river of Babylon, a tributary of the Euphrates.

I preached a series of sermons on the book of Daniel and used him as a backdrop for our worship. I'd often correlate the fact that Daniel probably didn't wish to be there any more than we did but in his faithfulness he continued to serve well, as did we. The history of the Old Testament came alive along the rivers of Babylon. I'd get stopped during the day and was asked questions on the history of Babylon and its biblical impact. Along with these many questions you'd never guess that Marine Corps officers would stop me and ask, "Hey, chaplain, who came first the Akkadians or the Assyrians?"

As you can imagine, there were many questions on Christian apocalyptic literature that always make for a very good theological exchange. The inquiries into prophecy and apocalyptic literature also helped to usher people from the realm of the magnificent to that of a personal reflection. When asked if we were in the end times I'd concur but usually expand the conversation to make the point that regardless of what and when God might plan for earth's final chapter right now the fact remains that if they died today the world would end for them. The greatest apocalyptic question is not always do you know what will happen next as much as it is do you have a personal relationship with God and are you prepared if it happens to you today?

At the rivers of Babylon I learned from the curators that they found our interest in Babylon curious because though they understood its impact in world history they had not associated it with our religious history. I'd often sit with the curators to discuss our faith journeys. I gave each curator a Bible and marked the areas that mentioned Babylon, Nebuchadnezzar, and ancient Iraq. I shared stories that I'd assume were familiar to them but in fact were not part of their faith lexicon. I spoke of the Assyrian empire and how God sent Jonah to speak to them in Nineveh, the great seat of power during its time. They didn't know all of the details of the story surrounding Daniel and the writing on the wall. They'd also heard partially the events of Daniel and the lion's den. One day when we traveled into town and I stopped to look at one of their huge fiery furnaces for brick building, they wondered why I was so intrigued. I shared with them the account of Shadrach, Meshach, and Abednego with the fiery furnace.

I'd swing by daily and sit with the staff in the late afternoons under the large tree in the courtyard after the heat would break and tours were over to debrief the day. We'd review the day and discuss business but we always delved into friendly conversations. In exchange for my faith stories they shared stories of the great Ali and his mighty sword or the stories of Gilgamesh. It was during these times when I learned that some of Iraq's scholars are concerned that a move toward religious fundamentalism by the Shiites may in fact prove to be more damaging to the ancient sites than the war. They shared that many fundamentalists didn't care to preserve history that predated Mohammed in Iraq and as such this jeopardized their scholarly efforts. If the government moved toward a fundamentalist regime they feared that they would lose support and in fact the over 10,000 archaeologically rich sites in Iraq could be abandoned or left unguarded to provide access to more black marketing.

It was also here in one of our warmhearted exchanges where I came to understand that the divisions between Iraqis were not so clearly distinguishable. We as Americans tend to divide them into

215

clear groups delineated by religious creeds such as Shiite, Sunni, Kurd, or Christian but the reality is that their loyalties are much more complex due to regional alliances, tribal affiliations, and other factors to include socioeconomic outlooks. We'd tend to think that a Shiite in Iraq would be closer to a Shiite in Iran than to an Iraqi Sunni but that is not the case. An Iraqi Shiite is Arab and they grossly mistrust the Persians (Iranians) regardless if they are Shiite or not.

The late afternoons in Babylon were my favorite times. In the relative peace of the courtyard, we would easily forget that we were brought together because of this war. It was usually a wonderful time to share experiences, ideas, concerns, theology, and stories. It was a time where we shared about family and our dreams for tomorrow. It was the perfect time for me to share the stories that drew our hearts to this place.

It was during one of these sessions when Amira was excitedly sharing a story with the other staff members and I joined them. "Chaplain, chaplain you must hear what was said to me by my friend in Al Hilla." I wondered what could rise out of communal gossip in Al Hilla and yet be of interest to me.

She mentioned the name of a family, whom I unfortunately never quite captured at the time, "[unnamed family] hold funeral yesterday. The entire town of Al Hilla [which was a bold exaggeration] join them in the procession for funeral. The family and friends came to intersection and they found Marines [pronounced Marreens] there. The Marines were walking in patrol with helmets and many weapons. The funeral stopped. The Marines stopped. Many were afraid then the Marine took off his helmet. The other Marines took off helmets. They showed respect to dead — it was wonderful," exclaimed Amira to the rest of the group.

It warmed my heart to learn that the Marines on patrol had enough presence of mind to show respect to the townspeople but I didn't think much of it. Amira, on the other hand, along with the others, raved about it for the next three days about how good this was. They talked about how this showed the Marines were gentlemen and they had respect for Iraqis. They spoke of how it honored the family. I didn't really understand the grand impact of this initially but I could see it in their delight, in their faces, and in the way they spoke about it so I thought it would warm the command's heart to learn that we were making a positive impact. I shot off an email to Colonel Coleman and he forwarded it to General Stalder and General Conway.

Years later, while attending a conference, I heard General Conway, now Commandant of the Marine Corps, retelling the same story with a few different details and what impressed me is that he did his homework and was able to identify those Marines by name. I didn't know the Marines but I saw firsthand that afternoon how they touched the lives of regular Iraqi townspeople by being gentlemen.

The rivers of Babylon also came to serve as a sanctuary, a place of respite for many who would just pause during their duties and take a breather during the week. The camouflage netting provided a sense of semi-privacy and as the river flowed south it drowned out the sounds of the world around us. Across the river and a little to the north sat another one of our camps but directly across from the chapel were some tall palm trees and a long road running parallel to the river. On quiet evenings I would sit in the chapel and watch Iraqi children gather on the other side of the river to play. Occasionally, fishermen would float by in their small, thin boats or cows would be led past for their evening wash. The skies seemed to always be bright blue and for those short moments, the rivers of Babylon allowed me to escape to a place of serenity.

The Iraqis we worked with saw the river as pure, an image that was hard for me to imagine since it was clearly not on the top ten or for that matter the top hundred of the cleanest rivers I'd ever seen. They insisted that they didn't like the bottled water we provided them because it had been processed and it had too many chemicals. To them the waters from the Euphrates were a gift from Allah and in their opinion it was better for them than what we had to offer. I didn't want to offend their sensibilities since they attributed the waters to Allah but I tried to explain that our reversed osmosis water purification units would draw so much bacteria and crud from the Euphrates that the usually recyclable filters had to be discarded after only a few uses.

217

The museum staff invited my staff and me to join them for a traditional Iraqi meal one afternoon after the usual round of tours. We returned later that afternoon to enjoy the late afternoon snack and found a blanket lying out under the large tree in the courtyard covered with a wide array of fruits, rice, chicken, and fish. They went on and on about how fresh the fish was and insisted that I have a piece of the fish. I asked where the fish was from and they responded, "Allah's river, the great Euphrates."

I tried desperately to hide my reservations and made a big fuss about the rice, chicken, and fresh fruits which were delicious.

At one point Amira turned to me and asked, "Chaplain did you try the delicious fish?"

I could not lie, so I thought I was being sly when I replied, "Amira, no I haven't. I've filled myself up with this delicious chicken and rice and I don't need the fish."

She retorted, "Chaplain, Chaplain you must have fish." She reached down on to the platter and with her fingers she broke off a piece of fish and placed it on my plate. Farah smiled and urged me to enjoy the fish.

I made the excuse, "I don't eat much fish."

Farah replied, "Just a little, Chaplain." All of their eyes were now on me. I smiled and took a small piece of the fish the size of a quarter.

The minute it touched my tongue I almost gagged. The only way I could describe the taste is by saying that it tasted as strongly as algae smelled. It was a putrid taste yet I smiled and swallowed the fish as they smiled along with me. RP2 Maria Hernandez knew what I was trying to do and she lit up a wide smile as to say, "Busted!" When she was asked to try the fish she just clearly stated that she doesn't eat fish. They let it go at that but I had no such fortune. I followed my fish with some fresh fruit and knew it wasn't going to sit well. It's funny how some things are just predictable. I spent the next hour just fine with the staff but a few hours later upon my return to my quarters I felt deathly ill in my stomach. Thank God for being neighbors with the medical section and CIPRO.

The rivers meant a lot of things to many people here. They wind through this desolate land and bring forth life to a barren place. To the left and to the right of the winding riverbanks and the expanding tributaries greenery explodes out of a brown dry desert making it a beautiful oasis. As you follow the rivers, you find crops growing, livestock abound, and towns and cities bustle with people. Since the days of ancients the rivers were signs of life and fertility as they also invited the human soul to reflect and ponder before this force. Before the quietness of the river, people have dreamed, aspired to great things, and have been touched by the soul of God. In the same fashion it has been before the flow of the very same rivers where others have come to look deep inside of their spirits and found themselves weeping, gnashing their teeth, and imploring a new fate. In Psalm 137, the lament reads, "By the rivers of Babylon we sat and wept when we remembered Zion."

By these same rivers, the Jews who had been carried away from Jerusalem lamented their condition in captivity under Nebuchadnezzar's rule. Thousands of years later, the Shiites lamented their condition under the iron fist of Saddam's rule as he oppressed them here in the southern regions. Abdul shared that where the current modern Babylonian palace sits today there once stood a small village of over 2,000 people. Saddam supposedly bulldozed the village and displaced them in order to make room for his palace and his new compound so he could look over the ruins and his river.

It was here, also, where some paused for a moment of reflection to rediscover their faith and hope but then there were those who sat by it and shed a tear in privacy along the river of Babylon. They sat in quiet desperation as they dealt with a failing marriage, the death of a loved one, or the pains associated with the heart growing fonder of a missed one so far away.

The living river never rests and never sits. When we pause by its banks it reminds us that we must never stop. It doesn't matter whether we stopped to shed a tear in joy or regret it reminds us that life goes on and so must we. With faith and determination, trust and confidence, hope and commitment, we, too, can break through the desolation in our lives and the aridly dry places of our heart and spring forth new growth.

By these banks I spoke to many Marines and Sailors who opened their hearts to me as they faced the challenges in their lives. There was the young Marine reservist who without hesitation responded to his call to service after September 11 and left behind his new business to discover that he left it in the hands of partners who had now destroyed him financially. The young woman who tearfully struggled with an unsupportive husband back home who made her feel guilty every chance he could for leaving him and the children behind. There was the painful guilt of the loving husband whose wife was battling cancer while he was thousands of miles away. Then there were the new fathers who had not seen their new babies and feared dying before they returned. The sacrifices of these young lives were many as they placed their lives on hold in order to answer a call they felt came by nation and God.

It was by the rivers of Babylon where I held the Marine Corps first Warrior Transition briefs as we began to send our troops home in small groups. It was an effort by Navy chaplains to gather Marines and Sailors together and allow them a place to reflect, feel supported, and begin to address the issues about returning home. The program was centered on three questions, quite simple but yet very profound: "Where have you been?" "Where are you now?" and "Where are you going?" The intent was to give Marines permission to begin to think about their transition back home to their families and to wrestle with their own expectations. Part of the training provided education to help them go through a process of self-assessment and identify trouble signs early on in their transitions back home. It also equipped them to assess their friends with the hopes of encouraging them to intervene early at the first signs of trouble. In the end the true intent was to convey that as an organization we cared and we were here to help because the effects of this journey will remain with us for a long time to come.

By the rivers of Babylon we celebrated. It was here where we greeted the movie stars that came to visit us, grilled hamburgers and hot dogs, drank cold sodas, and created a piece of Americana in Iraq. We celebrated Memorial Day and the Fourth of July by the rivers of Babylon.

It was by the rivers of Babylon where five Marines gave their all and we each left a little bit of ourselves.

---

1. Website commemorating these Marines: http://www.purplefoxyladies.com/ mem_news.html#lamont.

Chapter Eleven

Inshallah

For it is God's will that by doing good you should si-
lence the ignorant talk of foolish men.

— 1 Peter 2:15

Speak to an Iraqi about almost anything and they will share their opinion, vision, or conclusion with you, but in the end they shall end it with a popular phrase, *Insha Allah* pronounced by many as one word, "Inshallah." I found the practice remarkably similar to the practice of Puerto Rican Christians who end their phrases, *Si Dios quiere* (If God wills it), a practice common from our Roman Catholic heritage but probably rooted in an Arabic and Moorish past.

I recall as a young man saying to my mother in Spanish, "To-morrow I'm going to the movies with my friends." Her immediate reply would be in a passionate Spanish, "Are you a heathen? Do you control the events of tomorrow? Are you the Lord of the heavens? It will happen only if God wills it! So say it, 'If God wills it.' " I, in turn, would mumble back the amendment to my sentence and de-clare, "If God wills it." The sentiment is exactly the same in the Muslim-Iraqi culture. It is an implicit way of surrendering to the will of God in everything that you do. It is meant to be a sign of faithfulness, a sign of trust in God and God's overarching provi-dence over humanity. It is believed that the more secular version of this very word is the Spanish word *ojala*, which is believed to come from its Moorish roots in *Insha Allah* that today translates to, "Let's hope so."

Trusting "God's will" can be a tricky thing. It implies many things. It is a statement that perceives God as an active agent in humanity. It is a worldview that declares God's will is transparent to those who follow faithfully. To believe that events happen if God wills it is to proclaim trust in the providence of God but it also presents one with challenges. How do we know God's will in our lives? Is God's will, or in secular terms, "fate," predetermined in such a rigid pattern that our contribution is preprogrammed into the outcome or does it interact with our free will in an interplay of wit, compassion, and strategy? What does it look like when we live a life according to God's will?

I came to learn that theologically *Insha Allah* was an act of faith and public obedience but sometimes in practice it takes on another, perhaps unconscious, meaning. In this unconscious expression, *Insha Allah* seemed to reveal insight into their hearts and the hopelessness that resided deep within them as they used it to resign themselves from any real expectations in an almost fatalistic fashion. When I spoke with the staff of the efforts that were to be made on behalf of the museum and the insurmountable red tape that we had to overcome or when I spoke to folks like Ja'far of the future they would declare, *"Insha Allah"* as to convey, "We will see." If not careful, their tone could easily resort to allowing *Insha Allah* to become interchangeable with our American version of "whatever"! This is a statement that implicitly expects nothing and arbitrarily resigns to inactivity. In its most negative form it can even be defined as a means of expressing incredulity.

"If God wills it" is an expression that resorts to honoring God's sovereignty over all things. It implicitly suggests subjection to God. Explicitly, in our Western works-centered society, it calls for action. It demands an effort on our part to attempt and understand God's will. A "will" that we believe is transparent to humanity and revealed through the study of scripture. Such a quest in scripture reveals the person of God. Our quest then is to seek to align our actions, our motives, and our hopes with those of God's. This process shouldn't be confused with the selfish attempts to manipulate or coerce God to supporting our agendas. It shouldn't be confused with the dishonest attempts of some to reinterpret scripture, rationalize theology, or engage in *eisogesis*, the act of reading one's own agenda into scripture. Instead it is a call for genuine change on our part. It is an explicit act of subjection to the will of God through the process of self-reflection where we consciously and intentionally conform to the values of God. It ultimately becomes a call for realignment. Ideally, if we realign ourselves with the will of God, the act of realignment in itself can reveal to us that what we've asked of God is either appropriate or inappropriate. This process allows us to place ourselves in the proper position for further discernment that will inform us if we have to act further or simply wait on God. It is revelation through relationship.

In the military we call this the Commander's intent. It is every Marine's responsibility to insure that we understand the mission and the Commander's intent behind the mission. Marines are not given detailed instructions on how to accomplish every particular objective. Instead, what happens is that the Commander's intent is made clear and, in turn, the subordinate Marines set out to accomplish the mission while adapting to unforeseen circumstances to the best of their abilities and resources while remaining faithful to the intent behind the mission.

Insha Allah, unfortunately, and perhaps due to the oppressive environment that has existed in Iraq for the past thirty years, has been simplified to such a degree of passivity in some Iraqis that many allow it to take on a whole new meaning. Within some of the Iraqi context it seems to imply, "If God wills it" then God will make it happen. The explicit action on humanity's part is no action, an act of passivity. So if we wait and nothing happens it means that God intended it this way and it must simply be accepted. There is no self-reflective process to see if our desires are aligned with God's or if we must learn to do other things to prepare us to receive what God wills in our life. It rests on a "let's see" perspective. It becomes very difficult to inspire people toward action when they believe that they have no authority to engage in such activity.

In the summer of 2003, Camp Babylon hired local workers from Jumjuma to collect trash, sweep the streets, and perform general maintenance duties throughout the camp. One day a young man, about eighteen, was hired to collect trash along with a group of other men. On their way to collect trash, they hopped onto the back of a seven-ton truck and began their rounds. The seven-ton truck is the workhorse of the Marine Corps. They are huge diesel trucks with tires that stand almost four feet tall. Enroute through the camp, the pin that holds the rear gate locked into position either broke or came loose and this young man who was leaning against the rear gate fell backward off the truck and onto the asphalt street below, severely banging his head on the street. The Marines immediately dispatched him to medical and cared for him over the next few days and then sent him home with his family. About a week into his time at home, LtCol Lebidine, a few other officers directly involved with the incident, and I went to Jumjuma to visit the family. The Marines insisted on visiting to check up on the young man's condition because it was the right thing to do. They were very concerned about his health and even his future. We wanted to offer compensation to the family and make ourselves available. We had announced our intention beforehand and anticipated an angry response.

On the designated evening a small cadre of Marines drove into Jumjuma and parked on the outskirts of the village. The officers walked to the appointed house of the tribal leader in order to demonstrate our respect and adhere to the proper customs. We were received by a group of men, one of them being the boy's father, who invited us to enter. Inside we sat around a large square room where tables began to be placed and trays of delicious foods were brought out. The large platters revealed roasted lamb and chicken, a wide array of colorful vegetables, yellow rice, breads, and plenty of watermelon.

The large, square room had a large window opposite of where we were asked to sit. It was covered by a curtain on the other side. It became obvious to me that the women and young ladies were gathered on the other side of the glass. The curtain would often flutter with activity and we could see the corner of someone's eyes peering through the windows behind the curtains. On occasion, a very young girl would violate protocol and simply swing the curtain back and peer into the room only to be corrected by an older kin. The men before us ignored their antics and continued to speak fluently in Arabic in the manner that men do in such social affairs.

The council of men treated our visit as if it were an official delegation. They shared their concerns with the war, complained of the many assessments that were made and the lack of action that was taken, and spoke of learning to trust us. The constant theme that undergirded every conversation with a Shiite was trust. They openly admitted to not trusting us because in 1991 President George H. W. Bush encouraged them to rise up against Saddam Hussein, implying our support. We left the region and never came to their aid. Life since then had been hell for them. As the night went on, the conversational tone got softer. We shared a meal with little talk from our part and only lots of smiles. The meal was delicious and in the end the experience was grand. Our translator attempted to keep up with their conversation and relay their meaning to us but it proved futile to attempt to really engage.

Following the meal we were escorted through the village to the home of the young man who had been injured. We entered into what appeared to be a one- or two-bedroom house with a large common room on the first floor and a set of stairs leading upstairs. The room was barely lit. We found the family huddled around the young man who was stretched out on the floor over a large blanket. He was suffering from massive swelling in his head and we were very concerned for him. We entered their humble abode and joined them on the floor as the young man lay there motionless. He was conscious and would follow our remarks with his eyes but he seemed void of any energy and could not speak. We braced to receive the family's wrath as we would in a similar situation in the US but instead we received a very mild response from his father, "*Insha Allah.*" The translator voiced, "It is God's will and it is what was meant to happen. Who are we to question Allah?" I looked over at the XO and he looked back at me in amazement. Paul Lebidine reiterated that we were extremely sorry for the accident and we desired to be informed if there was anything we might be able to do. They nodded in understanding and waved us good-bye as we exited their home that evening.

Outside the home there had accumulated a crowd of children curious to see the visiting Americans. The town was used to seeing us drive by the town while entering or leaving our encampment but very few of them, with the exception of the vendors and those who worked in the camp, had any real contact with us. Some of the children had more contact than their parents did because many Marines carried candy or trinkets in their cargo pockets, and they frequently slowed their vehicles to share them with the children. It was a common practice I thoroughly enjoyed.

It became clear to me that this small town was much more populated than I had imagined. Our melancholy mood quickly dissipated as the children greeted us with large smiles. We walked out amongst them and began to say, "Hello, hello" in response to their greetings. We worked our way deeper into the alleys of the small village and the crowd got larger and larger around us. The children came by our sides, held each of our hands, and soon we were surrounded by children and men alike welcoming us to their village. There were easily over sixty people on the street and droves of children around us.

We had Marines with weapons across their chests walking behind us but they, too, were overwhelmed by the children. Our security team couldn't drive into the town so they were trying to position themselves closest to us by asking one of our Marines over the radio where we were at regular intervals. They repositioned themselves along the road just outside the town as we moved through the labyrinth of alleys and small streets. We passed the small one-chair barbershop that sat more outside of the shop than in and a grocery hut no bigger than an American broom closet. We passed the simple, one-room homes of some of the men who worked at the base or as vendors at the market. I wondered if any of the looted chandeliers from the palace found themselves into these small humble homes.

Before we knew it we were being led in our own little parade down their main street, perhaps more appropriately their main alley. The cool night air was filled with giggles, laughter, and mimicking as we said, "Hello" and they repeated our salutations. Paul Lebidine looked at me and facetiously said, "Tomorrow *Stars and Stripes* is going to report on the stupid Americans who were shot for holding hands with a bunch of children in a village" expressing concern over this extemporaneous act. What started out being a very solemn occasion turned into a very pleasant and unexpected surprise. This was a time to be enjoyed so I turned to the XO, laughed, and mumbled under my breath, *"Insha Allah."*

Sitting under the large tree by the courtyard I spent many good hours with Moussawi, Abdul, Mahmoud, Amira, and Farah along with a band of others. Under this tree we dared to dream of what might become of this place once peace has found it and made it its own. Abdul joked and said we needed to stay in touch so that after the war I could start a business where I would send Americans to Al Hilla for tours of Babylon and Ezekiel's tomb in the old Jewish market. Moussawi and the others would chime in and say it was a very good idea. We'd take the thread of imagination and follow it through exploring ideas of how we could offer great Mesopotamian and biblical tours to include Ur, Babylon, and Nineveh.

Moussawi, who by his figure attested to his great love for Iraqi food, would go on about how wonderful Iraqi food and hospitality would be in those days. We'd dream of bringing back the Mesopotamian celebrations and it was magnificent to see their faces light up as I saw them truly envision a world far beyond the present. They would stand and point to where the food stands would be, how the museum would be opened with many great original relics recovered from around the world, and what they would wear. Mahmoud exclaimed that perhaps Berlin would consider returning the original Ishtar Gate so it could sit in its proper place on the Procession Street. The ladies would comment on the beautiful fabrics and costumes that the workers could wear to make ancient Babylon come alive with color and splendor.

I shared with them that my daughter at the time was a classical history student at the University of Arizona and she had some interest in archaeology. "Chaplain, how wonderful it would be for your daughter to come and work here in Babylon with us," they would muse. It was a dream we shared. It was a time where we were transported far from this war and into a future laden with peace and hope. It was a dream that connected us beyond these circumstances and time. I told them that the next time I returned there would be peace, I would know more Arabic, and I would be accompanied by my wife and children. They would smile with me and walk with me through such dreams and say with a sigh when it was all over, *"Insha Allah, Insha Allah."* Yet, I would reply, *"Shuia, shuia,"* for I was once told it meant the equivalent of "little by little." A little something I would often say to encourage them forward and to help them envision themselves as participating members of their destiny.

By the time August 2003 came about, the souvenir shop, the main museum exhibition room, and the ticket office had all been renovated. CPA had contracts committed beyond the time of our stay promising to continue to fund other projects that would help them recover. I spent a great deal of time in liaison meetings with the Polish who were preparing to take over our base and the Spanish who were moving into other areas in the southern provinces that included archaeological sites. I explained to these foreign forces what had been done and passed on a list of things that needed to be accomplished. The Polish in particular seemed very excited.

Five months in Babylon had flown by tremendously fast in so many ways. When it became evident that we were leaving the staff from Babylon and the vendors were quite expressive of their gratitude. In our last days there, the vendors pleaded daily and asked us not to send the Marines away. They begged incessantly for us to stay every time they saw me.

Ja'far pulled me to the side, "Chaplain you cannot leave. The people love the Marines. They are generous. Polish are cheap. They buy nothing." But little did Ja'far know that the Polish were no richer than the Iraqis. In many ways they were also babes in a new democracy of their own. They wouldn't sit around the market and sing the praises of democracy while overpaying for a soda because that is a genuinely unique American spirit. We truly believe that for all its ills and shortcomings our country is the greatest country on earth, and we are evangelistic about sharing it with others. Our Marines understood that a dollar meant a lot to these people and that paying a dollar to an Iraqi during the day in the market probably meant that he wasn't an insurgent at night. Many Marines consciously overpaid for trinkets and souvenirs and it was perfectly fine with them because they understood "trickle down" economics. It was their way of contributing and planting the American dream in Iraq.

A few days before we left, Mahmoud and the staff threatened that they wanted to kidnap me and make me the mayor of Al Hilla.

"You are good man. Pure heart, white heart, and fair to all. Stay and be our mayor," he invited. I was humbled by their proposition and warmed by the affection that grew between us. It was a purely emotional offer rooted in no authority but it was one that warmed my heart. I prayed that the impressions I made as a Christian and as an American would stay with them long after we left. I learned years ago that an earnest outreach rooted in sincerity and left to the "will of God" is like a seed planted by the wayside. It grows and takes on a life of its own. I learned this lesson through experience as the benefactor of such outreach during my teen years.

A little over thirty years ago, I found myself caught in the melee that became the 1977 New York City blackout. My mother had taken her first trip in eighteen years to Puerto Rico. She took my sisters, Lizzy and Enid, with her, leaving my father and me to care for each other. When the city went black our neighborhood exploded into disarray. My father warned me to stay inside during the blackness of night. That night I witnessed the effects of the blackout from the confines of a second story apartment window in the Dr. Ramon Emeterio Betances projects. I stuck my head out often throughout the night attempting to capture what I was missing. I heard gunshots in the distance and received updates to the madness from those who had ventured out and now returned to the relative safety of our block.

The following morning, under the light of day, I got up early and set out to report to my Youth Corps summer city job as a street cleaner. When I got to the office it was closed. On my way to and from the office I saw the devastation that we brought into our own neighborhood as looters ravaged the tiny stores that represented the lives of our neighbors. I resisted the temptation to enter into these ravaged stores but it wasn't long before I began to rationalize why I shouldn't help myself when everyone else around me was "benefiting" from the opportunity. At one point, I ran into a shoe store and grabbed a pair of sneakers, checked for my size, and as I prepared to run out of the store with the shoes, all I could envision was my father's stern face asking, "Who gave you those shoes?" I knew he wouldn't approve so I dropped them where I stood, walked out of the store, and continued my trip home empty-handed.

The only thing that kept me from stealing at that moment was the fact that I had to be accountable to my father. The statutes or ordinances of the Great State of New York or even the moral imprint that had been set within me through all those years of church attendance never convicted me during that process. I never stopped to reflect on the impact it was having on the storeowner, our community, or even me for that matter. Choosing to be a looter was an opportunistic act that allowed me to simply serve my innate desires. It was instinctual, selfish, and strictly temporal as I lived in the moment and didn't think of the consequences — except of being confronted by my father.

Living in moral poverty has its own rules. Our neighborhood was deep in the South Bronx and often stolen cars would be dumped in our neighborhood. All the major components that the professionals desired would be stripped off the cars and the carcasses were left behind for the scavengers, basically the rest of us, to finish off. I recall when I was fifteen that my father needed a part for his car and there happened to be an abandoned car across the street that had a similar part. I grabbed my pliers, screwdriver, and torque wrench and went to work on the car in broad daylight. The piece I needed was under the dashboard so I positioned my head and shoulders under the dashboard and balanced the rest of my body onto what was left of the seat frame.

About ten minutes into my work I feel a tapping on my knee. I assumed it was one of my friends and I yelled, "Yeah, what you want?"

The tapping on my leg came again and this time it was followed by a deep voice I didn't recognize and I knew was not Hispanic, "What do you think you're doing?"

I peered out from under the dashboard and saw a white New York City policeman standing there lightly tapping my knees with his nightstick. I wrestled my way out from under the dashboard and explained that I was trying to get a piece for my dad's car from this junked car. The officer must have noted right away from my nonchalant answer that I had no clue that I was doing something illegal and hence the ethics class began. "Son, this car belongs to you?" he asked.

"No, it's just a piece of junk abandoned here," I retorted.

"That car was not abandoned. It was stolen and dumped here. Since it doesn't belong to you it means that it belongs to someone else — right?"

I thought on that for a split second and replied, "I guess so."

He proceeded, "Now since it doesn't belong to you and you are taking something out of it that is not yours, what is that called?" and he paused for me to fill in the blank.

"Stealing?" I embarrassingly replied.

"So you're not stupid after all. That's right. Just because it's on the street it doesn't make it yours. Now take your tools and get out of here."

Thus was my lesson in separating the ethics of the street from those of a law-abiding society. In order to not steal one has to actually think and seek to define their place in a society with others' vices functioning strictly from an innate self-serving perspective. A reality applicable not only to stealing but to every aspect of life as a citizen of a larger society.

On the day after the blackout, I found myself bored with inactivity so I thought it exciting to invite my friend's sister, Ruth Rodriguez, to walk with me down to Third Avenue in the Bronx to witness the madness firsthand. We walked from one end of the market to the other. It felt like one of those popular 1970s disaster movies as sirens blared all around us and people ran in all directions. It was the middle of July and we saw bands of teens walking down the streets with parkas and down jackets that made them look like Mr. Goodrich as they bopped down the streets after having obviously helped themselves at the local sporting goods store. It was total anarchy.

We came across a scene that could not be dreamed up. To our left stood a tall warehouse with the gate that normally covered the truck loading platform torn off and cast to the side. Directly across the street was a brownstone. A group of men were bringing furniture from the insides of the warehouse, crossing the street, and climbing the stairs while the residents inside the brownstone were ejecting old furniture pieces out the window to the cheers of onlookers. We stood there and watched as a carpet was brought in and then a couch. People ran out of the loading ramp with their arms wrapped around lamps, boxes, televisions, and an array of other things.

Curiosity got the better of me and I excitedly called upon my young friend, Ruthie, to come with me inside the warehouse. We climbed the stairs and reached the next level to discover that it was very dark inside. We could barely make out the figures that were moving about around us. There were a few windows facing another building so some of the natural light bounced off the adjacent building and rested before us, but it was still pretty dark. A guy pushed me out of the way as he struggled with a ten-speed bike down the narrow stairs and a group of five men were struggling to move a piano. I wondered what Bronx apartment that would brighten up? I soon came to my senses and reminded myself once again that if I were to grab anything my father would wrap it around my neck, so I turned to Ruthie and yelled in her ear over all the commotion to follow me on the way out.

We began to descend down the stairs when a mad rush of people began to push by us in the opposite direction. It was like a sudden onslaught of a wave moving against us. We wrestled past them and continued down the stairs. I broached the opening in the doorway to exit the building when a pair of arms reached into the darkness where I stood and flung me across the floor onto the loading ramp. There was about half an inch of water on the floor and I turned to curse when I realized that the arms that grabbed me belonged to a New York City police officer. Another officer approached me as I attempted to stand and told me to sit on my butt. I pleaded, "Officer, I didn't take anything! I'm only sixteen!"

He looked at my skinny frame, long hair, and shabby goatee and replied, "Sixteen, my ass! Sit down and shut up."

One of the officers grabbed Ruthie by the shoulder and yelled, "How old are you?"

She nervously replied in almost a cry and found the courage to say "fourteen" and he cast her to the side and allowed her to leave.

I sat there and witnessed a city bus full of police officers stop in front of this building and offload its army into the dark stairs. Radios crackled around me and I realized I was being carted off to jail. I retreated into myself and everything went silent for me. I was pushed into a line and rustled into a police van where about twenty of us were carted off. It all seemed surreal. It all unraveled in slow motion and all I remember thinking to myself was, "The Marines won't take me now. What in the world am I going to do? I've really screwed up this time."

We were offloaded in front of the famous 42nd Precinct popularly referred to as Fort Apache in the Bronx. They pushed us past a wall of police officers and into a large waiting room. In the room we waited for a few hours as they processed each person. A police officer in plainclothes came to me and told me to stand before the table on the other side of the room. I worked my way through the crowd and saw three police officers sitting behind a table. On the floor directly in front of them lay a pool of blood and splattered blood up the side of the leg of that table.

My only points of reference to what happens in jail were stories from others who had survived prison and Hollywood movies. I could only envision a potential scene of police brutality. I stepped up to the table overwhelmed with fear and began to answer the officer's questions. I was so afraid that I thought I was going to urinate in my pants. Early on in the questioning they asked me my age and once again I responded honestly, "sixteen." One of the police officers slammed his nightstick on the table and began to curse at me. He accused me of lying and told me it wouldn't get me anywhere. I swore to him I was sixteen and something in my quivering voice must have convinced him so he let me go with a warning, "If you're lying to me I'm going to kick your ass."

I meekly moved to one side of the room to wait for the next step. While I waited there someone called out in Spanish from within the room, "Oye [Listen], is there an Emilio here?" I raised my hand and he instructed me to look out the window. Through the wrought iron gate covering the window I was able to peer out and saw my father in the crowd behind the police barriers. When he saw my face I immediately saw the disappointment and sadness on his. I was more ashamed and embarrassed than anything else for clearly breaking my father's heart at that moment.

I knew my father was no angel but I honored him as my father. He had been imprisoned himself on numerous occasions for running numbers on the street. As a child he had been orphaned since the age of seven. He survived over the years by living with his elder brothers and scraping a living in the sugar cane fields of Puerto Rico or during bad crop years he earned a living by traveling through the southeastern US picking fruit or vegetables with waves of migrant workers.

In 1959, he married my mom, leaving behind a woman with two children, Neida and Samuel, whom he'd fathered, and set off to start a new life by abandoning them. Prior to them he'd fathered another child whom he never bonded with in any way. These were my brothers and sisters whom I never really knew.

Over the years, in his new life, he worked hard loading trucks for a plastics company in lower Manhattan. I saw him as the epitome of a man who lived by his hard work, his commitment to being a strong provider, and a firm disciplinarian. He wasn't much for playing or talking with us. Having had no real model to go by I really believed he struggled with how to interact with us as his kids. He was a likeable fellow who others enjoyed and befriended easily, but I learned this of him from observing at a distance and not by personal experience. In watching him, I learned a great deal about being inwardly strong, caring for others, and being part of a community. His mantra to me was, "Don't be like me. Get a good education and be a self-made man."

Standing at the window we both dismissed any dreams we may have shared for me and faced one another hopelessly. He had no money. By this time, the company he had dedicated twenty years to left him behind and moved to Canada. He was offered an opportunity to move with them as a foreman but he couldn't pass the English exam. He went on to find new work in the city but while at his new job he was injured and was destined to receive disability. Feeling physically weak and bitten by the bite of alcoholism he was on the edge of being defeated. The only semblance of hope that kept him alive each day was the dream of hitting the lottery and becoming rich overnight. He numbed his emotions with alcohol from sunrise to sunset. While he stood there and looked at me he was still my father, the man I learned to love and admire as a young boy and the man whom I had disappointed.

I was led to the cell rooms later that afternoon and seven of us were stuffed into a two-man cell. It was so crowded we could barely move. We shifted positions and everyone took turns sitting on the toilet, grateful to be off our feet for about ten minutes. At one point in the evening a police officer came by and turned on a garden hose and held it in front of the cell as we each took turns shifting around the cell to slurp our share of water from the hose.

The next morning I was shackled. Cold steel went around my wrists and my legs. Like a chain gang we were escorted to an awaiting truck and taken to a larger prison. It turned out to be the larger cells of the Bronx Central Booking complex out by Yankee Stadium. My deepest fear was that I would be sent to Riker's Island, well known for its violence.

I was fingerprinted, photographed, and then escorted through an array of iron doors. There is no emotion like that associated with hearing the loud clangs of steel doors electronically shutting behind you declaring your involuntary incarceration to all who see you enter. I was escorted into a new cell with ten other men in a cell designed to hold three men. I discovered that amongst my cellmates I had an accused rapist, an accused murderer, two with drug charges, and the rest were looters. I was the youngest in the cell and though I tried to mask my fear I was grossly intimidated.

Sometime that afternoon a corrections officer came by and began to pass out lunch. He gave each of us a bologna sandwich and a drink. Before I could unwrap my sandwich, a black cellmate who was twice my size grabbed it out of my hands and started to eat it. I had gone 24 hours without food. I didn't want to get into a scrap with anyone so I tried to disappear into the background silently whimpering with fear. Everyone soon had a place they found as their own. There were three benches that protruded out from the wall. I made my hole underneath one of these and this is where I slept and tried to stay out of the way like a pet dog on a front porch.

When night came they called out a series of names and took prisoners away. These few were taken to Riker's Island for overflow. I held my breath hoping they wouldn't call me and they didn't.

Early the next morning, I saw a group of prisoners escorted into an adjacent cell. I recognized one of the prisoners who was probably only a year or two older than I. He had been in an adjacent cell the night before, was taken to Riker's Island during the night, and now he was back. I noticed the bandage around his hand and soon learned that at Riker's Island someone had grown fond of his ring and attempted to bite his finger off.

I spent seven days in this prison. The days were like eternities. During the week people were being called and escorted off to court but it felt like I had been forgotten. No one came by to see me and I had no clue what was in store for me, now or in the future. My time was a time for reflection. I took to recalling Bible verses I had learned in Sunday school and writing them as graffiti on the wall with a pen. Ironically, the other inmates would often correct my scripture recall. I incessantly called on God to rescue me and in the process I realized that while God had reached out to me, it was I who had let go of God. In those days I turned to prayer and once again asked God back into my life. I pleaded for direction and purpose.

On the seventh night of imprisonment I was called out of my cell and escorted through a labyrinth of cell blocks to another awaiting cell. Here I learned that a group of us arrested on the same night in the same place would be charged as a gang. I had never known any of these guys before but tonight we were being made to stand before a judge as a group. I approached the corrections officer who stood by our steel door and asked, "What are the chances of being let go tonight?" He looked at me and said, "Not a chance in hell. Everyone that has come before the judge tonight has gotten a one-way ticket to Riker's Island." My heart sank at his words.

I sat in desperate anxiety anticipating what would become of me. While I sat, there a guy in his late twenties with a "wife beater" shirt or tank top came up to me and told me he knew my father. I had no idea who he was. He proceeded to ask me to give him my shirt because he had gang tattoos and he didn't want the judge to see them. He promised he would return the shirt afterward. I wore a black silk shirt I had borrowed from Sammy, Ruthie's brother. The guy begged me and reasoned with me that since I didn't have any tattoos I had nothing to lose. I looked at him and figured he was right. I also knew that if I refused it was going to turn into a fight and this was not how I wanted to get the judge's attention. I surrendered the shirt.

My name was finally called with six other men. I lagged to the back of the group and followed them in as they were led by a court officer. I entered the courtroom from a side door and immediately noticed the difference in color and aesthetics. The courtroom was covered with wood compared to the stale, cold steel and concrete walls in the holding cells. As I entered the room, I noticed the array of benches and my eyes caught sight of a large group of people sitting toward the back of the courtroom. It didn't take long before I realized that the group sitting there was composed of members from my mother's church. There in the front of the group sat my mother, Isabel, surrounded by her church.

My mother was in her thirties, ten years younger than my father. She had given her life to Christ about seven years earlier and it had transformed her life and ours. In light of my father's condition she had returned to work in a local factory where they made luggage and uniform parts for the military. She had only made it to the eighth grade. She couldn't afford the schoolbooks to continue on in her education. She was a young woman abandoned by her father and raised by family members in one of the poorest barrios of Puerto Rico. Today she was my provider, my spiritual leader, and my conscious. My heart broke when I saw her gasp in relief and then burst into tears when she saw me. I heard them say in Spanish, "Glory to God, there he is." My body walked toward the center of the courtroom but my eyes were fixed on the group. My mom's new pastor, Reverend Angel Luis Jaime, my youth pastor and interim pastor of the church, Reverend Roberto Rivera, and an array of church members were there that night.

I learned that night what a community of faith meant. Here was a community of believers who were cordial with me when I went to church but I never gave them any reason to befriend me. I was explosive in Sunday school, I ran through the church attic during the services, and at best was marginally interested in the church.

I'd gone through all the motions but my ethics were a clear example of how I had failed to integrate the faith into my life. Yet in spite of my lack of commitment they were here for me. I learned later that they had been camped out in that courtroom for days holding silent prayer vigils during each court session hoping I would emerge. Reverend Rivera was able to contact someone in the prison system and learned that somehow my records had in fact been misplaced and I had fallen off the radar of sorts. That was the very reason why I was never selected to spend the night at Riker's Island. In the meantime, these wonderful people had placed their lives on hold to physically support my mother, pray for me, and be present as the incarnation of God's community for me.

I turned to face the judge and he read off our charges. He scolded us for being opportunists during a time of crisis in the life of the city and assured us we would be fairly punished. He declared that everyone would be mandated to Riker's Island for further detention and when I heard this I felt so empty, like life escaped my chest. I dropped my eyes to the floor and felt the swelling of tears rising up within me. However, before he slammed his gavel he paused and said "Emilio Marrero will be released to the care of his pastor and his church." I stood there in shock. The others were whisked away and I turned to my mother and her congregation stunned with the developments of the night.

The unconditional love and support of that congregation made the Bible very real to me on July 20, 1977. I have never felt so loved and forgiven. I knew I did not deserve to be released yet I was granted grace. I felt shame for disappointing my parents yet I knew then as the prodigal son must have known upon his return that he was loved. My parents whom I resented as a selfish, young teen became my greatest supporters and encouragers. I realized my own callousness and selfishness. In the midst of this crisis, I felt God's touch through his people, their care, and their commitments.

In the days ahead, I felt God become more real to me than ever before and I responded to such with a commitment that I would dedicate my life to ministry. I want to dedicate my life to helping others discover the relevancy, the vitality, and the concreteness of God in their life the way my church did for me.

On the last afternoon when I hugged my friends in Babylon good-bye I felt a part of me remain with them. The last five months had been an adventure in building relationships, overcoming bureaucratic hurdles, and genuinely attempting to embody America and my Christian faith in a very real way. Most of all it was a time of sharing, building friendships, and sharing dreams for tomorrow. When we pulled out of Babylon that evening in our last convoy it was appropriate that the sun set on us, and we drove away with saddened hearts.

The people who sat in those court benches in 1977 had no idea what God would do with me but they knew very well what God would have them do, and they did it — they came to the courtroom and prayed. In my walk through Babylon I had no idea what God would make of the lives of those people, the museum, or their country but I knew what I needed to do. I believe that I, along with so many others, have done what was expected of us. I believe we continue to do so, conscientiously, today. So many times people are afraid to get involved, to step out in faith, or to support a new effort because they can't see the end. We have become so accustomed to seeing life in neat packages, beginning to end, that when we encounter those struggles that are bigger than us it is easier to quit before we start. In Hebrews 11:13, we are reminded that many of the heroes of the faith never saw their hopes fulfilled.

> *All these people were still living by faith when they died.*
> *They did not receive the things promised; they only saw*
> *them and welcomed them from a distance.*
> — Hebrews 11:13

This perhaps is the greatest challenge for us while at the same time being the greatest exhibition of faith. In the end, it shall be God's will, but in the journey we need to be open to allow God to use us to build a path. Others may come in behind us and see the vision to fruition but the fact that we can't see the end from where we are does not in itself negate the necessity to begin the journey, to start the project, and to pave the way. In our context, it may only be a random act of kindness but in the larger scheme it may be the master's stroke that brings it all together.

In my brokenness there is much I have done to go against God's plan as a sinner. When I place myself in God's hands I do pray that as God took this looter out of the streets of New York City and changed his life that he would take these simple acts, these modern-day "fishes and loaves" that we've offered up during our time in Iraq, and use them to take the looters of Iraq, the oppressed and fearful men, the women of Iraq, and the generations to come and walk with them into a journey of discoveries, reflections, and new beginnings. May God walk with them through the hardships that lie ahead and forge a time of peace and promise for them as he has done with me. May the example, the testimony, and the sacrifices we, as Americans, made alongside so many Iraqis prove someday to be the seeds of a new society rooted in a new vision for this region. In the end, this venture has proven to be much more complex than we could have imagined and at this point we may find that the only place where this can be made right is in the hands of God. Thus we might say, *"Insha Allah"* as we wait hopefully while the Iraqis step forth and say, *"Shuia, Shuia."* In the meantime, I pray, stand ready to serve and trust in the Lord.

Addendum

RP1 Stephens was Chaplain Marrero's assistant and mentioned frequently in *A Quiet Reality*. RP1 Stephens returned in December 2008 from a second tour in Iraq where he served as an Individual Augment with Multi-National Coalition Forces Iraq and provided this update in January 2009:

> *During one of my latest missions we flew to an Army camp and there was an area set aside for local merchants to sell their goods. One of these places had "Babylon" spray-painted on the front of the building. I went in there and the guy running store began to smile and said, "I have a picture of you in my home!"*
>
> *I asked him where he would get something like that and after looking him in the eyes, I realized he was one of the merchants from Babylon in 2003. We embraced and I asked him about the guys there in Al Hilla. He said most of them had stores and are living in the Baghdad area.*
>
> *To hear this from him was the highlight of this second tour. I had always wondered in the back of my mind if those guys were doing okay and to know there were well really made my deployment.*

RP1 (FMF) Donnell Stephens, USN
USS Enterprise (CVN-72)
7 January 2009

243

Appendix A

Personalize Your Relationship With God

Did you know that according to the Pew Research Center over 80% of Americans claim a belief in God? It is an amazing statistic because it affirms a truth that we all feel intrinsically deep within ourselves. If your faith in God is undefined or unexplored I'd like to encourage you to discover God and enter into a personal relationship with God. Let God be real in your life.

My faith in God has evolved from taking on the faith of others based on their experiences and understanding to embracing a very personal relationship with God. The God of Christianity is not meant to be engaged via metaphysical reasoning or the projection of ideas but rather it is an investment in concrete reality similar to a relationship with anyone else. It is about discovering one another. It is about engaging objective truth in your life. In other words, God is not conceptual. God in the Christian community is very real and very personal, and he is engaged in the world today. I believe that the Judeo-Christian scriptures, commonly known as the Bible, reveal to us a loving God who desires for us to have an abundant life dedicated to unity and service to one another.

We who are strong ought to bear with the failings of the weak and not to please ourselves. Each of us should please his neighbor for his good, to build him up. For even Christ did not please himself but, as it is written: "The insults of those who insult you have fallen on me." For everything that was written in the past was written to teach us, so that through endurance and the encouragement of the Scriptures we might have hope.

May the God who gives endurance and encouragement give you a spirit of unity among yourselves as you follow Christ Jesus, so that with one heart and

mouth you may glorify the God and Father of our Lord
Jesus Christ.   — Romans 15:1-6

I'd like to share some summary thoughts and scriptures with you and encourage you to come into community with God as a Christian. Herein lies a path on how to become a Christian as outlined by the Billy Graham ministries.

God's Purpose: Peace And Life
God loves you and wants you to experience peace and life — abundant and eternal.

The Bible says ...

> *We have peace with God through our Lord Jesus Christ.*
>   — Romans 5:1

> *For God so loved the world that He gave His only begotten Son, that whoever believes in Him should not perish but have everlasting life.*   — John 3:16

> *I have come that they may have life, and that they may have it more abundantly.*   — John 10:10

Why is it that most people do not have this peace and abundant life that God planned for us to have?

The Problem: Our Separation
God created us in his own image to have an abundant life. He did not make us as robots to automatically love and obey him. God gave us a will and a freedom of choice.

We chose to disobey God and go our own willful way. We still make this choice today. This results in separation from God.

The Bible says ...

> *For all have sinned and fall short of the glory of God.*
>   — Romans 3:23

For the wages of sin is death, but the gift of God is
eternal life in Christ Jesus our Lord.
— Romans 6:23

Our Attempts To Reach God
People have tried in many ways to bridge this gap between themselves and God.
The Bible says ...

There is a way that seems right to a man, but in the end
it leads to death. — Proverbs 14:12

But your iniquities have separated you from your God;
your sins have hidden his face from you, so that he will
not hear. — Isaiah 59:2

No bridge reaches God ... except one.

God's Bridge: The Cross
Jesus Christ died on the cross and rose from the grave. He paid the penalty for our sin and bridged the gap between God and people.
The Bible says ...

For there is one God and one mediator between God
and men, the man Jesus Christ. — 1 Timothy 2:5

For Christ died for sins once for all, the righteous for
the unrighteous, to bring you to God. — 1 Peter 3:18

But God demonstrates his own love for us in this: While
we were still sinners, Christ died for us.
— Romans 5:8

God has provided the only way. Each person must make a choice.

247

Our Response: Receive Christ

We must trust Jesus Christ as Lord and Savior and receive him by personal invitation.

The Bible says ...

Here I am! I stand at the door and knock. If anyone hears my voice and opens the door, I will come in and eat with him, and he with me. — Revelation 3:20

Yet to all who received him, to those who believed in his name, he gave the right to become children of God. — John 1:12

That if you confess with your mouth, "Jesus is Lord," and believe in your heart that God raised Him from the dead, you will be saved. — Romans 10:9

Where Are You?

Will you receive Jesus Christ right now?
Here is how you can receive Christ:

- Admit your need (I am a sinner).
- Be willing to turn from your sins (repent).
- Believe that Jesus Christ died for you on the cross and rose from the grave.
- Through prayer, invite Jesus Christ to come in and control your life through the Holy Spirit. (Receive him as Lord and Savior.)

How To Pray

Dear Lord Jesus, I know that I am a sinner and need your forgiveness. I believe that you died for my sins. I want to turn from my sins. I now invite you to come into my heart and life. I want to trust and follow you as Lord and Savior. In Jesus' name. Amen.

God's Assurance: His Word

If you prayed this prayer, you can be assured God will listen to you.

The Bible says ...

Everyone who calls on the name of the Lord will be
saved. — Romans 10:13

Did you sincerely ask Jesus Christ to come into your life? Where is he right now? What has he given you?

For it is by grace you have been saved, through faith
— and this not from yourselves, it is the gift of God —
not by works, so that no one can boast.
— Ephesians 2:8-9

Receiving Christ, we are born into God's family through the supernatural work of the Holy Spirit who indwells every believer. This is called regeneration or the "new birth."

What's Next?
This is just the beginning of a wonderful new life in Christ. To deepen this relationship you should:

- read your Bible every day to know Christ better.
- talk to God in prayer every day.
- tell others about Christ.
- worship, fellowship, and serve with other Christians in a church where Christ is preached.
- as Christ's representative in a needy world, demonstrate your new life by your love and concern for others.

If you take this step in faith please feel free to email me at emarrero@a-quiet-reality.com, so I can include you in my prayers and welcome you to the community of believers.

Appendix B

How To Become
A Navy Chaplain

Ministers are people of the "calling." The calling is the urging of God to draw us to use our talents and strengths to care for God's people in a variety of settings. The calling comes to us and we respond to church settings, hospitals, counseling ministries, community development, and chaplaincy.

The Navy chaplaincy can be an exciting ministry for those pastors called to service in a nontraditional setting. In the Navy you will have the opportunity to minister on the high seas with deepwater Sailors on aircraft carriers, ships, and submarines. You can be a pastor to America's 911 Force as you join US Marines in the desert, in jungles, and in foreign lands as they train or respond to this nation's needs. You will also have the wonderful opportunity to be a pastor to pilots and highly trained technicians on the flightline who maintain the Navy and Marine Corps' most modern aircraft such as an F-18 and the V-22 Osprey. Ministry in the Navy will also have you preaching in local chapels, engaging in Pastoral Care Residency programs, or pasturing with your family overseas in places like Japan, Spain, and Italy.

Ministry is always exciting and challenging as you care for this nation's greatest asset — its people. You will have an opportunity to share with the unchurched, disciple the churched, and exchange ideas with others of differing faiths and cultures.

In combat and peace I feel like God has tremendously blessed me to be part of such a great community of professionals who are at the cusp of history. If you've received a calling to ministry and think that it might include the Navy Chaplain Corps, I invite you to explore via the web at *http://www.navy.com/careers/officer/clergy/* and take the plunge. We would love to have you serve the heroes of this nation's sea services in the Navy, Marine Corps, Coast Guard, and Merchant Marine Academy.

251

Here are the basics:

- The Navy accepts clergy from over 100 denominations and faith groups. Qualified applicants must be US citizens at least 21 years of age; meet certain medical and physical fitness standards; hold a BA or BS degree, with not less than 120 semester hours from a qualified educational institution; and hold a post-baccalaureate graduate degree, which includes 72 semester hours of graduate-level course work in theological or related studies. At least 36 of these hours must include topics in general religion, theology, religious philosophy, ethics, and/or the foundational writings from one's religious tradition. Accredited distance-education graduate programs are acceptable.
- Chaplains then attend the Navy Chaplain School in Newport, Rhode Island, for a basic orientation course.
- The Navy also has a "Chaplain Candidate Program Officer" (CCPO) program for seminary students who might be interested in obtaining a commission before completing their graduate studies. The CCPO program offers significant pay advantages once a Chaplain enters active duty. The program also includes on-the-job training under the direct supervision of an active-duty Chaplain.

Appendix C

Churches Support Your Troops

The US casualty rate in Operation Iraqi Freedom is slowing down as peace filters its way through the various provinces of Iraq. The casualty rate in Afghanistan fluctuates with the level of operations. These facts may draw us to conclude that the worst is over.

In *A Quiet Reality* I indicate that the impact of war goes well beyond just the physical threats that burden a small percentage of those who have been wounded. The fact is that everyone who is deployed into a combat environment is greatly impacted by the experience but may show few signs of such an impact. Learning to live in an arduous environment such as the desert for six months to a year while also being exposed to possible threats, being separated from loved ones, and missing "life defining" moments often impacts much more heavily than one would ordinarily imagine. The work environment, even in relatively safe havens, is often grueling. It is not uncommon to work eighteen to twenty hour days, seven days a week, with just a few hours off on occasion. Everything that is processed or developed was due *yesterday* and has "real time" impact for someone else whose life may depend on it.

It is important to note that exposure to this type of high stress operational condition wears on the human body, the human soul, and the human psyche.

Today researchers and journalists are very eager to float high statistics on the impact of Post Traumatic Stress Disorder or PTSD. A recent study sponsored by the RAND Corporation indicated that as many as one in five suffer from PTSD or 20% of all deployed forces.[1] I take issue with this aggrandizement of such a condition. While I believe strongly that our forces are impacted by the conditions of such long-term deployments, I do not believe that these studies reflect the reality of what is happening within our ranks.

I concur with the fact that the data shows that upon return from deployments 20% of our troops may be suffering from PTSD

253

symptoms such as lack of sleep, nightmares, inability to concentrate, and more. However, exhibiting PTSD symptoms is very different from being classified as having PTSD in accordance to the DSM IV manual. It takes months under the care of a mental health care professional to accurately determine PTSD as a disorder. It is akin to a person having symptoms of flu such as sneezing, chills, and so on, but through further diagnosis it can be determined to be some other type of illness and not flu. This is the quiet reality related to PTSD. There are many who may be experiencing symptoms but in the long run may in fact not be experiencing PTSD *per se* but there are those who make a mad dash to immediately label them with the diagnoses of PTSD.

The vast majority of our returning warriors may indeed have symptoms of PTSD due to the high tempo of operations. We in the Navy, Army, and Marine Corps call this combat or operational stress. This stress stems from the conditions of deployed life in the field, being exposed to dangers, dealing with issues of death and mortality, and compassion fatigue as we attempt to empathize with the local populace. These are all factors that wear away at the human soul. The symptoms are closely related but Operational Stress does not always develop into acute cases of PTSD.

Matters become more complicated when we realize that many of our Marines, Sailors, Soldiers, and Airmen are being selected from within their ranks to go serve as individual augments to assist other commands and even other services. This means that the unit cohesion that has proven to be a major factor in developing resiliency against stress and PTSD is being undermined by sending them off by themselves. The very individualistic transitory experience endured by Individual Augments can in fact place them at high risk. With this comes higher levels of concern as they now embark on this journey alone and have to encounter fitting into a new unit while also attempting to fit into a new job in a combat environment. Along with these factors they no longer have the community of the unit to care for their families. Their families experience a higher level of isolation and disenfranchisement during the deployments. This is true in the active community and in the reserve community.

The Rand Corporation study states, "[r]ates of PTSD and major depression were highest among Army soldiers and Marines, and among service members who were no longer on active duty (people in the reserves and those who had been discharged or retired from the military). Women, Hispanics, and enlisted personnel all were more likely to report symptoms of PTSD and major depressions, but the single best predictor of PTSD and depression was exposure to combat trauma while deployed."

All of this means that there are hundreds of thousands of US veterans who served in Iraq and Afghanistan who are journeying with getting back to normal on their own. For some "normal" will no longer be "being as before the deployment" because such a quest is an impossibility. This is due to the fact that they have been shaped and impacted by their experience no matter how sublime their experience might have been. Many of these veterans and their families are in your communities today attempting to return to normalcy. In fact, they may be experiencing difficulties with their relationships, communications, sexuality, sleep, anger, and/or intimacy to name but a few issues. Some, due to their experiences, may resort to attempt to alleviate their symptoms through self-medication with alcohol, over-the-counter drugs, or illicit drugs. Others will experience an "out of sortness" deep within them and may resort to high-risk behaviors such as high speed driving, frequent and casual sex, high-risk sports, motorcycling, or other events in order to either quiet the demons or feel adrenaline once again.

The fact is that the vast majority of these returning veterans will find peace in their lives on their own by reconnecting with their own social networks and resources. Churches and local communities can be of assistance in this journey. I ask that churches, in particular, make an effort to support our veterans and their families by providing a venue of support. Here are some things that can be done:

If they are preparing to be deployed, or are already deployed, consider the following:

- Bring them forward to the altar and pray for them. Don't let them slip away.

- Many will have family members who are currently concerned about a deployed service member. Please support them by checking on them monthly. Please include moms and dads who have single children deployed. Ask about "Johnny" or "Jane" and ask them to convey your gratitude to their child.
- Begin a letter writing campaign to those who are deployed. It doesn't have to be every day but occasional news from home lifts the spirits up.

If they are returning from a deployment, or have already returned from a deployment, consider the following:

- Use a patriotic holiday at least once a year in the church to recognize those who have served. Upon my initial return this was particularly healing when my home church celebrated Veterans' Day and had us all stand and receive a standing ovation by the congregation. This is also a great way of identifying those who have deployed and are settling back into their lives. A note of advice, it doesn't have to be a militaristic or patriotic event within the context of the church. If you feel comfortable doing this feel free to incorporate it but be conscious about going over the top with this. Don't turn a worship service into a Fourth of July concert. Church is always about Christ first, however, use the opportunity to pray over or honor those who have served within your congregation. It can be a spiritually healing process for service members and their families.
- For those who have returned, allow them a few weeks and don't be afraid to ask, "How are you settling in?" A great way to know how well they are doing is by asking, "Are you sleeping through the night yet?" Some vets can take up to six months to get back to healthy sleeping habits. Vets who have made multiple deployments or have deployed for twelve to eighteen continuous months can take even longer. Sleep is a crucial piece to recovery so don't be afraid to ask

or to encourage them to seek assistance from a medical professional.

- Pastors, make yourself available for counseling and devote the time to listening. Allow them to tell their story and encourage them to journal. Don't attempt to fix them but guide them. Realize that the entire story will not come out at once. Part of this is due to the establishment of trust but a very real part can also be due to suppression. With time and sharing, they may actually begin to remember details they have suppressed for a variety of reasons.
- Faith counseling often involves confession, redemption, and forgiveness. There may be moments of the past that invoke guilt and second-guessing. While this should never be assumed, it is imperative that God's grace always be made available to help veterans deal with their emotions and guilt — even if it is perceived guilt. This guilt can be because of something that happened in theater or it can be guilt over a mix-up of priorities, broken relationships, or failure to perform to expectations. Never presume, don't fill in the blanks, but allow them to explore these emotions without judgment and always offer a safe place to share. Offer access to share; offer love, offer grace, and offer God's forgiveness.
- Be aware of the hero/nonhero complex. Be aware of the fact that the vast majority of our troops were not kicking doors down or firing off their weapons. Many were in support roles where they were turning wrenches or some served in areas that were pretty peaceful. For these reasons they often have difficulty seeing themselves as heroes. Heroes to those who serve are often those who made the ultimate sacrifice or those that lost a limb in combat. It is helpful when average Americans redefine this term and help our troops understand that a hero is one who volunteers and who answers the nation's call. The very fact that they placed their life on hold and went forward whether for one tour or a career, makes them courageous, selfless, and a hero. A community that redefines this definition of hero and helps

a service member come to terms with their role will greatly help to affirm and heal a soul.

- Church pews are filled with veterans ranging from World War II to Desert Storm. Use these veterans to reach out to the new veterans and encourage them to socialize. This is one of the healthiest forums for veterans to share their stories and find understanding from others who know where they've been.
- In the 1990s Promise Keepers was big — it was an opportunity for men to gather around and discuss what it meant to be a godly man. These types of prayer groups or study groups can prove to be very helpful. Use these venues to address issues about anger, pornography, faithfulness, courage, and purpose in life. It can prove to be a venue for young men to express their concerns and seek counsel.
- Identify mental health providers in the area who have experience in dealing with acute stress and PTSD. Keep their names handy and be ready to hand them to veterans who may be hurting and need a referral in your community. Put together a list of referrals that include mental health, veteran's information centers in the area, Veterans Administration contact numbers, and local reserve center family resources in the area.
- Provide similar support for women — in today's service women share the burden and experience equally. Rally around them and support them.
- Identify chaplains or veterans and bring them in for a prayer breakfast or to preach in your churches.
- Always remember Joshua 1:9, for once they have been strong and courageous God promises that He will go with them wherever they may go. That's a promise worth reminding.

Have I not commanded you? Be strong and courageous.
Do not be terrified; do not be discouraged, for the Lord
your God will be with you wherever you go.
— Joshua 1:9

1. Warren Roback, Rand Corporation, 17 April 2008. http://www.eurekalert.org/ pub_releases/2008-04/rc-sfo041708.php.

About The Author

Emilio Marrero, Jr.
Captain, Chaplain Corps, United States Navy

Chaplain Marrero is from the South Bronx in New York City. He is a 1982 graduate of Eastern College, St. David, Pennsylvania. He received his Masters of Divinity from Eastern Baptist Theological Seminary in Philadelphia in 1985 and completed his Doctor of Ministry in Religious Education from Claremont School of Theology, Claremont, California, in 2000.

Chaplain Marrero enlisted in the United States Marine Corps Reserves in January 1980 by way of Parris Island Marine Corps Recruit Depot, South Carolina. He served as a young Marine in the reserves for almost three years until he completed undergraduate studies when he was transferred from the United States Marine Corps to the US Navy's Theological Student Program as an Ensign. While serving in the reserves he was pastor for the First Hispanic Baptist Church of New Brunswick, New Jersey, and as Assistant Director, The Open Door Outpatient Alcohol Treatment Center, New Brunswick, New Jersey.

On September 6, 1986, Chaplain Marrero moved to San Diego, California, and began to serve as a Chaplain on active duty. He has served in a series of diverse tours to include the Ship's Chaplain to the *USS Tripoli* (LPH-10); Tactical Chaplain, Brigade Service Support Group, 1st Marine Expeditionary Brigade, Kaneohe, Hawaii; Group Chaplain, Direct Support Group-1, 1st Force Service Support Group during Desert Shield and Desert Storm; Chaplain Recruiter, Navy Recruiting Area Eight, Oakland, California; Postgraduate Studies at Claremont School of Theology, Claremont, California; Staff Chaplain, Naval Air Station, Keflavik, Iceland; Group Chaplain, Marine Aircraft Group-13, Yuma, Arizona; and Command Chaplain, Marine Corps Air Station, Yuma, Arizona. He served with the 1st Marine Expeditionary Force, Camp Pendelton as the I MEF Headquarters Group Chaplain, I MEF Forward Force Chaplain, and Deputy Force Chaplain during combat operations in Operation Iraqi Freedom (January-October 2003) and Operation Iraqi Freedom II (February-July 2004). Chaplain Marrero recently served as the Wing Chaplain, 1st Marine Aircraft Wing, Okinawa, Japan, and is currently serving as the Force Chaplain, Navy Expeditionary Combat Command in Little Creek, Virginia.

Chaplain Marrero is an advocate for community involvement and an integral approach to the employment of Chaplains. In his years on active duty he has paved the way for Marines and Sailors to be involved in the local community. He led the effort in joining his command and a local school in the Partners in Education Program. The *USS Tripoli* (LPH-10) became the first afloat command to sponsor the Adopt-A-School program in 1986. This effort resulted in an exciting tutoring program for community children that increased reading and math scores as high as two grade levels. He spearheaded numerous Project Handclasp and community relations projects overseas with deployed units in the Philippines, Korea, Okinawa, and Thailand. He volunteered as a guest speaker to Oakland inner-city schools during his tour as a recruiter; supported local orphanages and community agencies in San Diego, Oakland, and Yuma; in Babylon, Iraq, he spearheaded efforts to secure, preserve, and reconstruct Iraq's National Treasure of Babylon Museum, which includes the archaeological site of Nebuchadnezzar's Palace along with sponsoring a souk for out-of-work Iraqis.

He and his wife, Wanda, were the founders of a community child development center in Yuma, Arizona, serving over 100 preschool at-risk children and Juniper Tree Academy, the first K-8th Grade Arizona State Board for Charter School sponsored in the City of Yuma with over 400 students.

His personal awards include: Legion of Merit Medal, Bronze Star Medal, Meritorious Service Medal (three awards), Navy Commendation Medal (four awards), Navy Achievement Medal, Combat Action Ribbon, and over twenty campaign and unit awards. Chaplain Marrero also received Nueva Esperanza's first "Spirit Award" for outstanding service during his ministry in Iraq during the 2004 National Hispanic Prayer Breakfast in Washington DC.

Captain Marrero and his wife, Wanda, have been married for over 26 years. They have two grown children, one grandson, and a granddaughter due to arrive in spring 2009. Their son-in-law serves as a Staff Sergeant in the US Marine Corps.

Note: Many photographs of the material featured in *A Quiet Reality* can be accessed on Chaplain Marrero's website: www.a-quiet-realilty.com.

Ten percent of the profits from the author's sale of this book will be donated to the INJURED MARINE SEMPER FI FUND. The mission of the SEMPER FI FUND is as follows:

"Semper Fi" means "always faithful," and that is our pledge to the heroic OEF/OIF Marines, Sailors, and other OEF/OIF service members assigned to Marine forces who are injured in the line of duty or face life-threatening illness while protecting our nation.

Mrs. Annette Conway, wife of General Conway, was instrumental in helping spouses get together and create this charity.